REVIVAL IN THE CITY

MCGILL-QUEEN'S STUDIES IN THE HISTORY OF RELIGION

Volumes in this series have been supported by the Jackman Foundation of Toronto.

SERIES TWO   In memory of George Rawlyk
Donald Harman Akenson, Editor

SERIES ONE
G.A. Rawlyk, Editor

Revival in the City

The Impact of American Evangelists
in Canada, 1884–1914

ERIC R. CROUSE

McGill-Queen's University Press
Montreal & Kingston • London • Ithaca

© McGill-Queen's University Press 2005
ISBN 0-7735-2898-9

Legal deposit third quarter 2005
Bibliothèque nationale du Québec

Printed in Canada on acid-free paper that is 100% ancient forest
free (100% post-consumer recycled), processed chlorine free

This book has been published with the help of a grant from the
Canadian Federation for the Humanities and Social Sciences,
through the Aid to Scholarly Publications Programme, using funds
provided by the Social Sciences and Humanities Research Council
of Canada.

McGill-Queen's University Press acknowledges the support of the
Canada Council for the Arts for our publishing program. We also
acknowledge the financial support of the Government of Canada
through the Book Publishing Industry Development Program
(BPIDP) for our publishing activities.

Library and Archives Canada Cataloguing in Publication

Crouse, Eric Robert, 1960-
   Revival in the city : the impact of American revivalists in
Canada, 1884–1914 / Eric R. Crouse.

(McGill-Queen's studies in the history of religion ; 35)
Includes bibliographical references and index.
ISBN 0-7735-2898-9

   1. Evangelicalism–Canada–History. 2. Evangelists–Canada–
History. 3. Evangelicalism–United States. I. Title. II. Series.

BV3777.C3C76 2005   270.8'1   C2005-902006-7

Typeset by Jay Tee Graphics Ltd. in Sabon 10/12

Dedicated to the memory of George Rawlyk

Contents

Acknowledgments

My interest in American revivalism began at the University of Calgary with a fourth-year undergraduate research paper on nineteenth-century evangelist Dwight L. Moody. Under the inspiring supervision of David Marshall, I wrote my MA thesis on Moody's impact in Canada. Later, as a doctoral student at Queen's University, my work explored other American evangelists in Canada. After the tragic death of my supervisor, George Rawlyk, as a result of injuries suffered in an automobile accident in 1995, Marguerite Van Die (Queen's) and Mark Noll (Wheaton College) agreed to complete the final year of supervision of my doctoral study, providing exceptional direction and support.

I am also grateful for the fine work of the interlibrary loan staff at Queen's University and the University of New Brunswick (Fredericton) and the archival assistance I received along the way, particularly from the Moody Bible Institute Archives (MBIA), the Billy Graham Center Archives, the University of Georgia Libraries (UGL), the United Church Archives (Toronto), and the University of Manitoba Archives. Joseph Cataio (MBIA) and Nelson Morgan (UGL) provided excellent photograph service.

In the transition from doctoral study to book, I gained from the insights of many people. I appreciate the feedback from the anonymous readers of two of my earlier essays published in *Ontario History* and the *Journal of Presbyterian History*. I thank these two journals for granting permission to republish material found in "Revivalism for the Working Class? American Methodist Evangelists in Late Nineteenth-Century Urban Ontario," *Ontario History*, 91, no. 1, (spring 1999): 21–37, and "Great Expectations: J. Wilbur Chapman, Presbyterians and Other Protestants in Early 20th-

Century Canada," *Journal of Presbyterian History*, 78, no. 2, (summer 2000): 155–167. I am exceedingly grateful for the astute and wise comments and criticisms received from the anonymous readers of McGill-Queen's University Press and the Canadian Federation for the Humanities and Social Sciences. This book has been published with the help of a grant from the Canadian Federation for the Humanities and Social Sciences, through the Aid to Scholarly Publications Programme, using funds provided by the Social Sciences and Humanities Research Council of Canada.

Colleagues and staff at Tyndale University College have been supportive in many ways. Providing numerous hours of computer assistance and proofreading, Al Hounsell deserves special mention. My deepest thanks also go to McGill-Queen's University Press editor Roger Martin for his guidance from the very beginning. Once the manuscript received approval for publication, Joan McGilvray kept me on the right track and Curtis Fahey did an excellent job with the copy editing.

At home, the love and support of my wife, Ann-Marie, and two daughters, Emily and Elizabeth, continue to allow me to pursue history. Their love for books is a bonus.

Finally, I wanted to write a book that would have met with Dr Rawlyk's approval. As he did, I care about revivalism and economic justice for workers. He, however, might have questioned my position on the secularization thesis (I see a decline in the prominence of biblical principles in Canadian society). In the early twentieth century, the Toronto *Daily Star* and its editor, Joseph Atkinson, provided stunning support for evangelical revivalism, but one century later the Toronto *Star* ignores evangelicalism or arguably is hostile towards it. And yet polling data over the past decade indicate a rise in the percentage of evangelicals in Canada (15 per cent in 1993 to 19 per cent in 2003 (Ipsos-Reid)). I wish Professor Rawlyk were here to help sort out this incongruity. In the end, I wanted to provide an overview of American revivalism in Canada in a manner similar to Rawlyk's work. I hope that this book, even with its shortcomings, encourages others to explore the topics of revivalism and evangelicalism and better understand the religious passion and faith that ordinary working people embraced and continue to embrace. Rawlyk's studies on revivalism did so for me.

In Chicago, Dwight L. Moody (back row, left) with his Sunday school class of working-class youth (Moody Bible Institute Archives)

Front-page coverage – Brantford Welcomes Moody (Brantford *Courier*, 23 October 1897)

Dwight L. Moody (Moody Bible Institute Archives)

Georgia Evangelist Sam P. Jones (University of Georgia Libraries)

Sam Small (University of Georgia Libraries)

Reuben A. Torrey (Moody Bible Institute Archives)

63RD YEAR. NO. 19　　TEN PAGES

TORREY AND ALEXANDER GREETED BY THOUSANDS

Opening of Great Gospel Campaign Was Most Auspicious—7,000 Attended the Night Meeting At Arena

Dr. Torrey Preached Plain Simple Sermon With Much Force, Made Marked Impression on Multitude.

Mr. Alexander is a Great Singer and Large Choir Responded in Fine Style to His Leadership.

The Torrey-Alexander mission opened in Dey's arena yesterday afternoon and judged by the enthusiastic interest shown, the large attendance, the powerful preaching and the admirable singing the special meetings will be a great power for good in the Capital.

Dey's rink where the meetings are held is excellently suited for the purpose and the acoustic properties for both the singing and preaching are highly satisfactory. The raised platform for the choir is at the western end of the rink while a raised stand in front is used by Dr. Torrey while speaking and by Mr. Charles M. Alexander in singing. In addition to the regular seats at the end and sides, over two hundred seats are placed in the center of the rink so that there is ample room for a very large audience. The rain storm in the afternoon thinned against the attendance, still there were about 2,800 people present and nothing was lacking in the way of interest. The afternoon audience included a party of eight from Rideau hall.

Seldom, if ever before, has there been in Ottawa such a strong evangelistic aggregation. Rev. Dr. Torrey is a clear, logical, forceful speaker. There is no undue appeal to the emotions but an outspoken presentation of the truth and a radical invitation to higher things. His plan of campaign in Ottawa is the same as in other cities. In the afternoon a discussion to professing Christians, in the evening an appeal to the unconverted.

One cannot soon forget the way Mr. Alexander captivates and dominates his audience and choir alike. He is magnetic, irresistible. His intense earnestness energizes every atom of his being down to his never resting finger tips. Following the singing of a simple hymn he gives out a song with a more modern swing, a typical revival melody and then begins the work of teaching the audience to sing. With

Continued on Page Ten.

Dr. Torrey—"Every Christian should make soul-winning the business of life with Jesus Christ."

Front-page coverage – "Torrey and Alexander Greeted by Thousands" (Ottawa *Citizen*, 11 June 1906, Courtesy of Ottawa *Citizen*)

Chapman is Coming

Undoubtedly the greatest evangelist since the days of Moody. Chapman has carried on a campaign of revival and reform throughout the length and breadth of the United States. The churches of all the larger cities have united and extended a call to him to come and help them. In every case success before unheard of has attended his efforts. Vast crowds have flocked to every meeting place, so that from each centre there have been as many as five and six overflow metings. Chapman's methods are unique. He does not promote a revival in one congregation or in one denomination only. He works in all the congregations of the city and all denominations work with him. The whole city is enthused and awakened. The chief centres for his Winnipeg campaign will be the following churches:

Augustine   **Central Congregational**
St. Andrew's   **St. Stephen's**
Grace   **Macdougall**

> **Do not fail to hear America's greatest living Evangelist. Be present and help.**

REV. W. SPARLING, D.D.   **GEO. R. CROWE**
Chairman Executive   Chairman Finance Committee

Advertisement in working-class paper – "Chapman Is Coming" (*Voice* (Winnipeg), 18 October 1907)

Torrey Revival Has Closed With About 800 Conversions

Two Monster Meetings at the Arctic Rink on Sunday Notwithstanding the Inclement Weather--- Afternoon Crowd the Largest of the Campaign and Was Estimated at 3,000 -Dramatic Story of His Life Told by Mr. Jacoby---Dr. Torrey and Others Left For Home Today The Financial Report.

Revival conversions at Torrey campaign in Fredericton, New Brunswick (Fredericton *Daily Gleaner*, 13 June 1910)

WONDERFUL REVIVAL OF RELIGION

Result of Chapman-Alexander Services in Orillia.

Enormous Crowds Attend Meetings.—The Singing a Special Feature.—How Campaign Was Organized and Conducted.

Messages from the Leaders.—Work in Orillia.—Some Special Phases of Work.—
Breadth of the Movement.—What Ministers and Business Men Say.—
The Chapman-Alexander Itinerary.

The two weeks' services in connection with the Chapman Alexander evangelistic campaign were closed on Tuesday evening with a wonderful meeting in the Palace skating rink. Successful from the opening night on September 30, the attendance daily increased, and there was an unwonted of the merits of a public speaker, looked at his questioner with an air of surprise. "Dr. Chapman? I don't know. In fact I didn't think about him at all; he made me think so much of the Man he was preaching about." Perhaps no truer verdict could be pronounced upon the leader of the

A Message from Rev. Dr. Chapman

TO THE PEOPLE OF ORILLIA.

It has been a great pleasure to labor for the past two weeks in Orillia. I have rarely, if ever, in my experience as an evangelist, received a more cordial welcome from people after they came to understand the work than has been accorded me by citizens here. The ministers have been as true as steel, and the support which they have given to me has been unexcelled. I know that the work is to be abiding. I am persuaded that the churches will feel the impulse of the meetings for months and years to come, but two or three things will be required if the work is to be all that we hope for it.

First. The Churches must carry it forward and every service must be in the truest sense evangelistic, for weeks to come. The people who have made a start for Christ must be carefully looked after and won for the church and for Christ.

Second. The ministers must be more faithfully supported than they have been in the past, great as this support may have been; and from all that I know of them I am sure that they will carry this work on to a great climax.

Third. The special and regular services of the church must have the enthusiastic support of the church people. If these suggestions are carried out just for three months the effect upon Orillia will be startling.

I wish to say farewell to the people of the town, and again to express my sincere appreciation for the many kindnesses shown to me.

J. WILBUR CHAPMAN.

Front-page coverage – "Wonderful Revival of Religion" (Orillia *Times*, 15 October 1908)

J. Wilbur Chapman (Moody Bible Institute Archives)

DR. CHAPMAN IN CHARACTERISTIC ATTITUDE "EVERY MAN SHOULD BE AN EVANGELIST TO HIS NEIGHBOR!"

"Dr Chapman in Characteristic Attitude" in the Toronto *Daily Star*, a major supporter of evangelical revivalism (6 January 1911)

REVIVAL IN THE CITY

Introduction

Before the sounds and images of American radio, talking movies, and television, there was an onslaught of American popular religion into the lives of a surprising number of English Canadians. As a result of the emergence of famous Protestant evangelists in the United States from the mid-1870s to the First World War, populist forms of American conservative evangelicalism flourished in Canada. Many English-Canadian workers embraced the revivalism and conservative evangelicalism of visiting Americans who held meetings from coast to coast in churches, roller rinks, halls, theatres, and other public urban spaces. The attendance exceeded one and a half million for the approximately eight hundred revival meetings held by the best-known American evangelists of the late nineteenth and early twentieth centuries.[1]

The popularity of the evangelists confirmed their belief in the validity of their message, method, and focus while also reflecting Canadians' desire for meaning and solace in an era undergoing change. Yet the full force of revivalism was brief. When it became clear that revival meetings failed to entice attenders to take the next step into church membership, Canadian church leaders questioned the usefulness of revivalism rather than their own shortcomings in reaching the unchurched. For church leaders who were wary of certain aspects of American revivalism, particularly a conservative evangelical message and the financial costs of meetings constructed to popular-culture tastes, it would not take much convincing to lessen their support even though many Canadians experienced revival.

There was transformation at revival meetings for those who experienced sorrow for sinful behaviour, humility before God, and redemption through Jesus Christ. Revivalism spread its influence in cities throughout the United States and Canada, in step with the desire of evangelicals to see a spiritual renewal of modern communities experiencing the promises and pains of growth. This emphasis on spiritual commitment was the heart of Protestant "evangelicalism," a movement defined by historians as "a reliance on the Bible as ultimate religious authority," "a stress on the New Birth," "an energetic, individualistic approach to religious duties and social involvement," and "a focus on Christ's redeeming work as the heart of essential Christianity."[2]

Earlier in the nineteenth century, many evangelicals in the United States upheld social-reform ideas and fought against slavery, poverty, greed, and other social ills of the day. A more dogmatic application of "evangelicalism" was late-nineteenth-century "conservative evangelicalism," which devoted much energy to negative refutation of Darwinism, higher criticism, and socialism and which can be said to have retreated from far-reaching social-reform ideals.[3] The conservative evangelicalism voiced at revival meetings was a blending of theological conservatism with a particular individualistic approach to social action.

Although there were some liberal evangelicals in America, it was rare to find an evangelist who was accepting of social-reform ideals. Conservative evangelicals or proto-fundamentalists (forerunners of the fundamentalist movement) maintained hegemonic influence into the early twentieth century. Until the first World War, the dominant message from Protestant America was a conservative evangelical one and the best promoters of this message were the evangelists who saw no barriers at the American-Canadian border.

American revivalism represented more than the citizenship of the popular evangelists, for it was a home-grown brand of revivalism infused with biblical certitudes, popular culture, and American ideals of individualism and self-reliance. In his study of British North American evangelical life, George Rawlyk argues that Canadian evangelicalism differed in that it did not carry the baggage of "the covenant ideal and possessive individualism." But American revivalism, with its Great Awakening and "democratization" heritage, was a powerful and influential force.[4] As masters of popular culture, the Americans had an advanced understanding of the idea of "revival as a big thing" and the importance of the mass media.[5] "The Americanization of Canada,"[6] which scholars debate in regard to social, political, and economic issues of the twentieth century, began to occur in the late nineteenth century as a result of the visits by well-known American evangelists who upheld conservative theological, social, and economic ideals.

In a cultural sense, the American-Canadian border became remarkably fluid, and, consequently, contrary to arguments that claim Canadian Protestant exceptionalism, the American Protestant experience played a significant role in shaping Canadian evangelicalism.[7] Central Canada witnessed a large number of American revival meetings, mainly because of the advanced development of its urban centres and transportation network. The Maritimes attracted fewer high-profile evangelists, but the region did experience major revival campaigns. With the exception of southern Manitoba and Victoria and Vancouver, American evangelism had a slight effect in the west. Still, throughout all of English Canada, the impact of the American evangelists was exponential since local Protestant clergy and evangelists often modelled their message and methodology after the well-known evangelists. Moreover, the proliferation of revival reports in local newspapers brought an American brand of popular conservative evangelicalism to many thousands of households in most regions of English Canada.

While the task of offering comprehensive treatment or scientific analysis of the impact of American evangelists on Canadian Protestantism is virtually impossible, one can see that many Protestant clergy and lay leaders found American revivalism appealing and they drew upon the energy of American-style revival meetings with enthusiasm. Baptist, Congregationalist, Methodist, Presbyterian, and other evangelical denominations and churches anticipated that the Americans would revitalize professed Christians, reach out to the increasing number of unchurched workers in the cities, assist in offering sound biblical guidelines for family and community life, and, all in all, address concerns related to what some scholars identify as the secularization of society. In many ways, a significant number of Canadians looked to mother Britain for cultural and national guidance (although this became less so in twentieth-century Canada), but, on the matter of religion, large masses of Canadian Protestants found American popular evangelists especially attractive.

Popular culture refers to the whole range of human products, beliefs, values, and ideals in society that attracts a mass audience. Like a mirror, popular culture reflects who people are; the popularity of a given cultural element (an event such as a revival meeting or person such as a popular evangelist) for a mass of people exposes much about human traits and character.[8] In this context, the old-fashioned Gospel message, the popular hymns, and the methods of the major American evangelists, all of which received such lavish press attention, also represented an expression of popular religion. Popular religion seeks to reject both the clerical mediation between humankind and God and an over-intellectualized form of religious practice.[9] It usually exists in tension with established religious groups, represents beliefs channelled by word of mouth or by popular literature rather than by the seminaries of established religion, and rejects the "modernization" that is accepted by "official" religion.[10]

With their own cultural and sociability forms, popular revival meetings led by American evangelists were conspicuous events that demonstrated the blending of religion, popular culture, and public life.[11] Dwight Lyman Moody, the world-famous evangelist of the late nineteenth century, packed churches, halls, and various buildings in at least thirteen major cities in Quebec, Ontario, Manitoba, and British Columbia from 1884 to 1898. Holding approximately two hundred revival meetings, Moody transformed public space and mesmerized thousands of Canadians with a simple, earnest, and popular message. Even before Moody arrived in Canada, Canadian Protestants had followed his revival exploits in the 1870s, through newspaper and church reports. Successfully fusing secular popular culture to evangelism, Moody was the first evangelical master of popular culture in Canada. Even more of a showman than Moody, Sam Jones, the flamboyant Methodist evangelist from the American south, joined by co-evangelist Sam Small on three occasions, held well-attended meetings in at least seven urban centres throughout central Canada in 1886 and 1887.[12] Large gatherings also welcomed world-travelled American evangelist Dr Reuben Archer Torrey, who conducted approximately three hundred revival meetings in Toronto, Ottawa, Montreal, Fredericton, Saint John, and Windsor, Nova Scotia, in the 1906-11 period. Preaching a conservative evangelical message to hundreds of thousands of listeners, Torrey and his revivals generated controversy on the issue of his dogmatism. As was the case with the other well-known evangelists, Torrey understood that popular culture offered both threats and opportunities.

The revival as spectacle survived in Dr J. Wilbur Chapman's campaigns. Chapman visited ten urban centres in Ontario, Manitoba, and British Columbia from 1907 to 1911, bringing with him a contingent of co-evangelists and workers to stage a series of simultaneous revival meetings.[13] At Chapman's final Canadian campaign in Toronto in January 1911, more than 400,000 people – and this is a conservative estimate – attended the month of meetings to hear his old-fashioned Gospel message.[14] This attendance number is particularly impressive in an age when an increasing number of theatres and other places of amusements competed for people's time and attention. Other lesser known American evangelists, modelled after Moody, also attracted large numbers of revival attenders in centres throughout English Canada. B. Fay Mills, for example, held campaigns in Montreal, Halifax, and Charlottetown in early 1894.

Of the evangelists who answered the call from Canadian Protestant leaders to bring their evangelical message to Canada, Moody, Jones, Small, Torrey, and Chapman easily garnered the most publicity. There were Canadian and a few visiting British evangelists who adopted the methods of Moody, but it was the Americans who usually stole the show, if press coverage in secular dailies and denominational publications is an accurate indication.

Kathryn Teresa Long's work on revivals in the United States clarifies the essential role played by mass-circulation dailies in the success of revivalism. Having accepted the "concept of news as a product for mass consumption," secular editors, from the mid-nineteenth century on, became "image makers" as they embraced the task of marketing revivals in the public arena. Simply put, revivalism sold papers.[15] For readers, there was voyeuristic appeal in revival meeting reports of famed evangelists, overflowing crowds, mass Gospel singing, the sharing of prayers, popular preaching, and touching confession and conversion stories which spoke to the emotional impact of revival.

In Canada, newspaper editors did "construct" American revivalism to suit their economic and moral purposes. They, like their American counterparts, were anxious to "re-moralize a civic space" experiencing the pressures of urban-industrial transformation.[16] Secular newspapers viewed a revival campaign as an attractive commodity to be sold, but they also manufactured "revival" to embody piety, power, and community. The visiting American evangelists, for example, were "instruments of God" with "marvellous power" who "stirred the community." If understood as an "orientational metaphor," revival is "up" and representative of something that is central, positive, and inspiring.[17] The newspaper language on Moody,

Jones, Torrey, and Chapman, promoting such themes, is staggering and an examination of revival rhetoric reveals much about the dynamics of revivals.[18] Without accepting the accuracy and impartiality of newspapers as canon, this study maintains that there is no better source for understanding the essential aspects of revivalism than the innumerable printed revival reports. Even if language and emotion in daily reports helped embellish meetings, manufactured revival rhetoric could not take hold and thrive in a vacuum; a strong evangelical foundation that supported sincere and genuine revival developments existed in the Canadian urban setting, and arguably there were newspaper reports that fell short in capturing the emotional and pietistic nature of revival meetings.[19]

In addition to the drawings, photographs, editorial commentary, printing of sermons and hymns, and day-to-day reporting on revivals, local newspapers often published letters to the editors from ordinary Canadians commenting on the revivalists and meetings. Because of a scarcity of competitors, the popular press had a virtual monopoly on interpreting and presenting daily news and information. As self-appointed moral guardians of society, editors believed that they accurately represented the voice of the people. Indeed, turn-of-the-century English-speaking newspapers, which overwhelmingly supported Christian goals, vied with clergy in their ability to connect with the hearts and minds of Canadians.[20]

Although Canadian denominational periodicals did not publish as much information on the revivals as newspaper dailies, they usually did offer insightful commentary on the meetings. Anglican, Baptist, Congregational, Methodist, Presbyterian, and other denominational publications were less likely to sensationalize the meetings, and their understanding of theological and church issues, even with their own prejudices, allowed them to be discriminating concerning the impact of revivalism. They were certainly cognizant of and sensitive to the spiritual force that the evangelists themselves believed was the true power behind any genuine revival regardless of the instruments and strategies used.[21] While the labour press provided no specific coverage of revival meetings, editors occasionally offered criticism concerning the popularity of the evangelists.

When revival took on the "shape of a commodity," astute evangelists became alert to competing commodities. Dwight L. Moody, for one, "was content to slug it out in the cultural marketplace with all comers." He and later evangelists were, therefore, often the ideological companions of businessmen; they understood how to achieve commercial success.[22] Indeed, Moody gave mass evangelism a dramatic rebirth – combining modern persuasion techniques of publicity, organization, and advertising with an old-fashioned Gospel message. Revival was "a matter of salesmanship" and, after Moody, became "a secular rite of the Protestant evangelical churches."[23] Other American evangelists packaged their revivalism and orthodox message with modern strategies to attract the largest numbers possible – including journalists – to the revival campaigns.

Beginning with Moody in the 1870s, professional evangelists adopted a revival format that underscored the importance of organization. Well-planned and managed, each meeting consisted of a team of at least two specialists carrying out the bulk of the duties: one preacher gave the main message, and a soloist sang Gospel hymns. A large building or church was chosen to hold the meetings, which sometimes occurred in the mornings, often in the afternoons, and always in the evenings. There were greater possibilities for growth when meetings took place in the most public of interior urban spaces. Otherwise, the alienation or isolation of religious expression in growing cities compromised outreach. Revival services were, without exception, free and attenders usually gathered in advance of the designated starting time. Journalists looking for a story followed the huge crowds that gathered at the revival site, usually located in the centre of the city. The evangelists placed a premium on media relations and, consequently, journalists received special treatment at meetings.

At their urban revival campaigns, evangelists took particular care to target the men of the community; they often held meetings for men only. It was the hope of sponsors that the revival meetings could attract males into the churches and counteract the feminization of the church community. Worrisome was the reality that fewer men than women participated in local church activities. Like Christian laymen organizations, revivalism offered a vehicle for Christian men to be involved in the growth of the church. Behind this ideal of Christian masculinity lay a profound ambivalence and even fear concerning the changing role of women. Seen as a threat to manhood, turn-of-the-century women faced restrictions in the male sphere of business and religious leadership.[24]

Evangelists' connection with prominent businessmen offered an opportunity to model an acceptable form of Christian masculinity. One strategy to "defeminize" Protestantism was to adopt the orga-

nizational and ambitious practices of "the masculine world of business."[25] In the commentary of secular and denominational
publications, the evangelists themselves embodied masculinity. For
example, Moody often preached a sentimental message but his
beard and stocky and large physique generated comments from
journalists impressed by his rugged manliness. If the evangelists
were to attract working-class men, many of them semi-literate, they
had to offer an optimistic, masculinized, and popularized brand of
evangelicalism. Although women dominated audiences at meetings
held earlier in the day, men had the upper hand in the evening
meetings.

Revival accounts suggest that, for many Canadian revival attenders, the evangelists' mixing of popular culture, expressions of piety,
and conservative evangelical sermons that attacked theological
modernism made the campaigns alluring. Only a small number of
opponents spoke disparagingly about the "Americanisms" of
revival meetings.

More is known about Canadian proponents of theological modernism than of visiting evangelists preaching conservative evangelicalism at the grass-roots level.[26] Scholars who pay some attention to
American evangelists offer conflicting perspectives. David Marshall
claims that evangelists, seeking to be successful in the "open marketplace of modern society," accommodated themselves to popular
culture in a manner that deprived Christianity of its other-worldly or
spiritual qualities.[27] Phyllis Airhart argues that Methodists became
increasingly wary of American revivalism and its conservative evangelical message, even as early as the 1880s. Though there remained
Methodists who expected that professional revivalism would help
solve the problem of evangelizing the city, a growing number of
Methodists had become suspicious of the evangelists' conservative
theology and concept of social progress.[28] A more recent study by
Nancy Christie and Michael Gauvreau, which focuses on
early-twentieth-century Protestant churches, concludes that "revivalism and social service actually were drawn into an organic relationship in which mass revivalism functioned as the instrument that
converted people to the newer tenets of social Christianity."[29]
Though this perspective confirms the vitality of revivalism at the
grass-roots level in Canada at the turn-of-the-century, a careful
examination of the press coverage of revivalism will underscore the
important role that conservative as opposed to "progressive" evan-

gelicals played in attracting American evangelists to Canada. Moreover, a more detailed examination not only of the means but also of
the revival message may indeed conclude that the popularity and
impact of American revivalists in Canada, particularly among the
working class, depended precisely on their preaching of a conservative evangelical message that maintained rather than sacrificed biblical truths. Lynne Marks and others demonstrate that the working
class embraced revival religion.[30]

The success that American evangelists had in attracting the working class was not simply the product of their commitment to an
evangelical message. They succeeded in the open marketplace of
modern society because they offered an emotional, pious, heroic,
and masculine image that workers found captivating and because
the revival meeting became a popular-culture expression of the era.
Heeding Michael Denning's reference to the "'proletarianization' of
American culture," one notes that the Canadian working class participated in and influenced American revival culture in Canadian
urban centres.[31]

Of course, one must be prudent when assessing the popular
response to revivalism and the conservative evangelical message
preached at meetings. Workers were caught up in the essential daily
tasks of employment and feeding their children. They were involved
in their jobs, families, unions, clubs, sports, and other cultural and
ethnic activities. But many of them found time to participate in
revivals or were kept abreast of the meetings through the extensive
newspaper coverage, if they read English. In addition to reli-
gious-based incentives, no doubt some people went to revival meetings out of curiosity, to be amused, to be entertained, or to be part of
something exciting. Others went as a result of social-group forces
and the desire for "social belongingness."[32] Sandra Sizer's study of
nineteenth-century revival sees prayer, testimony, and exhortation
used to create "a *community* of intense *feeling,* in which individuals
underwent similar experiences (centering on conversion) and would
thenceforth unite with others in matters of moral decision and social
behavior."[33]

No empirical data exist or can be accumulated that provide information on what motivated each individual to attend a revival. The
majority of revival converts themselves were "faceless" unknown
people "largely frozen in time," difficult to explore because few left
records of their spiritual journeys.[34] The revival experience is more

mysterious than conclusive. Still, the mass of newspaper accounts of American revivalism and insights drawn from studies on religion, rhetoric, popular culture, gender, and the mass media can support reasonable inference and informed speculation on the relationship between the Canadian working class and revivalism.

The relationship of the working class to revivals is particularly strong when one uses "working class," "working people," and "workers" interchangeably and follows a conceptualization of class in which those who sold their labour power represented the working class.[35] Even though American contemporary newspapers rarely used explicit language in describing the class character of revival attenders, American historians overwhelmingly categorize revival participants as mainly "middle class."[36] Such a consensus interpretation may be wishful thinking without precise empirical definitions and occupational data to substantiate it. The numbers who attended revivals was much too large to represent mostly merchants, professionals, managers, owners, foremen, and self-employed artisans. Even local churches unsatisfied with their working-class representation had a significant number of working-class members, which is especially impressive when one considers that many who attend regular church services do not feel the need to become official members. The point is that churches and revival meetings would be anaemic if they had only petty-bourgeoisie membership and attendance. The 1910 occupational profile of Jarvis Street Baptist Church, an established, healthy Toronto church, shows at least 50 per cent working-class membership.[37]

In Canada, much of church leadership was likely "middle class," but the bulk of the rank and file experiencing a revival meeting had to be working class.[38] Even the majority of middle-income earners attending revivals were more likely well-paid skilled workers than managers. In his recent study of Canadian Methodists, George Emery makes the important point that Canadian historians of religion "muddy the waters of [class] definition"; class analysis becomes pointless when the middle class includes almost everyone.[39] A recent American study argues that the usage of the term middle class "has become so overwhelmed with present-day concerns that it lacks sufficient analytical clarity."[40]

For the time period investigated here, there was no doubting the popularity of American revivalism among Canadian workers. Supportive press rhetoric and the masculine and popular-culture status of famous evangelists were obvious forces behind this popularity. When the accelerated pace of change tore at Canadian society, the American evangelists represented the paradoxical spirit of the era, maintaining past certitudes and adapting modern ways as they preached. Thus, in addition to popular culture, class, and gender issues, the "crisis-theoretic perspective" that defines revivalism as a reaction to change and challenge does, in part, help explain the revival experience in Canadian urban centres.[41] During the late nineteenth and early twentieth-centuries, American revivalism was a dominant element in a Canadian Protestantism buffeted by modern stresses.

Relying heavily on revival accounts by secular and church publications, this study seeks to contribute to a better understanding of the impact of revivalism and conservative evangelicalism in Canada without characterizing incidents of religious faith as nebulous and generic affairs.[42] Certainly, the interaction of revivalism and working-class experience has generated considerable debate among respected Canadian historians even if pietistic evangelicalism remains a "blind spot" for many Canadian social and labour historians.[43] The focus here is not a social history of a few specific revival campaigns and participants as offered by historians such as Lynne Marks, but rather a broader examination of many revival meetings across Canada. Although this study describes the planning and execution of American revivalism, future studies will, it is to be hoped, uncover more on the role of local organizing committees, if the necessary historical records exist. Patching together revival rhetoric, impressionistic reports, and fragments of documentary evidence relating to class, gender, and popular-culture issues, this study offers an introduction and starting point for additional inquiry into American revivalism in Canada. The major argument is that a significant number of Canadian Protestants continued to show considerable interest in a populist and conservative kind of evangelicalism until secular and other forces lessened theological and financial support for American revivalism.[44]

The full brunt of American revivalism in Canada was over before the First World War. The message resonated with the spiritual needs of ordinary working people who did not appear to fault visiting evangelists for their dearth of social understanding. But many churches may have floundered in understanding the alienation and apathy that many workers felt toward bougeois church life that lacked an alluring, welcoming, and conservative evangelical spirit found at revival meetings. Moreover, the Canadian experience was replete with unresolved tensions that existed in church leadership circles over the issue of professional evangelists. In the end, an increasing number of clergy leaders may have found the financial and theological expenditures of American revivalism, flavoured with popular culture, to be too costly to pay for and control.

CHAPTER ONE

Evangelists

The year was 1875. "The jam was terrible and the confusion inde-scribable," reported the New York *Times*. One of the headlines revealed much in few words: "FIFTY THOUSAND IN AND ABOUT THE RINK DURING THE AFTERNOON."[1] The place was the Brooklyn Rink, the event was a revival meeting, and the evangelistic team was Dwight Moody and Ira Sankey. As the *Nation* explained in its 1876 article on Moody and Sankey, the success of their work was that it was "an old-fashioned revival with the modern improvements," a backwoods camp meeting expanded and transplanted to the city.[2] Countless Americans commuted to late-nineteenth-century revival meetings, and newspaper reports captured the intensity of crowds seeking access to these gatherings. In another example, the Balti-more *American* reported one woman breaking her jaw as she jumped from a streetcar, impatient to experience a Sam Jones revival in Maryland.[3] The Chicago *Tribune* estimated that ten thousand people failed to gain admittance to one of Jones's meetings.[4] This was the beginning of a period of great revival activity, during which modern revivalism in the United States made such significant gains that the years 1875 to 1915 have been characterized as "the third great awakening."[5] Moody, Jones, and numerous other evangelists held countless revival meetings in cities, towns, and villages in all corners of the United States.

A striking element of this revivalism was its conservatism.[6] As a complex industrial-urban experience emerged with all its inequities, so did evangelists with a conservative evangelical message that rarely questioned bourgeois ideals. In the eyes of evangelicals, as Douglas Frank argues, the evils of capitalism – including starvation wages and periodic unemployment – were "side effects, not systemic and inherent in the very operation of the economy."[7] Born before 1860, when life was simpler, well-known professional evangelists believed that salvation of individuals alone was the cure of societal problems. The social message of the evangelists was lacking, yet large numbers of people nurtured in an evangelical milieu and compelled, in part, by group forces did attend the popular revival meetings. Often billed by the press as a spectacle not to be missed,[8] revival was a spiritually uplifting and sociable event experienced and valued by Americans seeking spiritual sustenance and what social psychologists refer to as "social belongingness."[9]

The first signs of modern revivalism can be found in the Second Great Awakening, which took place in the years from 1795 to 1835, an era when the predominance of Calvinism ended. One who captured the spirit of the age was lawyer-turned-evangelist Charles Grandison Finney, who had an intense conversion experience in 1821 that "was a matter of simple decision."[10] Finney wrote: "I had intellectually believed the Bible before; but never had the truth been in my mind that faith was a voluntary trust instead of an intellectual state."[11] In his book, *Lectures on Revivals of Religion*, he argued that revivals had ceased for many years because of Americans' fixation with doctrines that Jonathan Edwards and George Whitefield had preached in the eighteenth century. With the emphasis on the doctrines of grace, divine sovereignty, and election, Americans had become apathetic, "waiting for God to come and do what he required them to do."[12] As one study on conversion explains, "one no longer waited on the Spirit but instead arranged regular events at which it was hoped the spirit would move."[13] Finney also played an important role in the pioneering of revival preaching that used colloquial language spiced with theatrical illustrations taken from experiences with common people. Finney's success in the 1820s and 1830s "securely harnessed the spontaneous, ecclesiastically schismatic force of frontier revivalism to the institutionalized church system in America's rapidly expanding western towns and eastern cities."[14] It would be another forty years before an evangelist exceeded his impact on evangelicalism in America.

Dwight L. Moody was born on 5 February 1837 in the small village of Northfield, Massachusetts. At the age of seventeen, with approximately five years of schooling, he decided to seek financial opportunity in Boston. Despite efforts by reformers to have urban centres adopt the moral order of the rural village, the mid-nineteenth-century city was a harsh place for young, rural-born people such as Moody.[15] Having no success finding employment, an utterly discouraged Moody sought help from an uncle who owned a retail boot and shoe business. The uncle's conditions for employment included that Moody attend church and Sunday school and stay away from the vices a city offered to naive young people. Moody found regular attendance at Mount Vernon Congregational Church to be enjoyable, though, initially, the Bible was an unfamiliar book to him. In 1855 Edward Kimball, his Sunday school teacher, visited him at work to remind him of Christ's love. Without a second thought, Moody gave himself and his life to Christ. Although his conversion experience might be viewed as undramatic, he showed great religious zeal and immediately sought to direct his energy "in the forwarding of the Kingdom." At age nineteen, Moody moved to Chicago, where he involved himself in numerous Christian activities. He began recruiting children for Sunday school Bible classes, a venture that was so successful that he began holding classes at a public hall.[16] One admirer recounted his first meeting with a young Moody: "... the first thing I saw was a man standing ... holding a negro boy, and trying to read him the story of the Prodigal Son; and a great many of the words he could not make out and had to skip. I thought, if the Lord can ever use such an instrument as that for His honor and glory, it will astonish me."[17]

In 1860 Moody gave up a promising career in the shoe business in order to devote himself entirely to Christian work. Because of his religious zeal and fearlessness, many thought that he was unstable and some referred to him as "Crazy Moody." However, citizens who were approached by Moody on the streets of Chicago, whether they wanted to be or not, discovered that he was irresistible. A story goes that Moody approached one man and asked his famous question – "Are you a Christian?" – and the man replied that it was none of his business. When Moody said, "Yes, it is," the man countered, "Then you must be D.L. Moody," giving up the fight.[18] As one historian of revivals has asked: How could a mother refuse a man who relentlessly chased her daughter across city blocks and through saloons merely to have her attend Sunday school? And what could a father do when Moody began to pray earnestly for his welfare after having poured his best whisky down the sink? Given his track record, there appears to be much truth to the statement that "Moody's sincerity was so transparent that Pharisees as well as publicans and sinners were helpless before it."[19]

By the late 1860s, Moody had become heavily involved with the Young Men's Christian Association (YMCA). He kept to an exhausting pace, teaching Sunday school, organizing meetings, raising funds, recruiting people, and participating in Christian conventions, including three held in the British Isles during the years 1867, 1870, and 1872.

In 1871 Moody experienced great hunger in his soul, crying that he did not want to live if he could not have the power of the spirit for evangelism. After months of thirsting for spiritual power, something "almost too sacred an experience to name" happened: "I can only say that God revealed Himself to me, and I had such an experience of His love that I had to ask Him to stay His hand." Moody continued to preach the same sermons without any new truths but something was different – "hundreds were converted."[20] The following year in Great Britain, a revival gripped a north London church where Moody had consented to preach.

By 1873, he had taken up revivalism full time with intense devotion, employing hymn singer Ira David Sankey to accompany him to the British Isles for two years of revivalist meetings. Beginning in Scotland and then moving on to Irish and English cities, Moody and Sankey awakened great Christian interest within the church and community. The masses of people that Moody and Sankey attracted were phenomenal.[21] Moody's successful work in the British Isles caused his popularity to grow in North America before he set foot on American soil in 1875. American newspapers approved his desire to serve the unchurched masses in the cities. Days before his first American revival campaign, the New York *Times* reported that Moody sought to reach "those who belong to the vast field of non-attendants on worship."[22] Even in Canada, the Protestant community received reports of his progress and impact.[23] Referring to Moody's extensive and successful preaching in and outside the United States, one critic admitted that, "all in all, it is very probably [true], as his admirers claim, that he reduced the population of hell by a million souls."[24]

Moody was the best-known evangelist of the late nineteenth century, but the distinction of being the most controversial American evangelist in these years went undisputedly to Sam Jones. Jones was born on 16 October 1847 in Chambers County, Alabama. As a young man he decided to pursue law and, after a year of study, gained admittance to the bar. Married to Laura McLwain in November 1868, he spent much of his time at saloons despite her tears and prayers. Overcome with emotion at his father's deathbed in 1872, Sam promised him that he would become a Christian. He approached his grandfather, who was a Methodist minister, and declared that he would serve God. According to Sam's own testimony, he became "a reformed and changed man from that hour."[25]

Within a week of his conversion, Jones felt the conviction to preach and a successful first attempt in his grandfather's pulpit convinced him and others that he had the ability to be an effective preacher. By November 1872, approximately three months after his conversion, the North Georgia Conference of the Methodist Episcopal Church, South, had appointed him as a travelling preacher to a circuit of five churches within four counties. Demonstrating great enthusiasm, he passed the four-year probationary period that was a requirement before an applicant could be ordained.

In 1876 Jones rejoiced over his ordination, and his joy became all the greater when he realized that he had become fully ordained only two years before the Methodist Church required all candidates to complete extensive courses or to attend seminary. His antipathy and distrust of the theological colleges of the day was the position, as scholars demonstrate, favoured by many turn-of-the century conservative evangelicals and those who would later be termed "fundamentalists."[26]

Trusting exhortations from the heart rather than learned sermons, Jones revitalized the churches of his first circuit and went on to other appointed circuits. His fame grew steadily as he often assisted other clergymen in revival activity. Looking back on the 1870s, the Reverend J.W. Lee, a Methodist minister from the North Georgia Conference, stated that Jones "magnetized everybody" – whether Methodist, Baptist, or Presbyterian.[27] In 1880 Jones received greater freedom to hold revival meetings anywhere he chose providing he raised money for the Methodist Orphan Home in Decatur, Georgia. Not tied down with the responsibilities of pastoral work, he began travelling and preaching throughout the state of Georgia and, as his popularity grew, in other southern states. Successful campaigns followed, most notably his Nashville campaign of 1885, which secured his place as a nationally known evangelist; having filled a 5,000-capacity tent three times a day over four weeks, he earned his reputation as "the Moody of the South."[28]

Jones's success in the United States was impressive given that he was not always in the best of health,[29] perhaps suffering from manic depression. In addition to experiencing bouts of animated cheerfulness and oppressive pessimism, he was victim to stomach and other undisclosed ailments which occasionally prevented him from working.[30] Despite health problems, he still committed himself to begin the Toronto campaign of October 1886, joined by Sam Small, an evangelist who assisted Jones at various campaigns.

Small was born in 1851 at Knoxville, Tennessee. After college he worked as a journalist and as a court stenographer. All was not well with his family life, however, since Small had become an alcoholic trapped in the life of constant drinking and gambling. After he heard Jones preach at a revival meeting in 1884, his conscience responded to the Gospel message and, within three days, Small shouted words from a hymn: "Here, Lord, I give myself away; it is all that I can do." In gratitude for his deliverance, Small desired to acknowledge all of God's love and mercy and spread the message about how he escaped enslavement to alcohol. Upon the first day of his conversion, without a theological education, Small began to preach the Gospel.[31] Later, when Jones was seeking assistance, he turned to Small as the best choice for a co-evangelist. Retold many times on the revival platform, Small's story provided an inspiring and victorious message. For the Toronto campaign of 1886, the Toronto *World* predicted that, with the combined efforts of Jones and Small, "the Devil will be seized by both horns."[32]

Other American evangelists arrived in late-nineteenth-century Canada to hold revival meetings, but most failed to garner the same degree of attention that Moody and Jones had. B. Fay Mills, for example, held 1894 campaigns in Montreal, Halifax, and Charlottetown, but his lasting impact in Canada was modest because soon afterwards he strayed from evangelicalism, adopted liberal views, and fell out of favour as an evangelist in the United States.[33] If Mills was the least conservative of American evangelists, Reuben Archer Torrey was one of the most conservative, particularly on the matter of theology.

Torrey was born in Hoboken, New Jersey, on 28 January 1856. His well-to-do parents were Reuben Slayton and Elizabeth A. (Swift). Having a wealthy father enabled Reuben, at the age of fifteen, to enter Yale College where he took advantage of his freedom and lived a life of pleasure, including heavy drinking. As an eighteen-year-old college student, he woke in the middle of the night in a terrible state of agony and despair, seriously contemplating suicide. When he failed to follow through with this plan, he begged God for help. Because of this experience, Torrey resolved to obey God and preach even though he "did not know what it meant to accept Christ." Torrey made little immediate change in his lifestyle and, if anything, his life was wilder than before. It was over a year before he was ready to "come out as a Christian," an intellectual decision prompted by the reading of works such as John Seeley's *Ecce Homo: A Survey of the Life and Work of Christ*.[34]

After completing his degree in 1875, Torrey entered Yale Theological Seminary. At the time his own theology was anything but orthodox; he adhered to a liberal interpretation of Christianity, doubting whether Christ was the Son of God. His whole Christian foundation was crumbling away. In his final year at Yale, Dwight L. Moody arrived at the college to speak. Despite his admiration for Moody, Torrey continued to cherish the works of Theodore Parker and William Channing and he wrote his graduating thesis on transcendentalism.[35]

Though ordained a Congregationalist minister in 1878, Torrey lacked an understanding of preaching and the planning techniques required for his pastoral charge. Fortunately, he had read the biography and addresses of Charles Finney, realizing that the first step was to promote revival in his church. With much prayer, determination, and energy, he achieved success since he initiated revival not only in his church but also in the two other churches of the village. After fours years in Ohio, Torrey withdrew from his first pastorate to study at Leipzig and Erlangen under the direction of well-known German professors. Ironically, it was during his search for theological knowledge abroad that he began to question the liberal views he had acquired at Yale. As friend and biographer George Davis noted, Torrey acknowledged the falsity of his liberal views and gradually accepted the "old conservative doctrines." Although Davis did not define these old doctrines or explore what motivated Torrey to change his views, he confirmed Torrey's earnest desire to save souls.[36] Torrey departed Germany with a determination to preach the inerrancy or literal truth of the Bible rather than liberal theology.[37]

After returning to the United States, Torrey declined a position at a wealthy Brooklyn church, choosing instead a "poor" Minneapolis one. From his experiences as a pastor it became clear to him that church members trained to be winners of souls made a perpetual revival a distinct possibility. His eventual success in Minneapolis paved the road to a position as superintendent of the Moody Bible Institute (MBI) in Chicago, a position he held from 1889 to 1908. In addition to these administrative responsibilities, he also pastored at the Moody Church in the years 1894 to 1906. Before he arrived at the MBI, Torrey had already accepted the literal truth of Scripture, the premillennial belief of the end times – that the milliennium, or one thousand years of righteousness, could begin only with the physical arrival of Christ – and the full baptism of the Holy Spirit, defined when an additional religious experience followed conversion.[38]

While at the MBI, Torrey had a vision that he was to share his ministry to peoples of other nations, and he thus embarked on a world tour in 1902 that resulted in revival meetings in Japan, China, Australia, New Zealand, Tasmania, India, France, Germany, and Great Britain. J. Wilbur Chapman claimed that Torrey had "done more to establish Evangelistic Work than any man in this generation."[39] At London, for example, he filled the Royal Albert Hall for five months in 1905, a feat few, if any, could match. Accompanying him was the singer Charles Alexander, who captured the hearts of many. During the world tour, millions heard the message and an estimated 100,000 came forward to accept Christ publicly as their saviour, but Torry maintained that neither his preaching nor Alexander's singing could produce results without the outpouring of the Holy Spirit.[40] In June 1905 the Reverend Tom Hyde, a Congregationalist, and other Toronto Protestants invited Torrey and Alexander to their city.[41] Torrey returned to North America in December and began to prepare himself for the Toronto campaign to be held in January 1906.

The success of the Torrey's 1906 Canadian campaigns was due in part to Charles Alexander, who, by then, had gained the reputation of being one of the better known Gospel song leaders of the early twentieth century. Alexander was born in Meadow, Tennessee, in 1867 to poor, God-fearing parents. During his earlier years, he dreamed that someday he might organize exceptional choirs and become a skilful conductor.[42] As a young man, he attended a small college in Tennessee but left in 1887 before completing his degree to become a chorister for a Quaker evangelist named John Kittrell. When the arrangement with Kittrell ended, Alexander travelled to Chicago where he studied at the Moody Bible Institute and directed music at the Moody Church. After assisting Moody at the 1893 Chicago World's Fair, Alexander joined Milan B. Williams to form an evangelistic team that toured the midwest until Torrey asked for his assistance on an extended revival mission that, if true to God's plan, would see the saving of many souls in many countries around the world.[43]

Following his partnership with Torrey, Alexander joined the evangelistic campaigns of J. Wilbur Chapman, who later held one of the largest revival campaigns in twentieth-century Canadian history. Chapman was born on 17 June 1859, in Richmond, Indiana, to Lorinda and Alexander Chapman. At Grace Methodist Sunday School in Richmond, under the direction of his teacher, a teenaged Wilbur stood up with others to acknowledge Christ as his saviour. In 1876 he became a member of the Presbyterian Church in Richmond. Chapman began his studies Oberlin College but finished his degree at Lake Forest College north of Chicago. Dedicated to God in his infancy, brought up in a Christian home, and having made, as a teenager, a public confession of faith in Christ, Chapman was, nonetheless, unsure of his salvation. While at Lake Forest College he went to a Moody revival meeting in Chicago and this event marked a pivotal point in his life. After the meeting, Moody confronted Chapman and made it clear that if Chapman believed the words of Christ he should not doubt his salvation. From then on, Chapman "never" questioned God's acceptance of him.[44]

According to a classmate, Chapman's preaching was very evangelistic, much more so than any other student, and it came as no surprise in 1881 when Chapman, still a young student not quite twenty years old, received his licence to preach for the Presbytery of Whitewater at Shelbyville, Ohio. The following year was even more exhilarating for Chapman; he graduated from college and one week later married Irene E. Steddom.[45] In his early years, Chapman was a pastor at a number of churches, but in 1893 he took a break from the responsibilities of a pastorate and embraced revival work for three years, assisting Dwight L. Moody and B. Fay Mills in addition to conducting his own meetings, some with the help of an assistant by the name of Billy Sunday. During these years, he visited mostly moderate-sized cities including Montreal.[46] In 1895 Chapman became the corresponding secretary of the Presbyterian General Assembly's Committee on Evangelism and directed the activities of numerous evangelists throughout the United States. Ten years later,

Chapman again became a full-time evangelist when a wealthy Presbyterian layman offered to pay his expenses. In the early twentieth
century, Chapman developed and promoted a new method of urban
evangelism that divided a city into many districts, each with an evangelistic team for holding meetings.[47] While Moody, Jones, and
Torrey usually went into the central district of a city and rented a
large hall for meetings, Chapman preferred to hold simultaneous
meetings in churches throughout the city. Late-nineteenth-century
evangelist B. Fay Mills had likewise divided the city into sections,
but his meetings did not operate simultaneously. Chapman's innovative approach captured the attention of a number of Canadian
evangelicals seeking to reach the unsaved in the growing Canadian
cities.

The population and industrial growth of major American cities
easily outdistanced similar development in Canadian urban centres.
From the Civil War to 1914, the United States underwent a process
of profound change in which industrialism influenced almost all
activities of the American people. Increasing immigration, rapidly
growing cities, new forms of transportation and communication,
and the growth of industry caused a fundamental alteration in
American social and cultural life. To the dismay of some reformers,
this era saw increasing production and profit become the measures
of community success as intense, nationwide competition, replete
with capitalist exploitation, gained dominance over the relatively
stable, local business affairs of the past.[48] In the United States, bourgeois society "burst more powerfully onto the scene than anywhere
else."[49]

Americans were individualistic and market-driven and, in comparison of urban-industrial experiences, an enduring perception is
that conflict was far more common in the United States than in Canada. A leading Presbyterian journal wrote in 1894: "There are times
when the American eagle sits very quietly in a remote corner of the
aviary and refuses to indulge in his tendency to scream. It is when on
the one side of his cage he sees city mobs and factory lock-outs and
miners' riots and industrial armies; and on the other side he notes the
quiet and content of his Canadian neighbors." The journal asked:
"Are our friends north of the great lakes made of other flesh and
blood than we? Are they, speaking different tongues and bred in
opposite faiths more homogeneous?" The future for Canada was
positive: "It will be a day long in the future before any one will hear

of discontented masses seizing a train of the Canadian Pacific."[50] Concerned that "we suffer immigrant, tramp and desperado to go his own gait," the journal saw only signs of "anarchy" in the United States and peacefulness in Canada.[51] Other spokesmen of the urban elite feared that class warfare was imminent and, to protect law-abiding citizens against domestic insurrection, most American cities had built massive armories by 1890.[52] Of course, Canada did have class conflict and thus the image of a "Peaceable Kingdom" representing "Peace, Order, and Good Government" failed to represent reality.[53] Still, turbulent events in the United States do stand out as labour struggled for control of the workplace; it was during these years that American evangelists gained much popularity.

In the midst of the frustrations and upheavals taking place in American cities, Moody, Jones, Small, Torrey, and Chapman offered an old-fashioned Gospel message harkening back to simpler days.[54] In addition to the soul-winning component of revivalism that many people supported, the evangelists promulgated conservative theology and opposed the historical criticism that questioned the authorship and authenticity of the Bible. Moody's refusal to read books that could not help him understand the Bible was anti-intellectual but not irrational or emotional; his religious faith depended on "his rational comprehension of the biblical text rather than subjective apprehension of the divine."[55] On the matter of science, the evangelists claimed that evolutionary science was incompatible with the word of God. For issues relating to urban-industrial life, the evangelists eschewed social-reform ideas even in the face of growing support for progressivism among journalists. The excess of greed in society troubled these evangelists, but they did not directly challenge the enduring American "success myth" which held that a "decent" Christian who worked hard could achieve success. Included with the evangelists' focus on the sin of society and the saving truth of the Gospel was the American doctrine of self-reliant individualism.

While revivals remained popular and widespread in American rural towns, new methods and techniques were essential if revivalism was to succeed in the larger urban centres. The revival message of the evangelists remained orthodox but the methodology was modern, for successful evangelists understood the importance of making conservative evangelicalism more accommodating to modern popular culture.[56] For meetings in his home city of Chicago, Moody used mobile circus-like tents, theatre-like tickets, and the latest in consumer advertising. Evangelists could adapt the forms and technologies of popular culture without accepting its secular substance – a strategy successfully employed by twentieth-century fundamentalists.[57] They could be hostile to or sceptical of scientific theory but accept the comforts of technological advances without compunction. The evangelists gave mass evangelism a dramatic rebirth in the United States by combining modern technology, persuasion techniques, organization, and advertising with an evangelical orthodox message.

The possibility of reaching many in the city improved when evangelists commanded the language of popular culture and spoke the "commoner's tongue." Presenting an exciting Gospel message in a manner their listeners could understand, evangelists not only transferred the enthusiasm of small-town revivalism to the metropolis but furnished the urbanite – a villager at heart – a degree of the missing poetry of ritual. The revival meeting became an institution and refuge for those who needed reassurance that God was attentive to their hard work and personal obedience and, most important, cared for their souls.[58] The irony was that only through modern methods and merchandising could the revival and its conservative evangelical message succeed in the cities.

Moody's own experience in the competitive retail world of the shoe business provided lessons on how to reach the masses in the cities. Placed on a solid organizational basis, the operation of a revival meeting itself shared common ground with the running of a business. Starting precisely at the appointed time, Moody's meetings demonstrated careful attention to promptness and efficiency.[59]

Because American evangelists conducted their meetings by business principles and promoted a message that the Gospel of Christ could solve the problems of the city, they received the sanction and much needed financial support of the bourgeoisie in the American cities they visited.[60] Such assistance was essential since modern revival campaigns were costly ventures far beyond the annual operating budget of local churches. For example, the cost of Moody's Philadelphia revival from 21 November 1875 to 16 January 1876, without including donated services and materials, amounted to approximately $30,000. Having to operate within the vicissitudes of business cycles and donors' whims, evangelists understood the "ongoing difficulty of serving God and needing mammon."[61] A number of capitalists who had connections with Protestant organizations like the YMCA promoted Moody's meetings in the United States. Wealthy individuals who had close ties with evangelical Christianity and who assisted Moody included Cyrus H. McCormick, banker Jay Cooke, J.P. Morgan, John Wanamaker, a Philadelphia millionaire and department store owner, William E. Dodge, a prominent manufacturer, business magnate Cornelius Vanderbilt, Jr, John V. Farwell, a leading Chicago businessman, and hotelier Potter Palmer, owner of the famed Palmer House Hotel in Chicago.[62] Even Sam Jones, who did not have as many connections with nationally known businessmen, had his fair share of sponsors from business circles. His experiences as a lawyer prepared him to move among business and civic leaders with ease, and Jones, more so than most evangelists, enthusiastically embraced business culture and experienced no embarrassment over the acquisition of wealth.[63] After the success of his first large-scale revival at Memphis, Tennessee, in 1884, Jones's meetings in subsequent years throughout the United States witnessed endorsement by local businessmen, including a few high-profile individuals such as John W. Thomas, Jr, owner of the Western and Atlantic Railroad, tobacco magnate General Julian Shakespeare Carr, and wealthy horse-farm owner General W.H. Jackson.[64]

A number of well-to-do-laymen also threw their support behind Torrey and Alexander. Those who promoted Torrey included John Wanamaker, John H. Converse, president of the Baldwin Locomotive Works, and Henry P. Crowell, president of Quaker Oats. At the campaigns, prominent business leaders played a large role and usually shouldered the costs of the meetings. In the case of Torrey's Nashville campaign of 1907, the laymen's committee took a far greater role in the organization and direction of the campaign than even the local clergymen.[65] Chapman's simultaneous campaigns also had noted laymen involved, such as Converse and Wanamaker, and the finance committee of the campaign was usually under the control of a successful businessman. Since evangelists required the backing of a city's wealthy elite, they became so "bound to the business culture, they could not question it."[66] At least they did not question it directly, even as they came to the realization that there were rifts between religion and business.[67]

All the evangelists had the overwhelming support of most Protestant clergy in all American cities visited. Moody received backing from most Protestant circles, with only Unitarians and Universalists remaining aloof. In the south, Jones had the support of Methodists, Baptists, Presbyterians, and Disciples, who together represented almost 90 per cent of the church-attending population. Over the years Jones accumulated a large sum of money from lectures, but clergymen in the United States who invited Jones to conduct revivals in their cities did not resent this fact. The Gilded Age favoured the notion that one's value corresponded to one's financial success; the clergy saw Jones's fiscal gains as evidence of his importance.[68] Symbolizing the growing division within American Protestantism in the early twentieth century, the confrontational Torrey experienced attacks by liberal Protestants but had support from editors of more conservative religious journals.[69] Chapman and his simultaneous campaigns rarely received damaging criticism in the United States.[70] At his Philadelphia campaign of 1908, the favour of clergymen was evidently widespread since almost all denominations participated, including Quakers, Lutherans, Episcopalians, Moravians, and Mennonites. Protestant clergy elsewhere cooperated with Chapman, believing that the simultaneous meetings were an effective method in reaching the urban masses.[71]

Attendance totals of the major revival campaigns in the United States were striking and estimates for Moody's meetings in the late 1870s in New York (1,500,000) and Philadelphia (1,050,000) enhanced his reputation. The number of conversions was especially encouraging for those seeking to have evangelists visit their cities. The estimates for conversions at Moody's meetings always varied but even the lower estimates can be viewed as promising: Brooklyn (four weeks), 1,000–2,000; Philadelphia (ten weeks), 3,500–12,000; New York (ten weeks), 3,500–8,000; and Chicago (sixteen weeks), 2,500–10,000.[72] For Jones's one-month revival at Nashville in 1885, some claimed that 10,000 conversions occurred,[73] and at the 1886 Chicago campaign, which had an estimated 260,000 for attendance, one report stated that Jones's career total was "not less than 50,000" conversions. Jones even claimed that, in the twelve-month period before his Toronto campaign, he had added 70,000 to the membership rolls of the Methodist Episcopal Church. These claims appear to have been accepted by most Protestants despite lack of verification. Other conversion figures offered by Jones for campaigns included: Memphis (1884), 1,000; Cincinnati (1885), 2,000; San Francisco (1889), 1,200; Memphis (1893), 2500; and Boston (1897), 2500.[74]

The results of the Torrey-Alexander campaigns in the British Isles, in the 1903–05 period, indicate that the number of conversions in most cities reportedly surpassed those of Moody. Torrey's meetings in many American cities also attracted large numbers and the 1906 Philadelphia campaign, which occurred between the Toronto and Ottawa meetings, resulted in 7,000 converts.[75] Chapman's six-week long campaign at Philadelphia in 1908 lured 35,000 people nightly, 1,470,000 in total, and resulted in 8,000 conversions through the combined efforts of Chapman and his twenty-one pairs of co-evangelists. At the Boston campaign of 1909, over 700,000 attended, of whom almost 7,000 pledged themselves to Christ.[76]

The accuracy of conversion and attendance statistics for the evangelists are unverifiable, but an important point is that the majority of Protestants knew that thousands gathered at every meeting and conversions did occur, as press reports confirmed. As for unchurched workingmen, there was the belief that churches had little interest in workers and failed to present "enough plain gospel truth." Commenting on Jones's 1886 Chicago revival and the working class, the Chicago *Tribune* wrote: "[Jones and company] have drawn many hundreds of people who never go to church and who cannot be induced to listen to the regular preachers, partly because they do not feel at home in our wealthy churches, and partly because the ministers preach clear over their heads."[77] Six years later, the Reverend Charles Goss of Chicago asked: "Have the working classes fallen away from the churches or have the churches fallen away from the working classes?"[78] Evangelists competed to reach workingmen, but the follow up after a revival campaign was the domain of local clergy who rarely had close connections with the working poor.

Moody, Jones, Small, Torrey, and Chapman were born before the Civil War and consequently they had observed the considerable socio-economic transformation that had taken place in the United States. Their response to the complexities of modern life was the doctrine of self-reliant individualism. The evangelists disparaged collective efforts at reform: "Since all sin was personal, all reform must be personal. Regeneration, not legislation, changed the human heart, and until that was changed all else was useless."[79] Revivalism and conservatism appeared to have become synonymous. Those who wanted American-style revival meetings in their cities would also receive a strong dose of theological and social conservatism that preserved Protestant orthodoxy, American individualism, and free-enterprise capitalism. There were Americans concerned with the excesses of capitalism, but, initially at least, evangelists escaped damaging criticism for their limited understanding of urban-industrial life because in newspapers the term "revival" became a powerfully laden symbol both for the growth of God's kingdom and for urban improvement. The evangelists' adaptation of popular culture also proved to be beneficial. Canada beckoned.

CHAPTER TWO

Endorsement

In the 11 December 1884 issue of *The Week: A Canadian Journal of Politics, Society, and Literature*, a report on Dwight L. Moody stated that "he is offensively American – by which we mean that he is characterized by many offensive Americanisms in speech, style, and system. But, when all exceptions have been taken, he still remains a remarkable and perhaps even a great man." The *Week* believed Moody to be "too dogmatic, too literal, and too emotional" and a poor model for Canadian preachers but found it difficult to dismiss his charisma, which attracted masses of Canadians during the late nineteenth century.[1] Though there were some Canadians who found Moody unappealing, what is striking is how rarely his American brand of revivalism and conservative evangelicalism received criticism.

In the early 1870s, Canada had a total population of approximately 3,700,000, of which one third were francophones and roughly 60 per cent of British descent. Before the arrival of Moody, only the Maritimes, Ontario, and some centres in Quebec had well-established Protestant churches. The Baptists were particularly strong in New Brunswick, the Presbyterians in Prince Edward Island and Nova Scotia, and the Methodists in Ontario, with the Presbyterians and Anglicans close behind.[2] With the exception of the Winnipeg area, the prairie region remained the domain of aboriginal and Metis peoples, with a small number of fur trappers and missionaries located throughout. Isolated from the rest of Canada because of the Rocky Mountains and no transcontinental railway, British Columbia had fewer than 40,000 people in 1871.

Given the lack of large urban centres and underdeveloped communication and transportation, the visits of American evangelists before

Moody were mainly small affairs carried out by relatively unknown preachers.[3] In the United States, significant technological improvements to the urban daily newspaper came in the two decades after the Civil War, changes that opened the way for improved revival reports that reached a greater number of readers than ever before.[4] However, until Moody's arrival in the 1880s, the impact of American revivalism on Canada as a nation remained relatively insignificant. Canadian churches continued to develop "in some measure in the context of the intellectual evolution of British culture."[5]

With Moody's arrival on the scene, this began to change. Analogous to Kathryn Teresa Long's findings for revivals in American cities, journalistic reports in Canadian cities increasingly directed public attention to revival meetings, transforming them into full-fledged media events.[6] This was clearly the case with revival reports on Moody, who attracted large crowds, many of whom represented the working class. The press "image makers" were at work in every city Moody visited. His first Canadian revival campaign was in 1884 in Toronto, the second largest city in Canada with a population close to 100,000. Having established its prominence in marketing, manufacturing, and banking, Toronto's metropolitan economic status was second only to that of Montreal. Toronto welcomed Moody with open arms, one press report estimating that the three days of Toronto meetings in December 1884 attracted 45,000 people, with 15,000, or approximately one-sixth of Toronto's population, in attendance each day.[7] The reports in other leading newspapers told of the immense crowds and abundant confusion as people attempted to gain admission, many without success. The Toronto *Evening News* described a desperate but typical scene before a Moody meeting: "The gates were firmly secured by chains, and pickets were posted in every corner in the vain attempt to keep the immense throng from gaining admission to the grounds." However, "there were nevertheless those whose impatience led them to scale the high iron fence with the thought that once within the grounds entrance to the church was comparatively easy." But the risky climb, which left some with sore muscles the following day, was in vain "for every door was locked." Frustrated, they had no choice but give up and try again the following day.[8]

As in Toronto, Montreal Protestants gathered in large crowds to hear Moody at his January 1886 meetings.[9] Montreal had a population of about 200,000 people – the majority of them Roman Catholic and French speaking. Several months before Moody's arrival, the city had fallen victim to a smallpox epidemic that claimed the lives of at least 2,500 men, women, and children.[10] Church activity became paralysed with the cancellation of missionary meetings, church conventions, and prayer meetings. In a time of tears and enduring grief, people cried out to God in anguish. Seeking spiritual and emotional uplift weeks later, the Montreal Protestant community sought to unite in mass evangelical meetings.[11] In a city where the largest Protestant denomination was the Anglican Church, there was hesitation by some ministers to support a four-day revival campaign by Moody and Sankey.[12] But other evangelicals wanted to experience American revivalism. Despite the harsh winter days and poor condition of the city streets, many shivering people made their way carefully across ice and snow to the old St James Street Methodist Church – the largest available building – which unfortunately was too small for the numbers who gathered. The meetings were virtually suffocating, with people shoulder to shoulder straining to hear and experience every word.[13]

The American revivalism of Moody was a hit and the Protestant Ministerial Association invited Moody to return to the city the following year for a campaign throughout much of the month of October. The choice of a venue was superior to the 1886 meetings since a large skating rink, with a sawdust-covered floor and 5,000 seats, was ready for Moody's services. The Crystal Rink was large, yet not everyone could gain access and during evening sessions it was usual for as many to be turned away as those who gained admittance. Those who controlled the crowds could only apologize to the revival seekers who came too late. The Montreal *Daily Star* estimated that as many as 7,000 crowded into the rink, with no standing room left.[14] In addition to Crystal Rink, the Crescent Street Presbyterian Church, Knox Church, St James Street Methodist Church, and Methodist Theological College Hall were sites for meetings.

In 1888 Moody travelled to British Columbia, where masses of working people gathered to hear him and his helper G.T. Studd in Victoria, Vancouver, and New Westminster. Comprising about 15,000 people, Victoria welcomed Moody and his two-week campaign. Meetings were held at Victoria's Roller Skating Rink, where as many as 2,000 gathered, and at the Pandora Street Methodist Church and First Presbyterian Church. The campaign appeared to have a significant impact on the community, for meetings continued at the Victoria

Theatre and the Methodist church after Moody's departure from the island to Vancouver.[15]

Vancouver, with a population less than 13,000, was smaller than Victoria, but massive crowds gathered at the Methodist Tabernacle and the First Presbyterian Church for a week of Moody meetings. At the Methodist Tabernacle especially, there were impressive numbers who filled the "inquiry room" seeking spiritual salvation.[16] Even after he had left Vancouver to hold successful meetings at New Westminster, a small community of less than 7,000, "the revival wave" was being carried on by Moody's workers in Vancouver.[17] British Columbia newspapers judged that Moody's revivals were phenomenal, transforming affairs.

Into the 1890s, the popularity of Moody in Canada grew. In January 1890, acting upon the invitation from the Evangelical Alliance, the YMCA, and the London Ministerial Association, Moody held as many as four services a day over six days at the Grand Opera House and other sites in London, Ontario, a city of 30,000. Journalists might have been first puzzled over the impact of Moody, but they did acknowledge that he poured "the red hot shot of simple gospel truth into enemy's line."[18] The choice of militaristic and masculine rhetoric was fitting for a brand of revivalism and conservative evangelical message that captivated thousands of London working people. Typical of his experiences in Canada, the venues often were not spacious enough to accommodate everyone who sought admission.[19] After Moody departed, Canadian Methodist evangelists Hugh Crossley and John Hunter, who embraced popular-culture strategies, continued meetings that more or less followed the model of American revivalism.[20]

Moody's next major revival campaign occurred in November 1894 at Toronto, which had almost doubled in population since the early 1880s. The members of the executive committee of the Toronto campaign, who brought Moody and his assistant, the Reverend T.W. Swan, from Pennsylvania to the city, were six eminent clergymen and three high-profile lay leaders. The main meetings of the three-week campaign were at the recently built Massey Hall and Metropolitan Methodist Church.

To begin the mission, Moody held, in the words of one Toronto newspaper, "two monster meetings" which had a combined attendance of 12,000 people, although more than 15,000 had to be turned away at the afternoon meeting. Various clergymen pleaded for him to conduct services in their church, but he declined because he desired to remain in the neutral confines of Massey Hall.[21] Revival mania struck. According to the Toronto *Evening News*, for example, two hundred women shivered in the bitter cold for over an hour hoping to be allowed entrance into a men's meeting.[22] The most impressive feature of the meetings was that large numbers of Torontonians and area residents continued to attend the meetings, day after day, showing no signs of losing interest in the campaign.

Moody also visited nearby Hamilton, a city of about 50,000 people, where approximately 4,000 working people gathered for the first day of "two Great Moody Meetings" at Central Presbyterian Church in November 1894. Two meetings the following day also attracted immense audiences which listened carefully to his evangelical message.[23] Before returning to the United States, Moody visited Montreal, where he conducted one meeting at St James Street Methodist Church before a massive audience.[24]

Three years later, in 1897, Moody and his musical assistant, J.H. Burke, returned to Canada to hold meetings in nine urban centres. His first stop was at Montreal, with a population by then of 267,000, where he held three days of meetings at St James Street Methodist Church and American Presbyterian Church. The interest among Methodists and Presbyterians in Moody showed no signs of diminishing and the revival sites swelled to their greatest capacity.[25] Sponsored by the Ottawa Ministerial Association, he also held three further days of meetings in the capital city at the Rideau Rink, Dominion Methodist Church, Knox Church, and the YMCA. Almost all of the local clergymen came to hear Moody, along with as many as 7,000 people who crowded into the rink.[26] Reflecting on his star status, one press report disclosed that a man hitched up his horses and drove twenty miles, a half-day's journey, just to meet the man whose sermons he had been reading for two decades.[27] People of all walks of life – "one of the most representative gatherings the city has ever seen" – gathered at the rink.[28] In addition to the large number of skilled and unskilled workers, there were a number of merchants and managers.

Moody left Ottawa and travelled to Kingston, a city of just less than 20,000 in population, where he held two days of meetings at Sydenham Street Methodist Church and Kingston penitentiary. Like other working-class Canadians, Kingston workers responded with enthusiasm to his brand of evangelicalism; more than 1,000 people failed to gain access to a meeting, testimony to the influence of popu-

lar American revivalism even in centres known for their British-
ness.[29] Equally, if not more, striking was the response to his four
meetings at his next stop, Peterborough, a city half the size of
. Kingston. One meeting at George Street Methodist Church, according to one report, was "something unparalleled in the history of
Peterborough religious services"; fully 2,000 were present as "every
inch of standing room was utilized." When it was known that "the
great evangelist" was to arrive in the city, people suspended previous
commitments, made other arrangements, and came from Lindsay,
Omemee, Lakefield, Millbrook, Hastings, Norwood, and the far
backcountry. The rhetoric in press reports created an image of cohe-
siveness and common identity for participants arriving from all
points of the region. At St Paul's Presbyterian Church, "multitudes"
also attended both the women's meeting in the afternoon and the
men's meeting in the evening.[30]

As his 1897 Canadian revival tour shifted west of Toronto,
Moody and his musical assistant J.H. Burke also left their mark on
Brantford, another small city of about 16,000 people. Moody was
struck with the reception he received, stating that, in his thirty years
of evangelism, the Brantford audience was the largest he had ever
seen anywhere for a city of its size. On its front page, the Brantford
Courier declared that "magnificent is the only word which will fit-
tingly describe the audience which assembled last evening in the
Drill Hall to welcome the famous evangelist, Dwight L. Moody."
Long before the first Friday evening meeting commenced, people
began to gather and soon there was a steady stream of humanity
surging to quickly fill the 2,800 chairs placed in the hall. A large
number of people either stood or used the window ledges but at least
they had not been denied access, unlike many others.[31] At two
Sunday meetings, more than 6,000 gathered to see Moody and
approximately 1,500 people woke up in the early hours and came to
hear his final message at a special meeting in the morning before his
departure from Brantford.[32]

After Brantford, Moody travelled to Hamilton, where huge numbers
gathered at Association Hall to hear him,[33] and then to Toronto, where
"there was a wild rush, as the people poured in pell mell in their excitement to get seats."[34] A newspaper acknowledged that his "marvellous
power" in 1897 was as strong as it had been at his last Toronto campaign. His two meetings attracted more than 10,000 people eager to
listen to "the vital question of the welfare of the soul."[35]

Departing central Canada, Moody and Burke journeyed to the west for five days of meetings in Winnipeg and two days at Brandon. The once remote southern Manitoba region was establishing itself as a prosperous gateway to the prairies and by 1901 Winnipeg would have a population of approximately 42,000 and Brandon just over 5,000. When Moody arrived in Winnipeg by train, the large crowd welcomed him and many dashed forward to grasp the hand of the famous evangelist.[36] The revival rhetoric in Winnipeg was no less effective than that in other Canadian centres in reinforcing the image that revival represented an uplifting and pivotal event. Organizers wisely chose Brydon Rink for the main meetings and made sure that the doors were open early to meet the expected masses of revival attenders. According to press reports, with as many as 3,500 people crowding into the rink, the local leaders pondered on how to handle the large crowds until someone suggested the cutting of another doorway. Professors of theological colleges, city clergymen, and ministers throughout the region lent their support with their attendance. Pulford Drug Store symbolized community support by closing early in the evening in order for its workers to attend the revival.[37] Describing one meeting, the *Manitoba Free Press* wrote: "Never before in the history of Winnipeg was so large a gathering for religious worship seen at so early an hour as 9:30 o'clock in the morning."[38]

After an extremely successful week in Winnipeg, Moody and Burke held a two-day campaign at Brandon, a city that also benefited by having all of the meetings take place at the largest building – a skating rink. Aware of Moody's power, directors of the YMCA worked hard to supply the rink with 1,000 chairs and numerous benches in the remaining space. An estimated 1,500 came to the afternoon meetings and up to 3,000 for an evening service.[39] His last Canadian campaign was a one-week engagement in Montreal in January 1898. At least three times a day, he preached to the large numbers gathered at St James Street Methodist Church and American Presbyterian Church. As had been the case in all his meetings throughout Canada, the press provided full and positive coverage of his popularity.[40] Across Canada, newspaper versions of the revival meetings expressed the themes of piety, power, and community.

Moody was an innovator and a trademark of his revival meetings in Canada was the high degree of planning and organization well in advance of the opening meeting; he understood that religious success in a consumer culture depended on business-like efficiency.[41] Certainly, his Canadian sponsors found the carefully organized meetings appealing. With popular-culture flair, he missed few details, as was the case at the 1884 Toronto meetings, where a ticket committee not only "struck off" an initial supply of 28,000 free tickets but issued blue tickets for the mornings, red for the afternoons, and white for the evenings, as well as square, oblong, and round tickets for each of the three days.

To secure seats for male workers in the evening meetings, white tickets went to men only. Moody sought to reach men first and recent studies link him to manliness and "Muscular Christianity."[42] In the United States, "the concept of manliness was suffering strain in all its dimensions" as the quest for authentic manhood became more difficult and uncertain in a modern urban world that, unlike the society of the past, allowed fewer opportunities for individualism, competition, and ambition. More disconcerting to religious leaders, as Margaret Lamberts Bendroth notes, was the declining presence of males in church activities, to the point that there was a female majority on many evangelical fronts.[43] Revival meetings, therefore, witnessed efforts to "defeminize" Protestantism, with Moody and his Canadian sponsors taking special care to attract male workers in order to address the shortage of men involved in church life. Canadian denominational publications agreed that reserving the evenings for men prevented women from totally monopolizing the services; in their view, reaching a greater number of males was imperative. Moody realized that women complained at being excluded from some of the evening meetings, but he stated that "if we want to reach their husbands we will have to have them here. We have to have a working chance at our unconverted friends."[44]

Moody, however, also clearly understood the advantage of having women attend meetings. As Ann Douglas argues, the nineteenth-century minister regarded the female "influence" as a "prime channel of communication" to reach, with a Christian message, the fathers, husbands, sons, and brothers who controlled society.[45] American evangelists upheld the gender ideology that the home was a private and feminine domain and that the public male sphere was no place for women, but Moody knew that when he had the attention of the wives and mothers, he had the whole community as his audience.

Planned in advance, most meetings had an assigned location, starting time, opening speaker, and sermon topic. Aware of Moody's American track record, Canadian revival organizers showed enthusiasm in assisting in the preparation and running of the revivals. Once he arrived and took charge, each separate meeting usually followed the proven successful formula of choir and solo singing, prayer, reading of Scripture, more music and prayer, finally a sermon by Moody, and concluding prayer. In most cases, an inquiry meeting that further explained the steps of salvation took place at the front of the revival venue or in a private room for those listeners who responded to his appeal to accept Christ as their saviour.

Appraising the popular-culture aspect of church music, scholars demonstrate that the singing of Gospel songs, with simple and comforting lyrics void of theological complications, captured hearts in ways that sermons could not. Such music attracted many "common people" to the meetings and was a vital component of American-style revivalism.[46] Reporting on Moody's 1884 Toronto campaign, the *Canadian Methodist Magazine* wrote that the collective effort of "the grand congregational singing was a potent attraction and an inspiring influence. The melodies were simple and easily caught and the effect of the three or four thousand voices was sublime."[47] At the meetings there was also an organist present and Moody's musical associate. In Montreal in 1886 this was Ira Sankey but for other campaigns J.H. Burke was often Moody's musical specialist. There were songs sung by a soloist, by the choir, and by the audience. Each contributed to the success of the revival, and audience participation in the singing was especially important since it helped create an atmosphere of community solidarity.

After the singing of hymns and prayer, Moody came forward to preach; some of his favourite sermons used often in Canada were on faith, assurance, the new birth, grace, reaping and sowing, Daniel, and how to study the Bible. Though they were distinct from each other, they all voiced the simple plea for individuals to relinquish their sinful ways and seek salvation through Christ. As one early biographer wrote: "He had but one question, which he plied life with in a thousand forms: Are you a Christian? All other questions were unnecessary."[48]

At the conclusion of his sermon, Moody called for people in the audience to accept Christ. At one of his first Canadian meetings, Moody was at the front, on his knees, urging the mostly young audience to "stand boldly up" for salvation. His words to those who came forward were emotional and effective, asking them to repeat some well-known prayers from the Bible concerning God's mercy

and direction for sinners. Canadian assistants who volunteered at
the various city campaigns spoke to each individual. The converts
then gave their home address and stated the church they preferred to
attend and only when all were spoken to and prayed for did Moody
exit the building.[49] Respecting his wishes, organizers discouraged
church members from attending more than one meeting; they were,
instead, to recruit and "bring in the unsaved."[50]

For many working-class Protestants seeking simple and direct
preaching, Moody's conservative evangelical message was appealing.
If he could be said to have a "theology," it was evangelical in a broad
sense of the word: "Ruin by sin, Redemption by Christ, and Regeneration by the Holy Spirit." As explained by one Canadian evangelical
Anglican in 1884, Moody's message "was nothing but the old, old,
story ... told with a directness, simplicity and pathos which went
straight to the heart."[51] Adopting powerful rhetoric, the Montreal
Daily Star declared: "No wonder that the enquiry rooms were filled.
The awful truth, the awful earnestness, the awful simplicity of his
words were irresistible."[52]

The simplicity of Moody's sermons was not surprising considering
his attitude towards higher education and modern thought. At his
first Canadian revival campaign, he stated that if he had the choice
he would rather have O&O – "out and out Christian" – after his
name rather than DD or LLD.[53] Since he had no theological schooling
and was not bound to any particular denominational doctrine, it
seemed that the only thing that was certain about his doctrinal position was that he believed in the unchanging truth of Scripture.
Speaking to a Toronto audience about his belief that an immutable
Holy Word was to endure forever, Moody declared in 1894: "I see
every once in a while in the paper somebody attacks my theology.
They say I belong to the last century, that my theology is 100 years
old. If it were not nearly 1,900 years old I would throw it into the
fire and burn it up." Speaking against liberal Protestantism, which
held ground in only a few circles in the late nineteenth century and
had yet to acquire a strong voice, he stated, "I want to say right here
that I have no new Gospel or new theology and have yet to find a
man who has accomplished much that has."[54] In his eyes, an evangelical orthodox message was timeless, never out of date. Moody
appeared to be so driven to save souls that he rarely reflected on
social, intellectual, and scientific questions and he did not possess
the intellectual flexibility to concede that perhaps science sometimes

offered a more accurate interpretation of the world than his interpretation of the Bible. By his logic, portions of the Bible that he
could not understand were proof of its divine origin.

Kathleen Boone's work on the discourse of fundamentalists and
their support of biblical inerrancy and dismissal of secular con-
structs indicates that anti-intellectual attitudes were not necessarily
irrational. Rejecting subjectivism and relativism, Moody embraced
a rational comprehension of the Bible that upheld the "determi-
nacy" of meaning in biblical text.[55] Determined by God, biblical
meaning did not change, an understanding upheld by Moody and
his followers, including Torrey and Chapman.

In Canada, the response to biblical criticism was slow among
Methodists and Presbyterians, though by the early 1890s each
denomination had seen one heresy trial take place on the issue of the
divine inspiration of the Bible.[56] Moody often made his conservative
evangelicalism clear, telling his Canadian audiences to accept every
portion of the Bible and criticizing ministers who used the new critical methods to study it. At a meeting in British Columbia, he
declared that the Bible was true from Genesis to Revelation and
those who disbelieved any part of the text were infidels.[57] In
Peterborough and Kingston, Moody warned that tampering with
the Bible was the work of the devil.[58] As he told a Winnipeg audience, a Christianity not based on a literal interpretation of the Bible
had little chance to convict people of their sins. If people rejected the
Old Testament, before long they might reject Christ's resurrection.[59]

In connection with his literal interpretation of the Bible, Moody
occasionally spoke on the issue of hell and on this topic there was no
mistaking his conservatism. At a Victoria revival meeting in 1888, he
lamented that "ministers of to-day are afraid of offending cultured
people; never give the naked Gospel, never mention Hell. They are
not like vulgar common people, they want a different Gospel."[60]
Every individual "must either give up his sin and go to heaven, or hold
on to them and go to hell." Moody stressed that all faced the wrath
and the law of God and the three steps to hell for everyone were "'ne-
glect,' 'refuse' and 'despise.'"[61] Even respectable, church-attending
people could miss the door to heaven; having wealth had no direct
bearing on one's eternal fate. To an audience in Montreal, he declared
that a great many were going to hell, including church members,
because of their failure to relinquish the hypocrisy and sin in their
lives.[62] Moody had little patience for ministers who insisted on soften-

ing the message of the Bible: "If you have one who tones down God's message, and is oily-tongued, he is a devil-sent minister. He will cheat you out of heaven if you do not look out."[63] As one scholar notes, "if the power of any discourse derives in some measure from the quantity and quality of fear it can instill in its subjects, fundamentalism is supremely powerful in its doctrine of the everlasting, conscious torment suffered by the unsaved in the literal fires of hell."[64] The proto-fundamentalist Moody found it impossible to accept that God was too merciful to condemn murderers and other perpetrators of evil acts. For Moody, such reasoning suggested that God had drowned in the flood all the wicked world and took them to heaven, leaving a faithful Noah to wade through the destruction.[65] On a point of difference between Canadian and American evangelists, Hugh Crossley and John Hunter, the best-known Canadian evangelists of the turn-of-the-century period, rarely voiced the "fire and brimstone" messages that were common in American evangelist circles.[66]

Moody saw the world as wicked, but he had little interest in social matters outside the experiences of family life. He especially showed sensitivity to the plight of women, often referring to mothers, wives, daughters, and downtrodden women. His sympathetic attitude corresponded with his concern for the spiritual welfare of women: "Mothers, wives, daughters, if you are in trouble, if you are weary of the cares, the troubles, the shams of life turn to Jesus. He can sympathize with you. He knows what it is to be misunderstood, He knows what it is to be denied by loved ones ..."[67]

For Moody, the poor treatment of women often was the result of alcohol abuse by males, and while he did not openly promote a temperance agenda, drunkenness was a sin he targeted. In fact, late-nineteenth-century temperance unions approached the issue of temperance as a religious issue and not exclusively a social one.[68] Moody delivered touching sermons on women and children as the innocent victims of drunkenness and the importance of alcoholic husbands becoming "born again." He told his listeners that Canadian families should rely on the Bible for guidance; wretchedness and misery had come into so many families because they did not follow biblical teachings.[69] His understanding of family life followed his belief that a proper Christian home provided the direction for children to become upstanding citizens. He was often conscious of the role that a godly family played in the stability of the community, something achieved through Bible reading, hymn singing, and family prayer in the home. Like many evangelicals in Canada, he emphasized the critical role played by the mother in religious nurture.[70]

For Moody and other Christians, providing religious direction for young people was especially important by the late nineteenth century because dancing halls and dime-store novels were only two of a number of amusements that diverted young people from church activities. There was a culture-denying component in his conservative message and youth, in particular, required protection from modern (evil) forces.[71] The Young Men's Christian Association and Young Women's Christian Association (YWCA) were two organizations that played a vital role in providing religious direction for the many young working men and women who left the dull routine of family life to live in larger cities where an expanding factory system offered paying jobs.[72] Because of Moody's earlier involvement with the YMCA, he understood that the city could dissolve social and religious bonds and he often directed his Canadian audiences to replace the missing moral influence of the young person's home.

Moody's solution to urban strife followed an individualistic rather than a collectivist approach. His ideas for assisting the working poor were simplistic. He urged Christians to show sympathy to the oppressed woman, the drunken man, and the spiritually lost young men and women of the city and to go among the poor and lend a helping hand. At a meeting in Brantford, he directed his listeners to do good deeds: "Pour oil into heart wounds. Bind up the bruised. If you have a carriage take some poor hard-working woman out for a drive and some fresh air. Live your Christianity."[73] While representing good intentions, his message was, according to William McLoughlin, "escapist" because it did not grasp the changing nature of a society that was in need of social reform.[74] Although he seldom took sides in labour-management disputes, his sympathies were obvious. Concerning labour unrest in the United States, he stated that "either these people [striking workers] are to be evangelized or the leaven of communism and infidelity will assume such enormous proportions that it will break out in a reign of terror such as this country has never known."[75] Moody preached to Canadians that the only realistic solution to the problem of societal strife was to target people's sinful hearts with the Gospel. As he saw it, one was to sympathize with others and rely on God's power to realize an improved society. In 1898 his message to a Montreal audience concerning class conflict was overly optimistic: "I don't know anything that would do more to remove the prejudice between capital and labor than if the rich were to get out of their carriages occasionally and allow the poor to ride."[76]

Distancing himself from the social gospel movement that was gaining strength among some ministers in the United States, Moody often told his Canadian listeners that clergymen were not to preach science, literature, and social reform. Rather, their mission was to preach sin and salvation since the world could not survive without Christ.[77] To an 1894 Toronto audience he lamented: "There is so much talk of reform, reform, reform, till I am sick of the whole thing. What is wanted is to preach Christ in season and out of season."[78] He understood that the building of a Kingdom of God on earth was impossible to achieve because all people were corrupt. In Montreal, Moody preached: "We are naturally bad. Who in this audience would be willing to have his heart photographed with all its real thoughts and passions brought to light."[79] He desired that individuals reach for Christ's kingdom, but the kingdom he referred to was not a Kingdom of God on earth but rather almost exclusively the Kingdom of Heaven.

Moody endorsed a pre-millennial understanding of the end times – the belief that the millennium, or one thousand years of righteousness, could begin only with the physical arrival of Jesus – and he argued that churches were negligent in failing to preach the second coming of Christ.[80] His pessimism was contrary to the post-millennialism that many nineteenth-century Canadian Protestants accepted.[81] To an 1887 Montreal audience, Moody stated that, while he once thought the world would become better, he had changed his mind; now he accepted that it was going to get worse until Christ's return.[82] To Toronto listeners he declared: "We have lost spiritual life by being hand in-glove with the world, believers unequally yoked with unbelievers." Christians were to lead a separate life on the basis that Christ taught that "the world was at war with Him."[83]

The power that Moody's evangelical message had over his audience fascinated Canadian newspaper editors who, as self-appointed moral guardians of society, held considerable influence in an era when newspapers had a monopoly on daily news. Editors' propensity to criticize the performance of clergymen meant that revival meetings were fair game for criticism.[84] Fortunately for Moody, however, he had newspaper people mainly on his side, which is no surprise given the keen public interest in revivalism. The upstart Boston *Globe*, for example, had more than tripled its readership when it offered daily steno-graphic accounts of Moody's 1877 meetings.[85] His keen sense of salesmanship enabled him to understand the power of the press; he often publicly thanked the journalists for their good work. Moreover, he told his revival audience to purchase the daily reports that gave excellent coverage of the meetings and send them to friends in other towns and cities. The Montreal *Daily Star* said it best: "Mr. Moody has always been a favorite with newspaper men because he appreci-ates their efforts and regards them to a certain extent as co-laborers. He believes in the missionary powers of the press."[86]

Moody also received positive press because journalists respected and admired his ability to capture the hearts and minds of so many Canadians. The rhetoric of revival points to the press construction of revivalism as an extraordinary event. In October 1887 the Mon-treal *Daily Star*'s description of an early meeting suggested that Moody had cast some kind of spell over the Protestant community: his revival meetings were clearly successful given "the long rows of men and women of all stages of adult life" making their way to the rink. Even more impressive was "the marked difference in them before and after the meeting [which] speaks volumes for the renowned revivalist's power. Where there was laughing and chatting on the way toward the rink, there was quiet and serious thought on the way from it." Many who had arrived in small groups departed "alone, preferring meditation concerning the truths which they heard to conversation with others." When one revival attender expressed an unbecoming remark concerning the revival meeting, not only were people nearby surprised and hurt but the comment prompted his friends to chide him.[87] Many Montrealers appear to have adopted Moody as their spiritual mentor and his efforts had to be defended against criticism. In one afternoon meeting, a reporter detailed the crowd's intense anticipation of his arrival: "Whoever was present at the Bible class yesterday could not help but notice the anxiety with which Mr. Moody is expected." If he arrived a minute or two late "the excitement grows more and more intense. Strangers need not ask by what door Mr. Moody will enter the church. Nearly every face seems involuntarily to turn toward that one door."[88]

Other Canadian newspapers commented on Moody's ability to influence his audience. In 1897 the Ottawa *Free Press* attempted to understand the power of Moody but, like his audience, could only

admit that he had a profound effect.[89] According to the Kingston
Daily Whig, people "sway before his words as a ripened field of
wheat before a breeze."[90] A Vancouver *Daily News-Advertiser*
reporter wrote of his evangelical message: "each person thinks his
own individual heart is laid bare. And so it is. His shots, therefore,
are red hot and bury themselves. His arrows thus aimed never fail
the mark. Conviction of sin is forced home, then follows a turning
unto righteousness."[91] The Victoria *Daily Colonist* wrote that
Moody demonstrated a quality "akin to that of a person about to
impart some momentous news, whether of joy or sorrow, whose
very looks are electric, and who imparts a thrill to those whom he
seeks to address before he opens his lips."[92]

For a number of journalists, Moody's popularity with his audience
was mostly due to his preaching of the basic Gospel message in an
understandable language. The Victoria *Daily Colonist* claimed that
his sermons had an advantage over some ministers' elaborate essays
on subjects that people in the pews generally never bothered their
heads about. To fill churches with eager men and women to hear
God's word, clergymen needed to consider Moody's example; in
particular, they should study the human heart and speak the language of everyday life which people fully understand and appreciate.[93]

In one sense, the press manufactured Moody's "revival" into
something virtually sacrosanct. His revival sermons carried the
stamp of a special authority; his simple and conservative evangelical
message went beyond the mechanical sentiments of the revival meeting to represent "profounder depths of meaning and feeling."[94] The
Toronto *World* claimed that Moody "has done for religion what
Socrates did for philosophy – brought it down to the homes and bos-
oms of men. And this has touched the hearts of his hearers." Canadians were "shown that religion is no vague incomprehensible theory,
no shadowy system embodied in sublime phrases and profound
propositions, but a thing of hourly experience, built upon the common, trivial everyday duties of life."[95]

The evidence in newspaper editorials and reports suggests that
many Protestant Canadians in the growing urban centres wanted to
hear the preaching of uncomplicated biblical truths. Moody's evangelicalism delivered this. Like the Toronto "motorman" converted at
Massey Hall, listeners received spiritual sustenance.[96] "Men and
women who hardly enter a church from one year's end to the other,"

according to the Victoria *Daily Colonist*, came to see Moody.[97] In some cases, on account of the frustrations and upheavals of city life, newcomers to the urban environment wanted reassurance that God cared for their everyday physical and spiritual needs.[98] According to one sociologist, the emotion and testimonies of revivals provided "the fabric of individual and collective identity, purpose, and solidarity."[99]

Criticism of Moody's revivalism and conservatism did come, however, from a number of other sources. As early as 1875, at least one Canadian progressive and intellectual subjected Moody to scrutiny. Writing in the *Canadian Monthly* on the topic of Moody and Sankey's revivals, William D. LeSueur admitted that the revivalists "*may* be right" on the issue of eternal damnation but, if the Bible was accurate, "most educated classes of the present day have many, many steps to retrace." As LeSueur saw it, a revival based on biblical teachings was archaic since any "teaching that cannot rouse the conscience without insulting the intellect is not adapted to the nineteenth century."[100] Such highbrow criticism of Moody's conservative evangelicalism, however, was rare.

Another group of critics came from a much different quarter. At a Hamilton meeting of the Ministerial Association, a number of clergymen criticized Moody and S.H. Blake for their statements against higher criticism. Blake, a prominent lawyer and evangelical Anglican layman, was one of a number of well-known Torontonians who not only combatted higher criticism but developed strong alliances with conservative evangelicals in the United States. Identified as a "proto-fundamentalist" by one scholar, Blake participated in the Niagara Bible Conferences and sponsored Moody's Toronto revival meetings.[101] Upset with Moody's and Blake's orthodox evangelicalism, a certain Dr Lyle even went so far as to say that such ignoramuses should be censured since "the memories of higher critics will live when these wretched, sneering critics [i.e., Moody] are dead and forgotten."[102] During Moody's highly successful Toronto revival campaign of 1894, a Unitarian minister, the Reverend J.H. Long, argued that Moody did more harm than good in Canada. For Long, an American revivalist such as Moody was "generally an inferior and unlearned man, who preached the last century theology of a material hell."[103] With his university degrees, Long equated his own brand of Protestantism with cultural progress, a Protestantism much more enlightened than the conservative evangelicalism of American revivalism.

American revivalism especially struck a sensitive nerve with an Anglican publication – the *Canadian Churchman*. The arrival of Moody provided one more topic of contention between the so-called high and evangelical factions of the Anglican Church. During his 1894 Toronto campaign, the *Canadian Churchman*, representing the high church wing of Anglicanism, declared: "One wonders what kind of food of a spiritual kind these 'Moody-mad' people had been getting, that they take such immense trouble to 'hear Moody' – and they even go to considerable expense."[104] In another issue, the Anglican organ made comments on the gullibility of the crowds who gathered to hear Moody's message: "Any self-dubbed doctor has a better chance than an ordinary 'regular practitioner' with the stupid public, because so many have claimed recognition under new systems of physic, rivalling one other, that individual brass is the only really popular thing." Consequently, an American evangelist "may talk utter nonsense, and 'populus' is ready to swallow it wholesale – because they don't see his well-hidden self-interest in the 'proceeds'; their sight is bad!"[105]

Feeding the anger within some circles of the Anglican Church was Moody's evangelicalism, particularly the acceptance of instantaneous conversion. The claim that there was no such thing as gradual conversion was an outrage, one Anglican argued.[106] Other writers in the Anglican publication attacked Moody's "intensely mischievous" and "damaging" methods, stating rather that to reach people's souls one must appeal to their "higher faculties."[107] The *Canadian Churchman*, more so than any other denominational publication, consistently spoke out against the conservative evangelicalism expressed by evangelists like Moody. Perhaps the findings of a recent study that turn-of-the-century Anglicans fared lower in wealth/status measurements than historians had previously thought can help to explain the *Canadian Churchman*'s fears that too many Anglicans found Moody's popular revivalism attractive.[108] Whatever the reasons, the Anglican Church, with the exception of its evangelical members, could not promote a populist and American understanding of Protestantism which challenged the mediating role of the institutional church.

For others, Moody's greatest shortcoming was not his theological or methodological approach but rather his understanding of capitalism. The *Palladium of Labor*, a Hamilton working-class publication, missed the mark when it claimed that he owned a "splendid mansion" and lined his pockets for personal gain, but much of the journal's critique of Moody was more astute than the commentary in the bourgeois press: "We do not believe that any man professing to follow the example of Christ can be at once sincere and intelligent if he upholds the commercial Christianity of the day and fails to raise his voice in protest against the social injustices which render it possible for a few men to accumulate wealth at the expense of the toiling masses." Further, the *Palladium of Labour* asked: Had Moody ever condemned "the oppressions of the competitive system under which Labour is crushed?" Did he ever show an "understanding of the social teachings of the great Labour Reformer whose example he professes to follow?" No was the answer, according to the *Palladium*; he failed to tell "his rich and comfortable supporters, the well-to-do stick gamblers, bankers, profit-mongers, land speculators and capitalistic exploiters of various sorts that their luxuries and religious donations came from the robbery of the poor," and that their prayers "were a profanation and their gifts an abomination to the Lord."[109] Such criticism had merit, but the arguments of labour leaders failed to prevent large numbers of working-class people from attending the popular revivals. Without access to the views of virtually all the ordinary workers who attended revival meetings, one can only speculate that their attendance reflected their attraction to someone they, unlike labour intellectuals, perceived to be a "commoner" who presented a simple and powerful Christian message.

Given that the majority of Canadian Protestant leaders upheld the individualistic, competitive philosophy of modern industrial life, it is only to be expected that voices of protest against Moody's lack of understanding of or concern for the oppressive side of capitalism were rare in church circles. The Baptist, Congregationalist, evangelical Anglican, Methodist, and Presbyterian press showed no signs of withdrawing their endorsement of Moody during his revival campaigns in Canada over fourteen years. Canadian Protestant leaders agreed with him that an individual needed to experience conversion to Christ and most Protestants of the late nineteenth century promoted spiritual salvation over social salvation, since they believed that personal salvation was the first step for solving social problems.[110] The social gospel movement in Canada would eventually show its strength, but not until years after Moody's final visit.

There were few signs of disagreement from ministers concerning Moody's acceptance of the inerrancy of the Bible. Theological colleges discussed higher criticism, but most Canadian evangelicals never paid much attention to such matters. Salem Bland, an early leader of the social gospel movement, believed that controversy over biblical criticism rarely had any influence on the people in the pews.[111] The vast majority of turn-of-the-century Baptists "felt their religion – in other words, they experienced it – and they therefore saw no compelling need to intellectualize it."[112] An American brand of conservative evangelicalism had yet to be seriously challenged by Canadian Protestants. In step with Moody, most evangelical ministers and lay people accepted the Bible as the word of God and showed little interest in unsettling questions and intellectual perplexities.

During the period of Moody's Canadian campaigns, the many clergymen who expressed an opinion on his work continued their support of his evangelicalism because, nurtured in an evangelical milieu, they found his orthodox preaching familiar and, perhaps more important, inspiring. Praising Moody's revival efforts, the *Canadian Methodist Magazine* declared that both the clergy and laity heard him gladly and hailed his visits as those of an apostle, who travelled through the land awakening, encouraging, and inciting the Christian community to increased energy and zeal.[113] As the Presbyterian *Westminster* saw it, his arrival at Massey Hall in 1894 was heaven-sent: "Ministers were there, a hundred of them, earnestly desiring a message, a fresh inspiration, something to help them out of the rut, something to revive them in the fainting years. Were they disappointed? No. There was power."[114]

Indeed, Moody, with his simple words, was calling the faithful to new heights of spiritual ardour. This was an era when religious movements such as the Salvation Army were playing a role in revitalizing some communities.[115] Even better received was American-style revivalism. Seeing the fervour and popular religion that the Salvation Army promoted in its successful evangelistic work, late-nineteenth-century Canadian evangelical ministers underwent self-examination on the issue of popularizing their message.[116]

The arrival of American popular evangelists such as Moody was well timed. In the *Evangelical Churchman*, Dyson Hague saw the lesson learned from Moody's popular revivalism and evangelicalism: "Let preachers get off their homiletical stilts. Let them be more simple, practical, homely, human. Let them preach less to the head and more to the heart. Let them preach the Word." Rejecting the formalism and intellectualism that he saw stifling the growth of Anglican churches in Canada, Hague wanted ministers to preach a simple

Gospel message which ordinary people could understand and praise. It was true that Moody's cup was not of polished crystal, Hague added. Yet it contained living water and it was the water that people wanted.[117] The *Christian Guardian* found it striking that Moody held the attention of his audiences with sermons drawn from the lives of biblical characters and the lives of everyday ordinary folk.[118] Likewise, the *Presbyterian Record* claimed that his simple, plain, and forceful preaching held crowded throngs as no other clergyman could do.[119] Like their counterparts in the United States, apparently, many of the "better classes" in Canada were cool or openly hostile to Moody's revivalism, but what mattered most was the support of rank-and-file working people.[120]

Although Canadian evangelical clergymen seldom directly criticized Moody's work, some did at times voice indirect concerns. Methodist clergymen, for example, made it clear that evangelists employed by their churches should adhere to "Methodistic usages."[121] This meant that evangelists should be accountable to the doctrine and regulatory control of the Methodist Church. In letters to the *Christian Guardian*, both laity and clergy expressed some concern over the role that professional revivalism played in church life.[122] However, with only a few exceptions, Methodist critiques of revivalism rarely made specific reference to Moody. On the topic of Moody's theology, the editor of the *Christian Guardian* admitted in 1894 that he was not in total agreement with Moody. But he still gave his blessing to Moody's Canadian meetings.[123]

Within the Canadian Protestant community, Moody's revival activity could hardly do wrong. Although sociologist S.D. Clark saw the late-nineteenth-century rise of the Salvation Army and other sectarian groups as primary evidence of "the Great Revival of the City,"[124] Moody's revivals touched a far greater number of Canadian Protestants. Through the medium of revivals, he promoted conservative evangelicalism in a society undergoing modernization. Technological improvements in communication and particularly the growth of inexpensive newspapers gave Moody's Canadian revival meetings a high degree of publicity that visiting American evangelists James Caughey and Phoebe Palmer had not enjoyed in the 1850s. Aware of the popularity of revival meetings, secular newspapers increased their coverage to meet the demands of their consumers, thereby exciting the desire of many English Canadians to view the evangelistic exploits of American evangelists such as Moody.

These newspapers were not only providing revival information; they were, in a sense, placing their stamp of approval on American revivalism and conservative evangelicalism.

Moody preached that there was a hungering for the Bible and "nothing else would draw a crowd like the announcement of an address on the wonderful book."[125] Many Canadians agreed. During the 1894 Toronto campaign, the *Mail* believed that a city that failed to be spiritually moved by the American revivalist could be described only as "Gospel hardened."[126] According to the *Westminster*, Moody's preaching hit hard and caused wincing but he had the power of "the old, old story."[127] His message in Canada had a conservative edge in a theological and socio-economic sense, but his meetings attracted a broad consensus of support from evangelical clergy and laity. There is little evidence to suggest that his popularity in Canada diminished over the years. As will be further discussed later, the endorsement of American revivalism was a result of its success in attracting large numbers of working-class men and women to meetings and the perception, circulated in revival accounts, that the revivals contributed to church growth.

Canadians embraced the masculine and pious Moody and his revival meetings, with their many elements of popular culture. At all of his Canadian destinations, in Quebec, Ontario, Manitoba, and British Columbia, people, many of modest working-class roots, were receptive to his campaigns even though he said little about a flawed social order. Almost forty years after Moody's last Canadian campaign, Salem Bland wrote that while Moody preached, workers suffered. The story of Moody was one "of a great and good man who moved amid the appalling spectacle of this greedy, sordid, money-crazy, inhuman and oppressive business life and a political life corrupted by business men, with the unseeing eyes of a child."[128] He was naive, but his sincere preaching of Gospel beliefs – the old truths of sin and salvation – still appealed to many ordinary working people. The people embraced this simple, poorly educated man, overlooking or forgiving his shortcomings.[129] Both the clergy and laity believed that the impression he left was not temporary but "deep and lasting." As a result of Moody's late-nineteenth-century Canadian campaigns, supported by the image makers of the press, American revivalism and conservatism established themselves in the Canadian Protestant experience.

CHAPTER THREE

Limitations

Sam Jones, an American from the deep south, became a household name in English Canada largely because of the success that he and co-evangelist Sam Small enjoyed during their Toronto campaign in 1886, less than two years after Dwight L. Moody's first set of Canadian meetings. If the volume of press coverage is an accurate indication of Jones's fame, he was virtually an overnight popular-culture success in central Canada; at bookstores, and even on trains throughout Ontario, eager Canadian readers bought his evangelical sermons and sayings.[1]

To contemporaries like Toronto Methodist leaders, the Jones and Small 1886 campaign was an unqualified triumph, attracting larger crowds, over almost three weeks, than any other previous revival campaign in Canada. In the months after the Toronto campaign, Jones returned to Canada without Sam Small and held more lectures instead of revival meetings. But by the time the two returned to Canada as a team in August 1887, momentum had dissipated. The question of profit making, the preaching of a weak salvation message, and their hostile attacks on the labour movement were issues that dampened enthusiasm for the southern evangelists. Small's direct assault against labour unions and the press, something Moody did not do, was an especially important factor in preventing Jones and Small from having other revival campaigns in Canada that matched the success of their earlier efforts. The appeal of American revivalism and conservative evangelicalism remained powerful, but the story of Jones and Small in Canada indicates that there were limitations to a popular American revivalism that failed to maintain a working relationship with the press. Without the ongoing positive support of the image makers, piety deficiencies or other flaws in modern revivalism became conspicuous.

In the wake of Dwight Moody's successful three-day campaign at Toronto in 1884, Toronto Methodists were eager to invite Jones and his own brand of American revivalism to their city.[2] Although Jones visited Toronto in 1881, he had at that time been largely unnoticed. By 1886 this had changed. The Reverend Hugh Johnston, a Methodist representing the multidenominational Evangelical Alliance, wrote to Jones to see if the famed evangelist could hold meetings in Canada. Johnston had gone to Chicago to observe the best-known Methodist evangelist of the day and learned that the Georgian had the ability to reach the masses. Overseeing the Toronto revival activities were secretary Johnston, of Carleton Street Methodist Church, and two other well-known and respected Toronto Methodist clergymen: Dr John Potts, a minister of Elm Street Methodist Church and major Moody supporter, was chairman of the meetings, and the Reverend John E. Starr of Berkeley Street Methodist Church was chairman of the Committee on Spiritual Results, which was responsible for supporting the individuals from the audience who came forward at the inquiry meetings at the conclusion of the sermon. The Methodists were in an emotional state of excitement as they anticipated the arrival of Sam Jones and Sam Small. The press likewise showed enthusiasm.[3] Using masculine rhetoric, the Toronto *World* stated that Sam Jones and Sam Small promised "to do some heavy execution against the powers and patronage of Satan."[4] While Moody usually overshadowed evangelists who joined him on campaigns, Jones and Small were seen more as equals.[5]

In addition to Sam Small, Jones brought Marcellus J. Maxwell to be the musical director in charge of a choir of approximately three hundred from the various Toronto Methodist churches. Assisting Jones, Small, and Maxwell was Chicago soloist Professor E.O. Excell, a "big, robust six-footer, with a six-inch caliber voice," who could belt out hymns in a manly, folksy, and entertaining manner.[6]

Jones and Small attracted a large number of Torontonians to the meetings at Mutual Street Rink, which had extra chairs to accommodate comfortably about 4,000, and at the large Metropolitan Methodist Church, which could hold more than 2,000 people. The almost three weeks of Toronto meetings seemed to ignite an existing spiritual powder keg. On the first Saturday night of the October campaign, the Salvation Army, quite separate from the Jones and

Small meetings, was busy marching down Kingston Road and hundreds collected at each street meeting to hear the testimonies of Salvation Army members. Signs and expressions of popular religion were everywhere and most of the participants appeared to be of the working class.[7]

Early into the campaign, the leaders of the Local Committee of Methodist Pastors and Laymen happily announced that "a spiritual cyclone" was ready to envelop the community. Methodist leaders and the press worked together to construct the revival as an exceptional experience. When a *Globe* reporter asked a Methodist pastor if he thought the big meetings would last through the week, the pastor confidently replied that the meetings would continue to be packed throughout the campaign.[8] This prediction was quite accurate. The publicity, positive and negative, that Jones and Small received from the Toronto newspapers played an important role in boosting the public's interest in the meetings. During the month of October, no other conversational topic in Toronto matched that of the two Sams and so once again American revivalism had taken a Canadian city by storm. The *Globe* wrote that the two Sams were "as well known to very many people of Toronto as that of their own pastor, and when Wednesday arrives and the evangelists leave for their southern homes, many will feel that they have really lost a pastor."[9]

On the last day of meetings, the Reverend John Potts declared that the meetings were the most impressive ever held in Canada, a position few Methodists were likely to disagree with.[10] By 1886, Moody had yet to hold as large and long a campaign as the Jones-Small evangelistic team. According to the *Globe*, Jones and Small had attracted 180,000, or approximately one and a half times the population of Toronto. The newspaper based its calculation on the fact that every evening meeting at the 4,000-seat rink was overflowing (between 5,000 and 6,000 could squeeze inside), and other meetings at the Metropolitan Church and at the rink in the afternoon attracted an average of more than 2,000 people.[11]

In December 1886, not seven weeks had gone by when Jones and choir director Marcellus Maxwell, without Small, returned from the United States to hold several meetings at a few Methodist churches in Toronto. Long before Jones began to preach, Central Methodist Church became full and hundreds were shut out. According to the Toronto *World*, the meetings at three other Methodist churches

attracted so many people that fewer than half of the crowds could
gain admission. At the Elm Street Methodist Church, fully 5,000
people were unable to enter, causing a commotion and problem for
police wanting to keep the street open to traffic.[12] The press's earlier
image making was still intact. The *Globe* reported that among those
gathered to hear Jones were thousands of women and men who
would always regard him as their "first spiritual pastor."[13] Jones
conducted one meeting for women under the auspices of the
Women's Christian Temperance Union (WCTU). He held revival
meetings but also added lectures to his itinerary. Charging the audience a fee was a rather unusual practice for an evangelist in Canada.
At the Metropolitan Methodist Church, Jones's first lecture cost
individuals as much as fifty cents (fifty times the price of a newspaper) to be admitted.[14]

Jones's next visit to Canada took place in March 1887 when he held
meetings with his musical assistant E.O. Excell in Toronto, Hamilton,
London, Galt, Montreal, and Kingston. While Jones continued to
receive letters from others requesting his services, he could not accept
all invitations.[15] He arrived at Toronto on a Saturday night as a heavy
blanket of snow fell on the city, but, when word circulated that he
planned to speak at the meeting of the Young Men's Prohibition Club
at the Horticultural Gardens Pavilion, a huge crowd gathered. The
News suggested that perhaps "never" in the history of the club has a
meeting "attracted such a tremendous gathering."[16] Three meetings
that he held at the Carleton Street Methodist Church also drew overflowing crowds, despite no special advertising in Toronto.

The following Monday afternoon, Jones travelled to Hamilton, a
city of less than 50,000, where his first engagement was a lecture
given at Wesley Methodist Church to an enthusiastic audience
"ready to be moved either to laughter or tears, pity or indignation."
He did not disappoint. Described by a reporter as "a small, dark,
tired, and nervous-looking man," Jones, nonetheless, gave the
Hamiltonian Methodists an entertaining and rewarding lecture on
"Character and Characters." Over three days, he gave two lectures
and one sermon at the Wesley Methodist Church. His sermon on
"Christian purity" took place on a weekday morning and thus was
given to a largely female audience.[17] From Hamilton, he travelled to
London, where the *Advertiser* wrote that he was a noted American
who had achieved "world-wide celebrity." In London, which had a
population of approximately 30,000, Jones followed the same for-

mat as in Hamilton: two lectures over two nights with a sermon preached on the third morning of his visit. All three meetings held at Queen's Avenue Methodist Church attracted a large number of people.[18] The next night he was in Galt, a small urban centre, where people from Ayr, Berlin, Doon, and other points came to hear the American evangelist at the Methodist church.[19]

After Galt, Jones travelled to Montreal, holding meetings on a Sunday in the morning, afternoon, and evening at the St James Street Methodist Church, the site of Moody's meetings less than sixteen months earlier. At the final service of his first day of meetings, hundreds were unsuccessful in gaining access while those who were successful had to endure claustrophobic conditions which caused a number of women to faint and to be carried out into the fresh air. During his second day in Montreal, a large number of students from the Methodist Theological College, McGill College, and other colleges gathered at Convocation Hall to hear him speak.[20] A large crowd also paid the twenty-five cents admission fee to attend a lecture at St James Street Methodist Church.[21] Jones was received favourably, too, at Kingston, Ontario, where the *Daily News* described him as a truly remarkable man: though having good Methodist ancestry, he had been a slave to whisky drinking and profanity before experiencing a victorious transformation at his father's deathbed. The *British Whig* saw Jones as "A Man of the Times and the Best Known Evangelist in All America." He attracted 1,000 people to hear his one lecture at the city hall.[22]

Jones's next visit to Canada was in August 1887, when he and Sam Small held a few meetings at Grimsby Park, Ontario.[23] These meetings favoured those with money and so likely did not have a strong representation of working-class men and women. Interestingly, Grimsby Park had lost some of its religious heritage as a result of its focus on leisure activities.[24] Jones's quick visit to Toronto, the following month, was anti-climatic, since he spoke for only a few minutes at the conclusion of a lecture delivered by Sam Small at Carleton Street Methodist Church.[25] While Small stayed in Toronto for a short period, Jones and E.O. Excell travelled to London, where a crowd numbering about 2,500 gathered at the Princess Rink for Jones's lecture. Large audiences willing to pay to hear him were also at the rink for the next two evenings of lectures. Although both the *Daily Free Press* and the London *Advertiser* provided coverage of Jones's lectures, neither gave any indication when Jones departed from London about what his future plans were.[26] If Jones and Small held other campaigns in Canada, their meetings did not procure the publicity of the visits of 1886 and 1887.

Both the secular and denominational press had closely followed Sam Jones's revival meetings, especially those with Sam Small in 1886. Toronto Methodist clergymen were familiar with the well-known Canadian Methodist evangelists Hugh Crossley and John Hunter, but these evangelists were not from the deep south.[27] Jones's southern roots even set him apart from many of the other well-known American urban revivalists of the period, the majority of whom were from the northeastern and midwestern states. His Canadian supporters often defended his use of slang as a mannerism representative of southern culture. Given that the working class attended his meetings in large numbers, Jones's slang was not a deterrent in the eyes of those who brought him to Canada.

The Sams were products of the south, but Small was no Jones when it came to revival style and personality. Like Jones, Small had a slender build and a prominent mustache and voiced his words with a southern twang. Except that Small wore glasses, they looked so similar that readers had to look carefully at newspaper drawings to tell the two apart. On the issue of revival style, however, there was no confusing the two. A thinker and eloquent, polished speaker, Small was not entertaining in a humorous way and rarely received a smile from individuals in the audience.

Jones, by contrast, was a master at generating emotion. An example of the delight he took in revival enthusiasm was his statement to a Toronto audience that Methodists "were born in a revival, and they could only live by revivals – (hear, hear) – and the only way the other churches who did not believe in revivals lived was, that when it flowed over from the Methodists it ran into their old ponds. (Laughter.)" He stated, "If they would show him a church that did not believe in revivals he would show them a church that looked like an abandoned graveyard."[28] As Jones saw it, the Roman Catholic Church had a pope, the Baptist Church had water, the Presbyterian Church had starch and dignity, but the Methodist Church had nothing but religion.[29] He did not explain exactly what he meant, but an important point was his preference for the enthusiasm of popular religion over the dryness of formality.

The 1886 Toronto meetings more or less followed a schedule. Jones and Small held meetings early in the day, but the 7:30 evening meetings were the focal points of the campaign. Under the direction of Marcellus Maxwell, the choir, consisting of three to four hundred members drawn from local Methodist churches, usually opened an evening meeting with the singing of the doxology and other hymns. With extra chairs added throughout, the Mutual Street Rink (the largest auditorium in Toronto) comfortably accommodated the approximately 4,000 people who made their way into the building. Those who failed to find a vacant seat used "camp stools" which the ushers carried in to fill the aisles. According to a newspaper report, the 5,000 men who crowded into the rink for a men-only meeting were mostly labourers, mechanics, and clerks, with only a few merchants and lawyers present.[30]

Given that Methodism had become more self-consciously ostentatious by the 1880s,[31] the crude appearance of the rink presented an odd sight for Methodist leaders. There were no decorations, the boards overhead were without paint, and the interior of the building had a bare appearance, creating a "barn-like general effect." A journalist reminisced about the days of John Wesley, when Christians met in unadorned locations to share a faith that could easily lead to their persecution. The writer also could not help but think of Wesley's attacks on the formalities of the church establishment. One "Country Parson" commented that the meetings at the rink reminded him of the old-time Toronto revivals from the early 1850s.[32]

On the hour, Jones entered the building and the meeting officially began with Excell singing a sentimental hymn such as "The Lily of the Valley," which focused on the love of Christ. Before proceeding with his revival sermon, which he delivered at the rate of 140 to 200 words a minute, Jones made some candid, and even blunt, introductory comments. At his first Canadian revival meeting in 1886, he wasted little time in describing his "peculiar" methods to his Canadian revival audience: "My Christian friends and brethren of Toronto, it gives me great pleasure to meet you and greet you in the Lord. I come to you full of love to God and sympathy for souls ... My methods and manner are peculiar, and I will give you the secret. I am perfectly natural." Jones explained that there were men who were college-educated and there were those, like himself, who were natural. "Some preachers have one voice for the pulpit and another for the street. Now, I don't like that. The great thing needed in a preacher is sympathy with his people."[33] As Jones preached his revival message to Canadians, he often appeared irreverent, broaching sacred themes in a flippant manner and surprising listeners by the novelty and populism of his words. Yet, as the *Evening Telegram* saw it, Jones's "sayings and the quaint way in which they are uttered may be the feathers which guide his arrow to the mark at which the regular clergymen have been shooting in vain for years." He believed in using all and any methods to share his Christianity.[34] Relying on anecdote and illustration, Jones's true-to-life, popular-culture-like stories could be hilarious or they could be sentimental, but they were never dull. One thing for sure, Jones's performances gave the press an amusing product for mass consumption.

There was no mistaking Jones for anyone else. Considering himself a natural man, a man of the people, he wore this badge of self-identification proudly; and, indeed, it was his apparent honesty and his belief that he could initiate great results that went a long way in gaining the initial confidence of so many people. To many working-class Torontonians, Jones and his language did appear to be natural, but in truth his use of simple and often sensational language was a careful choice. When his audience was mainly women, he made adjustments and dropped slang altogether.[35] Moreover, Jones acted as if he had limited education, but his choice of literature suggested otherwise. He commented to Canadian journalists that he enjoyed literature by Shakespeare, Dickens, Scott, and Thackeray, that two of his favourite historians were Hume and Macaulay, and that he also read Ralph Waldo Emerson and the well-known Congregationalist preacher and writer Joseph Parker.[36] There was no indication, however, that the thought of these men informed his preaching. Jones often told his Canadian audiences that he disliked shams, but, consciously or not, he went to great lengths to fabricate the image that he was just a common man who preferred the everyday language of working-class folk. For example, with a touch of theatrics, he claimed that he despised theology and botany but loved religion and flowers.[37]

Jones's interpretation and delivery of the Gospel always captivated his Canadian audiences. There was often laughter but there were also periods of seriousness when listeners contemplated Jones's candid comments. When the message and music were still fresh in the minds and hearts of penitents, many filled out a "revival card" providing information (name, address, spiritual condition, church preferred, minister's name) that went to the appropriate churches and ministers, who were ready to welcome them into the fold and make sure that they received proper Christian direction. Attempting to demonstrate that the meetings were interdenominational, the Reverend Hugh Johnston clarified that Christian assistants faced dismissal if they attempted to influence penitents to join a particular church.[38]

As with Dwight L. Moody's meetings, organization was an important feature of the Jones and Small campaign in Toronto. During the October 1886 meetings, organizers arranged the rink into twenty sections, each with a clergyman and twenty lay helpers to instruct and pray for those who rose from their seats at the request of Jones. The lay assistants at his meetings played a more public role than was usually the case for Moody's campaigns. At the rink, there was no inquiry meeting for those seeking salvation and the helpers went among the crowd to the penitents who had indicated they wanted spiritual instruction.

Unlike Moody, Jones did not emphasize the need for an individual to have a born-again relationship with Christ. At the conclusion of the service, he often stressed that individuals should promise to be good Christians and not to succumb to sin. At one meeting, Jones asked those who came forward to repeat: "I renounce my allegiance to the devil, and God being my helper, I will serve Him." Similarly, Small asked penitents to come forward and "make peace with God to-night."[39] There were no specific statements declaring, as with Moody, that all could be forgiven through the atoning blood of Jesus.

With that theological emphasis missing in the preaching at revival meetings, it is not surprising that proselytizing was virtually non-existent at Jones's lectures; the lectures were a form of paid popular-culture entertainment, with instruction on how to lead a Christian life. To be assured a good audience, the lectures were always held in the evenings when Canadians had more time for leisure. At either a neutral site or a Methodist church, large crowds of both men and women paid to hear Jones lecture. The meeting usually began around 8:00 with a prayer and then some singing under the direction of one of Jones's musical assistants. The selection of songs varied and included "The Model Church," "Keep in the Middle of the Road," and "The Old Arm-Chair." The last was anything but worshipful, as can be seen from this stanza: "My grandmother she, at the age of eighty-three, One day in May was taken ill and died; And after she was dead the will, of course, was read. By the lawyer, as we all stood by his side."[40] Why it was sung at a London lecture is a mystery. Such music might enliven the crowd, but it could hardly be expected to make people feel closer to God.[41] Some of Jones's favourite lectures were: "Character and Characters," "The Battle of Life and How to Win It," "The Troubles of Life and What to Do with Them," "How to Win," and "The Ravages of Rum." The major thrust of these lectures was that individuals should exercise industry and self-control – bourgeois notions commonly expressed by leading members of the Protestant churches.

The lectures were at least an hour long and consisted of a collection of anecdotes spiced with Jones's wit, colloquialisms, embellishment, and bluntness, all effectively delivered to gain the attention of audiences. One Canadian journalist noted that, although Jones talked audaciously to his audiences, as he pointed out their faults, they appeared to enjoy it. His startling, unconventional phrases and illustrations were not only entertaining, they struck a note with Methodists who sought to attack all forms of unrighteousness in society. Combining humour and criticism, Jones, for example, warned men that if they spoke kindly to their wives in the morning, the wives would have to call in the neighbours to identify the men as their husbands.[42] A favourite line was his remark to an audience that their city had the prettiest women and the ugliest men of all the places he had ever visited. There was often side-splitting laughter when he used yarns to illustrate his points. On the theme of hitting hard at whisky sellers, Jones told a story about how a farmer defended himself from an attacking dog by spearing it with a sharp pitchfork. As the tale goes, the owner of the dog demanded why the farmer did not use the wooden end of the pitchfork, to which the farmer replied, "Why ... didn't your dog rush at me with his other end? (Uproarious laughter and applause.)"[43] As with all of his addresses, there was much hilarity and little sense of reverence.

Trying to understand Jones, the Galt *Reporter* struggled in its assessment of one of his lectures: "To one-half his hearers, perhaps, the lecture, with its rough wit and peculiar humor, its terse sentences and sharp points, would be a grand treat; to the other half, who look for dignity and reverence at the hands of ministers of the gospel and their sayings either on the platform or in the pulpit, it would be little more than a burlesque."[44] At his lectures there was neither salvation message nor an appeal for people to come forward; the conclusion came abruptly without a call for prayers or for an inquiry gathering. Jones's Canadian lectures, most of them delivered in 1887, did not generate the level of enthusiasm of his 1886 Toronto revival meetings. He offered entertaining stories, but, in the evangelical milieu of the 1880s, a revival meeting was a more entrancing commodity than a lecture devoid of Christ.

Jones's sermons differed somewhat from his lectures. The main theme in his revival messages in Canada was that godliness and good behaviour were analogous and conversion was a resolution to "quit your meanness." Accordingly, he placed much emphasis on the idea that a righteous individual was one who did righteous acts. Kathleen Minnix argues that Jones inverted the usual formula of finding Christ and living in a godly manner. Jones had given up his sins before he experienced salvation and, thus, he told his listeners that individuals do not become good by accepting Christianity, they get Christianity by first becoming good.[45] According to Virginia Lieson Brereton, men were more likely than women to emulate this message.[46]

Jones spoke largely of the sin in society and spent little time discussing theology. For him, it was vital that Christians both be aware of and be ready to confront worldliness; it was far more important to stress Christian living rather than dogma. To Torontonians, Jones proclaimed that, if his son ever wanted to preach, he "would not send him to a school of theology, but to a school of manology. Our preachers know a good deal about God, but very little about men."[47] Minnix suggests that Jones's style, including his attacks on liberal Protestantism, link him to the forerunners of fundamentalism.[48] Though Jones did not preach the imminent second coming of Christ, as did almost all of the forebears of the fundamentalists, his diatribes against sin in society were similar to the rhetoric of later fundamentalists.

Concentrating on the behavioural aspects of Christianity, he sought to shame Canadian Christians over their lack of compassion for the working poor. A girl from a rich family, Jones lamented, easily cried over Dickens's Little Nell, but she would walk by a barefooted and starving little girl on the street without a second thought.[49] In stating that it was morally irresponsible for an alleged Christian to treat servants unkindly, Jones also appears to have acknowledged that domestic servants were more likely than an employer to embrace Christ's teaching: "I am sorry for the home where there's more religion in the kitchen than there is in the other part of the house." Jones was also repulsed by the unchristian behaviour of a man behind a counter who smiled all day and provided polite service to every lady who entered the store, and then went home and treated his wife as if she were a stranger. On the issue of greed, he stated that the pursuit of money was like quenching thirst with salt water; "a fellow's thirsty, takes a glass, and in five minutes he wants more; and when he gets full right up to her, he's nearly dead for water. (Laughter.)"[50] Jones did occasionally attack the avarice displayed in contemporary society, but overall his notions of improvement failed to appreciate working-class grievance and need. Like Moody, he did not offer a critique of industrial capitalism at a time of social upheaval and class tension.

With wit and humour, Jones was effectively able to present and denounce behavioural sins. On the "sin" of profanity, he stated that if one could not quit cursing one should "go like Robinson Crusoe and live on a desert island, with no one but goats to associate with. And a profane swearer is fit for nothing but to be butted to death by a goat. (Laughter.)" On the connection between the immorality of playing cards and the lack of intelligence, he acknowledged to one Toronto audience that "now and then you will find a smart fellow playing a game of cards; but he is an exception to the general rule, and he ain't here to-night, so we won't speak about him."[51] Employing such an irreverent manner, Jones was better able than a stodgy clergyman-professor to make a connection with working-class people.

Jones's fearlessness exuded a rough-edged masculinity that diverged from a Christianity that young workingmen, according to Lynne Marks, viewed as feminine.[52] Jones and an increasing number of conservative evangelical men identified Christianity with traditional notions of masculinity rather than with the feminized Jesus of liberal evangelical piety.[53] Adopting an aggressive demeanour, Jones clearly endorsed a strong, muscular religion rather than an "effeminate, weak, sentimental, sickly, singing and begging sort."[54] He declared that he would die in a pool of blood at his front door before worldliness entered his home.[55] It is fitting that he wrote a book entitled *Rifle-Shots at the King's Enemies*.

Jones also adopted a hardline approach on the issue of eternal punishment and he was critical of ministers who neglected to preach on the subject of a fiery hell. David Marshall argues that there were

late-nineteenth-century Canadian clergymen who had difficulty rec-
onciling God's love with God's punishment of the unsaved, and that
many Victorians regarded hell-fire banishment as morally offensive.
He concludes that "ethical concern and moral feeling," more than
scientific theories, caused the unsettling of faith of both clergymen
and laity in Canada. Late Victorians' softening of orthodox Protestantism allegedly made it difficult to embrace fully the doctrine of
eternal punishment.[56] But did the proletarian element attending the
revival meetings find hell-fire preaching morally offensive? Whether
or not Marshall is correct in general, press reports indicate that the
preaching of eternal punishment attracted large crowds of revival
listeners.

At the Toronto campaign of October 1886, Jones stated that the
biggest fool on earth was one who spent time trying to persuade others that there was no hell. Reciting the names of great Protestant figures such as Martin Luther, Jonathan Edwards, George Whitefield,
John Wesley, and Dwight Moody, he argued that every clergyman
who was an effective minister accepted the belief of "a real, burning,
brimstone hell." According to Jones, clergymen who did not believe
in a burning hell were "mighty little fellows" incapable of having
much influence over people.[57] A minister who did not believe in hell,
according to Jones, would himself reside there eternally, suffering
physical and spiritual torment in a place "where the worm dieth not,
and where the fire shall never be quenched."[58]

Sam Small also used sermons on hell in Toronto. In 1886 the
Globe provided extensive coverage of what it described as "Sam
Small's Great Sermon on Hell." Offering no criticism on the content
of the sermon, the newspaper recorded that more than 4,000 people
had packed into a Toronto rink to hear Small. The main themes of
the preaching were the existence of an eternal hell and the reality of
punishment delivered to an individual on earth, which could hardly
compare with the punishment inflicted on the immortal soul of one
who despises Jesus. Scoffing at the suggestion that science proved
there was no hell, Small argued that he did not know of a book, in
this world, that could disprove God's revelation concerning eternal
punishment. There were those who lacked the common sense to
believe in God, but, ultimately, there was only one destination for
them. "Take that husband out there," Small continued, who inflicts
pain and suffering on his poor wife and children. A person must be
an idiot to believe that this husband will receive his retribution on

earth. Rather, the real suffering will only occur when he goes to an eternal hell. In one sermon, "his picture of the future abode of the wicked was Miltonic or Dantean in its realistic materiality – the burning marl, the crested waves of burning sulphur and the flaming mountains casting forth lava down their glowing sides being freely used in his terrific portraiture of hell."[59] The rhetoric was aggressive and masculine. At the successful Toronto campaign of October 1886, both Jones and Small made their conservative position heard as they appealed to their mainly working-class listeners to escape the awful doom of an eternal hell.

The interest in the Jones and Small October 1886 campaign was largely due to the comprehensive coverage of the meetings by the Toronto press, especially the reports that captured the excitement generated by the evangelists. For example, in its report of the last meeting of the October campaign, the Toronto *Evening News* related that total chaos appeared to prevail as thousands tried unsuccessfully to gain entry to an overflowing rink that had far too many inside already: "'Get in we must, and we will somehow and sometime, if we stay all night,' was the feeling, and so the crowd thumped at the doors and pried at the windows, and begged and entreated and threatened and coaxed the doorkeepers ..." The mob had even crushed the policemen in its efforts to gain admission. The scene became so chaotic that "it seemed that the living wedge, if it ever got an entrance at the door, must either rend the building or something." There was no mistaking the signs of revival in the city: "The tide of religious enthusiasm and zeal that has for nearly three weeks been steadily rising in the tabernacle on Mutual street and the Metropolitan church, last night culminated in a tidal wave of excitement which surged for hours around the gifted evangelists, who have been almost idolized by a large number of their hearers, and would not subside till it had bestowed upon them its parting token of affection and regard."[60]

According to the *Globe's* report of the same service, inside there was a potential safety crisis since, not only were some policemen crowded out of the meeting, but 6,000 people crammed into a space that accommodated 4,000.[61] Some men and women were half-suffocated and a couple of women fainted before someone broke a window, allowing approximately two dozen men and women to escape for some much needed fresh air. As they staggered outside, there was a rush of about one hundred people seeking to gain access through the broken window, but only three reporters, Methodist clergymen, and a few others made it into the building.[62] From the press reports, the meetings were popular, exciting, and tumultuous events that had greater appeal to the masses than to members of the bourgeoisie.

The *Evening News* reported that one stuffy, old Presbyterian who vowed never to attend the Jones campaign went reluctantly as a personal favour for a friend and became one of the more notable supporters of the campaign.[63] On this one night alone, a reporter claimed that he could provide a dozen similar examples. He explained the revival excitement with the metaphor of harvest time: "It has come at last. Sowing time is over, the reaper is in the field, the sickle of Providence is reaping the ripened grain, and the door of salvation stands open to receive the harvest." As the reporter described the meeting, the rink's doorways filled early, with many more outside on the muddy street staring in, much like a starving beast looking at a good pasture.[64]

Because of the extensive newspaper reports, many details of the Canadian revival meetings and of the evangelists themselves became common knowledge among an increasing number of Ontarians.[65] There was a voyeuristic appeal to the letters sent to the *Globe* editor from "Observer," "A Lover of Justice," "A Christian," "Globe Reader," "Fair Play," "Hibernian" in Erin, an "Old Subscriber" in Meaford, a "Constant Reader" in Listowel, and "H.W.B." in Collingwood, all praising the Toronto newspaper for publishing full reports of the meetings.[66] One proposal received by the *Globe* was that the railroad companies should offer inexpensive excursion fares for the many other Ontarians who wanted to attend the Toronto meetings. An awakening was in progress and even in regions far from Toronto there was a belief that an unprecedented religious feeling was washing over communities.[67] In one letter, a person reminisced about the seven months of Toronto revival meetings held by the Reverend James Caughey in 1851–52, stating that the meetings of Sam Jones had triggered vivid scenes and memories of his own experience in being called by the Holy Spirit to "stand upon the walls of Zion."[68] In a letter to Jones, a W. Calvert wrote: "Let nothing daunt you, you have truth and heaven on your side. You have the sympathy of all true hearts and their prayers. The Lord only knows what amount of good you may do in this great and proud city."[69] The Toronto *World* related a story that, when one man in a barbershop argued that Jones was a fraud and the meetings a farce, two of the barbers who had been converted at the campaign immediately came to Jones's defence, informing the customer that he should see Jones for himself.[70] As was the case for Moody, the press rhetoric presented themes of piety, power, and community.

Of those who made a commitment to Christ, many appeared to represent the working class. One letter written by a John Risk celebrated that two printers of the *News* and one printer of the Toronto *Mail* were turning their faces Zionward owing to the work of Jones and Small. Another friend of Risk's, who had been wayward and reckless, also committed himself to God. Risk wrote that "they must feel, with many, that Jones, Small & Co. are doing something that reflects credit upon their own heads, and everlasting renown upon these young men who have suddenly abandoned their erratic and miscellaneous life, at the expense of irritating a few and gathering the blessings of many."[71] In the wake of these stories of workers influenced by revivalism and the widespread support for popular religion, the *Globe* stated: "The world is sick and tired of formalism all around."[72] There was yearning for the removal of the formalism and institutionalism that was smothering the growth of Christianity. For those who bothered to investigate, there was an abundance of evidence that workers were not generally supportive of formal and ostentatious churches.

For some community leaders, Jones's iconoclasm was seen as an effective way to highlight the need for ethical and moral guidance. Simply put, revival could "re-moralize" civic space. Assessing the impact of the October 1886 campaign, the *Globe* praised Jones, his unrefined speech, and his ability to stir the community and encourage many to examine their characters and live "a better life."[73] Similarly, an *Evening Telegram* editor wrote that there was too much meanness in society and that "it will be a blessing if a percentage of profane, drinking, immoral or debt-owing individuals can be induced to carry out their good resolutions and keep in the right track." Although it is not clear whether the editor was referring to the rough element of working-class life, he noted that it was "a grand thing for the revivalists even to have succeeded in inducing a number of men and women to make up their minds to reform."[74] Jones and Small, despite their faults, were on the side of sobriety, morality, and truth and their efforts to awaken the consciences of people offered the potential for ample improvement since "the better the individual the better the community at large."[75] This assessment was a timely one given the many strikes and episodes of class conflict occurring in Toronto at this period.

Initially, the response of Methodist leadership to the work of Jones and Small was positive. Phyllis Airhart argues that revivalism and the commitment to a basic evangelical message not only helped define Methodism but also sparked the transformation of Canadian Methodism into the largest Protestant denomination of the second half of the nineteenth century.[76] In its report of the Jones and Small 1886 campaign, the *Canadian Methodist Magazine* suggested that, on account of the weeks of revival, Toronto experienced a spiritual awakening more intense than that ever experienced by any other Canadian community.[77] The *Christian Guardian* also lavished ample praise on Jones and Small, stating in one issue that the crowds for the Jones meetings were twice the size of those that had gathered at Dwight L. Moody's three-day Toronto campaign at Metropolitan Methodist Church in 1884.

The daily attendance seemed all the more impressive when it became clear to the editor that few other ministers outside the Methodist fold supported the campaign.[78] But did the lack of clergy support for Jones's and Small's crude manner matter? Were not the packed rink meetings, in large part, a result of a grass-roots phenomenon of extensive working-class interest and curiosity? The *Christian Guardian* did acknowledge the impropriety of some of Jones's expressions; however, a far more important point was that his message, delivered in a pragmatic manner, had made a direct connection to the working masses.

Besides, as the *Christian Guardian* saw it, clergymen who had never promoted revivals were in no position to criticize the work of the evangelists.[79] This posture by the Methodists found strength in reports that a significant number of conversions had occurred at the meetings and that newspaper descriptions of the Toronto campaign were generating religious enthusiasm throughout the country.[80] There was also the point that sixteen Toronto Methodist churches planned to continue revival services after the departure of Jones and Small.[81] To no surprise, the *Christian Guardian* printed a positive report of Jones's December 1886 return to Toronto.[82]

The commentary in other denominational publications varied. Evangelical Anglicans showed some sympathy for the work of Jones and Small. As the Toronto campaign of October 1886 was in progress, the *Evangelical Churchman* declared: "To condemn them out-

right is at least a great mistake." Noting that Jones and Small treated
Christianity in a light and frivolous manner, the *Evangelical Churchman* nevertheless defended the evangelists on the basis that their language reflected southern culture, that their methods were reaching
the working class, and that some newspaper reports not only exaggerated the irreverence of some of their statements but could not
accurately capture the evangelists' deep earnestness.[83] The *Canadian
Independent*, a journal published by Congregationalists, also
pointed out how different the religious mind of the American south
was from Canadian religion. Acknowledging that there were Christians in Toronto for and against the evangelists, the publication, in
late 1886, gave their revival style its cautious approval, stating that
they were "using such means and utterances for the glory of God in
the conversion of souls."[84] While the *Presbyterian Record* and
Canadian Baptist appeared to have ignored the southern evangelists,
Presbyterian clergymen W. Frizzel and Baptists Dr Thomas and Dr
Cassels were on hand at the Toronto campaign in 1886. There were
also hundreds of non-Methodist lay people who were in attendance
at all of the meetings of the October campaign.[85]

Still, in comparison to Moody, Jones and Small received less support in church publications and from church leaders of other denominations. The *Dominion Churchman*, a strong traditionalist Anglican
publication, declared that "the quips and cranks of speech, the forced
humour, the slangy phrases, the sneering, the personalities, which
form the staple of the 'Reverend' Sam Jones' discourses, smack
strongly of the whisky saloon." Unwittingly providing the revivals
with public-relations material that might have enticed additional curi-
ous working-class people, the *Dominion Churchman* stated that the
delivery of the evangelists "seems to require as fit accomplishments
the clinking of glasses, the fumes of the dirtiest tobacco, and the inces-
sant use of the spittoon." Pained by the vulgar preaching of Jones in
Toronto in October 1886, this journal argued that members of the
Salvation Army were grotesque but at least they did not wilfully
"indulge in vulgar jests to draw a crowd."[86] Viewing popular revivals
in general as evanescent, many Canadian Anglicans were not about to
support the work of Jones. One year after Jones's first Toronto campaign, the *Dominion Churchman* was still speaking out against Jones
and others who made revivalism a trade.[87] Of course, the Anglican
publication was also critical of revivalism in general, such that even
Moody did not escape denunciation.

No other denominational publication was as critical of Jones and Small as the *Dominion Churchman*, but the relative silence of some publications on the subject of the evangelists made it clear that they had their reservations. With the exception of some Anglicans, Protestant leaders were generally willing to give the revivals of Jones and Small the benefit of the doubt; in the mid-1880s, there was an evangelical Protestant consensus on the issue of urban revivalism, and thus the Baptist, Congregationalist, evangelical Anglican, Presbyterian, and Methodist churches were all largely supportive of revival meetings. The fact that the brief visits by Jones and Small to Canada, in 1887, did not receive much treatment from Methodist or other denominational publications, cannot, therefore, be attributed to lack of support for modern revivalism; rather, it was a result of misgivings about several aspects of their work which contrasted with the work of Moody a short while before.

Daily newspaper correspondents criticized Jones for his appalling sensationalism, slang, and vulgar anecdotes. Early into the 1886 October campaign, the Toronto *Mail*, in response to a letter from a Canon J.B. Worrell arguing that the newspaper ought to cease printing Jones's revival reports, proclaimed that such a move would "impede a movement which, with all its blots and imperfections, is contributing not a little to promote the spiritual welfare of publicans and sinners."[88] The *Mail* – a Conservative organ – had received a fair number of letters of criticism of Jones from its readers, but the Tory paper recognized that the Jones-Small campaign was a good story that sold newspapers. In any event, responses from those defending Jones soon followed Worrell's letter, such as one communication from John A. Carrol, a medical doctor in St Catharines, who quoted Jesus: "Forbid him not, for he that is not against us is for us." In the same newspaper, "Torontonian" suggested that if Worrell attended one of the services he would not likely ever criticize the meetings again.[89] In another letter referring to Worrell's letter of protest, "W. Calvary" wrote that men with commonsense saw that Jones's slang is purity compared to "the deep-dyed, devilish spirit manifest in that letter."[90]

Worrell, himself, re-entered the debate with another letter castigating popular religion: "If the language of the saloon and bar-room, disregard for the sanctities of the family, fierce denunciation of our fellow-creatures, arrogant exaltation of self, gross familiarities with the name of the Almighty, are evidences of casting out

devils then Dr. Carrol's idea of Christianity and mine is very different." Strongly implying that Jones was a charlatan, Worrell added
that intelligent young men were able to detect the deceit and false-
hood of these miscalled revivals.[91] Agreeing with Worrell, Walter
Dillon protested against Jones's vulgar and abominable language
and declared that true and lasting religion consists of reverence
rather than screaming and laughter.[92] One Montrealer suggested
that Jones's vulgar anecdotes were harmful to "refined and
pure-minded people."[93] Similar concerns on the issue of reverence
found expression in editorials of the *Week*, a journal whose intellectual and political content catered to the refined and well educated.[94]
Even in its defence of Jones, the Toronto *Mail* admitted that his
methods were more suitable for the working class.[95]

Another issue that received some attention was the evangelists'
use of tobacco, a habit that the Canadian Methodist church opposed
forcefully.[96] Reformers warned that smoking, no less so than alcohol, corroded "character, intellect, and body."[97] In his October 1886
letter to the *Globe* editor, Dr Aylesworth of Collingwood, viewing
tobacco as a great evil, questioned the wisdom of a Methodist who
smoked.[98] J.W. Cunningham, in the Toronto *World*, focused his
attack on Jones, who preached a gospel of self-denial yet yielded to a
polluting tobacco that made him an affront to cultured women and
men.[99] Rushing to Jones's defence, "Justice" was angry that
Cunningham hurled his tirade of abuse just when Jones and Small
were trying to bring their successful Toronto revival to a glorious
conclusion.[100] During his October 1886 campaign, other letters followed that argued both for and against the smoking of tobacco.
Jones's image began to suffer among "respectable" Protestant Canadians who preferred not to see an evangelist indulging in the use of
tobacco, but he did not appear to worry that his smoking would
have a detrimental effect on his character and ability to reach working people. A *World* reporter asked him if he smoked and he allegedly replied: "As to my habits ... it is no more the public's business
than the color of my socks."[101] In the opinion of the Toronto *Mail*,
Jones's strutting around his hotel corridors, puffing contently on a
cigar, was casting suspicion on his sincerity to do the Lord's work.[102]

Some criticism on this issue came from more compassionate
sources, such as one young Canadian woman who attempted to res-
cue the revivalist from the evil of tobacco. Nellie Smith, who
attended a Hamilton meeting in March 1887, wrote a letter to Jones

arguing that he should quit the use of tobacco since his smoking was a stumbling block for others. In a ten-page, heartfelt letter to Jones, Smith began by stating that she was happy "to shake hands with one who is courageous enough to hold his principles & faith in the face of being called a crank ..." Then, presenting personal, religious, and health reasons for quitting the use of tobacco, she assured him that through God's strength he could eliminate his desire to smoke. Smith trusted that he would make the correct decision and overcome this "fleshly lust."[103]

Jones's sensationalism and smoking likely did not have a serious impact on his ability to attract the masses. More serious shortcomings concerned the issues of profit making, his weak salvation message, and, more importantly, Small's direct attack on the labour movement.

The spectacle of Jones and Small making large sums of money from their Canadian visits, especially when so many workers experienced overwork and poor pay, caused much controversy. The *Grip* approached the money issue in a light-hearted manner: "'Sam' Jones has gone, bad – no, let us say good luck to him. With 'Sam' Jones has gone 'Sam' Small. Good luck to him also. And with them both have gone two thousand five hundred Toronto dollars. May they speedily return! – N.B. – The dollars, that is."[104] Comments from others were more straightforward. In a November 1886 letter to the editor of the *Irish Canadian*, S. Smith argued that "the whole motive and aim of all so-called revival movements is 'Money, Money,' nothing but Money."[105] Information published on the huge amount of money presented to Jones and Small for the 1886 Toronto campaign compelled the *Palladium of Labor* to declare: "We should think that by this time some of the workingmen and others who have denied themselves comforts to contribute to these overpaid humbugs must begin to realize that they have made fools of themselves."[106]

In October 1886 a Toronto *World* editorial also raised the issue of money, arguing that the business of revivalism – the selling of revival sermons and songbooks – adopted sound financial principles and was lucrative.[107] Jones was open to attack, particularly for his acceptance of a cheque for $2,500, a huge sum of money, from Toronto Methodists for the October campaign.[108] Workers who attended the Toronto meetings of 1886 had no idea that the evangelists would receive such a large sum at the conclusion of the campaign. The question of moneymaking was even more of an issue the following

year when Jones delivered more paid lectures than free sermons.
While it was common for clergymen in Ontario to give lectures to
raise money for various causes, it was peculiar to have admission
charged for an address by an evangelist.[109]

Had Jones become more of an entertainer than an evangelist seeking to save souls? In March 1887, at the beginning of a lecture in
Hamilton, Jones attempted to deflect criticism of his charging a fee
for lectures by arguing that he had a wife, family, and an orphan asylum to support. Stating that a great many people wanted him to
preach instead of lecture for money, Jones declared: "I tell you if
some of you had to carry the load I have to you would run around
lecturing a little too."[110] Newspapers rarely defended his charging of
admission.[111] During his lecture campaign at London in September
1887, Jones hinted that there had been some criticism concerning his
acceptance of $100 per sermon at Grimsby Park. The *Daily Free
Press* reported that Jones's alleged – less than modest – response was
that he "was cheaper than the small fry they had around them at
camp meetings."[112] Whereas Moody and other evangelists refused to
use their status to turn big profits, Jones was unapologetic over his
accumulation of wealth. Unfettered by ethical restraints and equat-
ing material and spiritual blessings, he amassed a considerable fortune from preaching.[113]

Another criticism was the lack of a salvation theme in his message,
a valid point when Moody's revivalism is used as a reference. In his
October 1886 address, reported in the *Globe*, Dr Samuel Nelles
honoured Sam Jones and Sam Small "so long as they keep in harmony with the spirit and teachings of the New Testament."[114] While
Nelles did not specify what he meant, the Toronto *World*, at the conclusion of the October campaign, argued that Jones did not teach the
importance of "the Cross."[115] His revival message differed from
Moody's since Jones tended to speak more of Christian ethics than
of personal salvation. The piety theme evident in initial press reports
showed signs of unravelling. During his 1887 visits especially, Jones
rarely mentioned the atonement of Christ, and, consequently, he
offered too little to many of the working class who, according to
recent scholarship, tended to favour other-worldly and soul-saving
preaching that shared common ground with the emotionalism of an
earlier pietism. In the months after the successful October 1886
campaign, the issues of profit making and limited pietism likely
began to undercut some of his support among the common people.

Jones had little to say about the exploitation of labour, but when he confronted "the question of capital and labor" he focused on violent episodes and not on their roots. Some contemporaries praised Jones for referring to current events and for placing considerable emphasis on moral reform, but his approach was naive. Within weeks of the Haymarket Riot in 1886, Jones stated, "When you come down to bed-rock, all this communism and Anarchism are based upon the liquor traffic. Where did the Chicago Anarchists hold their secret conclaves? In the back part of barrooms."[116] As he saw it, many economic problems would disappear with prohibition and an injection of Christian principles. He was critical of a capitalist's love of money, but he also believed that the worker who did not indulge in whisky, idleness, and other immoral sins had the freedom to achieve success. It was simple – workers needed only to exercise ethical and moral behaviour. Regardless of his distaste for greed in business practice, Jones's message appeared to reinforce employers' assumptions about the inherent soundness of laissez-faire industrial capitalism.

More so than Jones, Small spoke directly about labour issues to Canadian audiences. As his sermon to "working girls" near the end of the 1886 campaign demonstrates, Small was aware of class struggle: "Capital and labor are in antagonism. There are feuds and strikes, and contentions, and disturbances between the men who labor and the men who furnish the money and means for these enterprises. There is something abnormal, something radically wrong with the system on which business is done, or else there would be peace and harmony and community of interests between these people." But why was there struggle? "I do not assume to say it is the fault of the capitalist," Small declared. Rather, contentious "relations of capital and labor" were a result of the lack of Christian principles in society. According to Small, "social reformers" and "social agitators" were following a sinful and false path; his advice to those complaining of injustice in the workplace was to "cease your antagonism" and seek "righteousness," to come "from a condition of servitude, pain, suffering, and injustice, to a high place of justice, whence you cannot be shaken."[117] Although not winning favour with labour activists, Small's message represented the views of many Canadians.

More damaging were Small's statements at his Toronto lectures in September 1887, and especially his lecture at Carlton Street Methodist Church, chaired by businessman R. Irving Walker, where Small presented his thoughts on "Society Thugs." Whisky sellers and ministers did not escape his barbs, but his commentary on newspaper editors and "labor agitators" was particularly striking. Without clarifying his position, Small argued that much of the conflict and unrest among "the masses" was the fault of newspaper editors who not only failed to voice public opinion but pandered to the "low and debased." "Labor agitators" fared no better in his estimation: "The state has no greater enemy than one of these nineteenth century labor agitators. I am not a worshipper of wealth; nor am I a sycophant to approve of these men who labor – with their mouth." As Small explained: "Labor is honourable, and I always feel a sense of dignity in grasping the hand of the honest laborer. But the man who organizes a strike should be sent to the penitentiary, and the man who leads a boycott, the only fit jewellery is a ball and chain."[118] The following evening, Small repeated his diatribe against labour organizations, singling out the Knights of Labor.[119] The friction caused by Small's lectures soon became apparent.

Small's attacks distressed the revival image makers, especially, no doubt, when he criticized their handling of labour issues. A *News* editorial labelled him insincere because, on the evening he attacked labour organizations, he allegedly accepted an invitation to the Canadian Shorthand Writers' Association, a trade union whose members, the Toronto daily explained, "are well-to-do and wear good clothes, which makes a mighty sight of difference." The union's president responded immediately, declaring that the provincial association had received Small. There was no confusion where the district assembly of the Knights of Labor stood on the issue of Small. On 23 September, under the chairmanship of Master Workman Samuel McNab, the assembly challenged Small to a public debate with a representative speaker, stating that his unfair and unjust attack on the Knights' platform "should not be allowed to pass unquestioned."[120]

There was much at stake for both labour and capital in this highly publicized confrontation. As Gregory Kealey and Bryan Palmer demonstrate, the Knights of Labor in Toronto – which played a key role in protecting labour from employers determined to cut wages and increase the pace of work – had experienced a decline in membership and importance from its high-water mark in 1886. Capitalists themselves fretted over the labour upsurge of the 1880s and any legitimation of union activity.[121]

Small's anti-union actions resulted in lost support from the *Globe*, which had been supportive of Small in the past, given his work with Sam Jones: "While it is the duty of journalists to refrain from criticism of pulpit utterances delivered with due regard for the sacred responsibilities of the preacher's position, it is no less the duty of journalists to denounce preachments tending to bring the pulpit into hatred and contempt. That disagreeable duty we have performed in Mr. Sam Small's case." As the *Globe* pointed out, "that clergymen are too neglectful of the miseries and strivings of the least comfortable classes is, unhappily, too much the belief of those classes already. Should they come to think that the comfortable Christian laity can approve of clergymen who denounce legitimate associations of workingmen as 'Thugs,' good-bye to the hope of bringing the masses to the churches." The long-term prognosis was similarly bleak: "Good-bye also to the hope of maintaining the churches themselves, for workingmen and workingmen's children of today will occupy nearly all the comfortable and powerful positions twenty-five years hence, and carry with them the feelings as to religion with which they may now be imbued."[122]

The *Globe* was not alone. Another Toronto daily, the *News*, also took the side of labour in its dispute with Small. Referring to the Knights of Labour's challenge of a public debate, the *News* stated: "If Mr. Small refuses, the public will justly conclude that he has taken advantage of the immunity from reply afforded by the pulpit and the lecture hall to make assertions which he knows to be incapable of proof."[123]

And so, even if not all informed workers questioned Small's attack on labour unions, at least two important Toronto dailies showed their displeasure. Worse still from his point of view, Small's welcome among the Toronto press as a whole ran out immediately after his comments in September 1887, and since the successful promotion of modern revivalism depended, in large part, on newspaper coverage, there was no longer any prospect of a major Jones-Small revival campaign in Toronto.

In summary, Jones and Small did not have the same degree of sustained success in Canada as Dwight L. Moody. If Moody shared their views of labour organizations, he chose not to voice them publicly. Unlike the southern evangelists, Moody did not give lectures and there was less suspicion of his making money from his meetings. He also had a much broader base of support among the evangelical

churches. Jones offered a conservative evangelical voice for many
Methodists concerned about sin in society, but he differed from
Moody by not focusing his message on the heart of a revivalist theology, the means of achieving a personal relationship with Christ. As
measured by Moody's earlier and later successes, Jones's failure on
this account may well explain his relatively ephemeral presence in
Ontario. Immediately after Jones and Small's great Toronto campaign of 1886, the *Christian Guardian* asserted that, in order to
have revival, there must be "earnest preaching of the more prominent doctrinal teachings of the Bible. What is wanted is to make the
unconverted feel their need of a Saviour; that they cannot live a right
life in view of eternity, unless they are converted and have God's
help."[124] By this standard, the preaching of Jones and Small was
deficient. In two separate reports on the October campaign, the
Christian Guardian wrote that, although the evangelists did attack
sins pervasive in society, they did not spend enough time "explaining
the way into the kingdom."[125] The preaching of Small and Jones
failed to conform consistently to the type of pietistic revivalism that
attracted Canadian Protestants, particularly those representing the
working class.[126]

Both Jones's and Small's manly attacks on sin in society assured
them the notice of many English Canadians during a time when
there was a groundswell of conservative evangelicalism at the
grass-roots level and when a large number of American and Canadian evangelists were holding revival meetings in cities, towns, and
villages across the country. Despite their considerable popular-culture appeal, however, Jones and Small revealed the limitations of
revivalism in capturing the attention and hearts of the urban masses,
particularly when press support for their work faded.

CHAPTER FOUR

Resurgence

The Canadian campaigns of Reuben Torrey began approximately two decades after Dwight L. Moody's and Sam Jones's and Sam Small's first revival excursions into Canada. The interval is significant. First, Torrey's message was much more clearly a conservative evangelical message than Moody's. The offence of modernism, which Moody had treated lightly, was central in the sermons of Torrey. But, second, despite the new emphases in Torrey's message, his sustained popularity among Canadian Protestants as measured by the press accounts was considerably greater than the popularity of Jones and Small, and fell short of Moody's popularity by only a small margin. There was considerable criticism of Torrey and his message, but such attacks were not from working-class representatives.

Without wanting to over-generalize on only the basis of press rhetoric about visiting Americans, that press coverage nonetheless suggests that the traditional evangelical message, even when moving in a fundamentalist direction, had the power to attract support from many working-class Canadians. At this time, secularizing forces were at work in the Canadian churches, as David Marshall demonstrates.[1] In addition, the fissures within Protestantism that were becoming more obvious in the United States may have been exerting a similar force in Canada, a position supported by Phyllis Airhart's account of Methodist uneasiness with the intellectual revivalism promoted by the Plymouth Brethren.[2] That Torrey received more negative criticism than had Moody suggests some fragmenting. Yet many press reports of the campaigns expressed the themes of piety, power, and community and indicate that the nineteenth-century

Canadian evangelical consensus, which had supported Moody so completely while reacting relatively cooly to Sam Jones and Sam Small, still retained strength even in the late years of the Laurier era.[3] The resurgence of modern revivalism that occurred in this period was largely the work of Torrey, who, despite criticism from modernist circles, appeared to attract a significant number of working people to revival meetings.

From 1906 to 1911, when Torrey held revival campaigns in Toronto, Ottawa, Montreal, Fredericton, Saint John, and Windsor, Nova Scotia, the Canadian social scene experienced rapid urbanization and industrialization. Rural depopulation placed extra stress on urban centres and contributed to the rise of social problems; Canadians attracted by the opportunities of the city faced sweeping changes in their everyday lives.[4] In Toronto, for example, the population from 1891 to 1901 had increased by less than 30,000 but from 1901 to 1911 the increase was almost 170,000. The nation itself was growing by leaps and bounds in the early twentieth century, its population increasing by 34 per cent in the first decade. There was exceptional economic growth, too; however, that growth resulted in little evident improvement in the working and living conditions of working-class men and women. A number of studies show that increases in the Gross National Product at this time did not produce an improvement of the standard of living for most Canadian urban labourers. As prosperity increased among the ruling class, many workers experienced alienating work, a cycle of insecurity, poor health, and dispiriting living conditions.[5]

On the matter of Canadian religious life, Airhart argues that sweeping social transformation signified the beginnings of a fracturing of the old evangelical Protestant consensus; some Protestant leaders appeared to spurn modernism while another group embraced a more forward- looking approach to Christianity. But she also points out that many denominations still retained their confidence in mass evangelism.[6]

In June 1905 the Reverend Tom Hyde, a Congregationalist, and Toronto leaders representing a variety of churches extended an invitation to Reuben Torrey and Charles Alexander to visit their city of more than 250,000.[7] In a demonstration of the high level of organization characteristic of modern revivalism, Massey Hall in Toronto had been rented for the month of January by leaders of the local evangelical churches. Approximately seven hundred people enlisted for choir service, three hundred for usher duties, and six hundred for the personal work of providing spiritual direction and instruction for new converts.[8] Assisting Torrey and Alexander with the overflow meetings was the Reverend Melvin Trotter, a Grand Rapids, Michigan, mission worker and former drunk who had almost committed suicide before becoming a Christian. Mrs J. Gordon, an evangelist of the WCTU and the Reverend Dr T.B. Kilpatrick of Knox College also assisted.[9] The Toronto press provided daily accounts, including reports that Massey Hall was unable to accommodate the overflowing crowds, who included visitors from all over southern Ontario.[10] No different than for Moody and Jones, the press often presented revival as a stirring and special episode able to transform the city for the better. As the Toronto *Daily Star* reported, Toronto was "experiencing a real religious revival."[11] During the twenty-five days of meetings, approximately 220,000 people had crowded into Massey Hall to hear a message of sin and salvation. The Torrey and Alexander campaign captured the attention of most Torontonians and, consequently, became the leading news item in the city throughout the entire month. Correspondents begged newspapers for space to voice their opinions on Torrey, a Toronto *World* editor writing that "more texts have been submitted to indulgent editors during the first four weeks of this year than are usually forthcoming in twelve months."[12] As a commodity to be sold, a Torrey revival campaign was a sure winner.

After Toronto, Torrey and Alexander departed to the United States and then returned to Canada in June 1906 for meetings in Ottawa, then a city of approximately 70,000. Moody had been the last high-profile American evangelist to visit Ottawa, and that had been nine years earlier. In a letter to the editor, L. Foote stated that the Ottawa region would do well if it could rise to a sense of its "responsibility toward God and His revealed truth, in view of such favored instruments of His divine approval coming to the city as they are now expected."[13] Both of Ottawa's major newspapers, the *Journal* and the *Citizen*, showed interest in the meetings. The Ottawa *Citizen* made it clear that it would do its part by providing verbatim reports of Torrey's sermons and the words and music of Alexander's songs. The newspaper planned to publish a daily series of Torrey-Alexander stories so that its readers could read "the wonderful story of the power of the Gospel to reclaim the most degraded ..." The *Citizen*, of course, would make money on the campaign; the editor encouraged people to subscribe to the newspaper with the best and brightest reports of the campaign.[14]

As in the Toronto campaign, clergy and lay leaders made preparations in Ottawa before the arrival of Torrey and Alexander. Representatives of various evangelical churches met at the YMCA to discuss issues including a suitable system for ushering the forthcoming immense masses. In a businesslike manner, ushers were to wear white satin badges, the choir members blue badges, and the personal workers red badges. The meetings were to be held at Dey's Arena, which could hold 3,000 people on the floor and another 3,000 in the galleries. Speakers and singers benefited from an elevated circular platform built to hold an assembly of 500 people. Canadian and British flags decorated the arena and above the platform hung a large banner declaring the Torrey-Alexander motto: "Get Right With God."[15] Perhaps sensitive to the encroachment of American revivalism, some revival attenders would be reassured by the presence of Canadian and British flags. Assisting in the music was Australian pianist Robert Harkness and American soloist Charles Butler, and Torrey's secretary, Mary Moody Parker, and A.P. Fitt, the son-in-law of the late Dwight L. Moody, also held meetings.[16]

The meetings in Ottawa always drew large crowds, often more than 5,000 people in the evenings. Even meetings in the afternoon, when many people were working, could attract a thousand or more attenders. The smallest evening service, when Ottawa was experiencing very hot weather, had more than 2,500 people present.[17] In light of this, the *Citizen* submitted that the critics – who had predicted that interest in the meetings would wane – "if honest, must admit their failure as prophets." That several thousands nightly crowded into Dey's arena was proof "that the gospel has not lost its attractions for Ottawans."[18] Audiences also came by the Canadian Pacific Railway from Arnprior, Renfrew, Buckingham, and other points, and excursions such as the one organized by the Christian Endeavors Union of Toronto brought large groups to the meetings.[19]

As early as June 1906, Torrey had met with Montreal revival planners to discuss the proposed mission in that city.[20] Ten months later, the Montreal *Daily Star* reported that Torrey, without Alexander, was on his way to Montreal for revival meetings, to be held at the St James Street Methodist Church, which had a seating capacity of 2,500 but could fit approximately 3,000 with the aisles and other spaces utilized. The article provided a picture of Torrey, a brief history of his life, and an introduction to the other leaders of the campaign. Charles Butler replaced Alexander as song leader and the Reverend W.S. Jacoby was there as Torrey's right-hand man. Mary Moody Parker, one of Torrey's revival assistants, was also present for meetings for women.[21]

Montreal had a population of approximately 400,000, of which 75 per cent were Roman Catholic. There were only about 100,000 Protestants, but the Torrey campaign began with 2,300 people attending the first meeting in the afternoon and approximately 3,000 in the evening. A snow storm on the third day of the meetings brought eight inches of snow and fifty-miles-an-hour winds, but, according to the Montreal *Daily Star*, the stormy weather cooled revival enthusiasm "if at all, only in a very small degree."[22] At the conclusion of the first week, the *Star* reported that the revival was gaining strength each day. A large number of people, for example, travelled from as far as the Eastern Townships to experience a Torrey revival meeting.[23] Near the end of the campaign, the *Gazette* reported that "with Dr. Torrey's approaching departure further stimulus seems to be added each evening to his powers as a drawer of crowds."[24] At the close of the revival, the Montreal *Daily Star* wrote of the revival's piety and power: "In a blaze of religious enthusiasm Dr. Torrey's evangelical campaign was brought to an end."[25]

By 1908, Torrey had temporarily suspended much of his revival activity, concentrated instead on his new responsibilities as a teacher at the Los Angeles Bible Institute. But in 1910 he was back in Canada for two revival campaigns in the New Brunswick cities of Fredericton and Saint John. The local Baptist, Methodist, and Presbyterian churches invited him to Fredericton, a city of approximately 7,000, to hold meetings at the Arctic Rink, which could hold as many as 3,000 people. Joining Torrey were two assistants, the Reverend W.S. Jacoby and Mary Moody Parker, singer Charles Butler, and pianist Mary Anderson. In addition to the main evening meetings held at the rink, afternoon services took place at the Methodist church. The coverage of the May and June campaign by the *Daily Gleaner* was comparable to what Torrey had received in other Canadian cities; the reports devoted significant space to the daily meetings. At the services, as many as 3,000 listeners gathered to hear the evangelists, with a number of people coming from outside the city, like the large excursion from Saint John. Early into the campaign, the *Daily Gleaner* wrote of the star status of Torrey's campaign: "To say that the revival meetings in the rink are increasing is to put it mildly. The people are just beginning to wake up to the fact that there is in our midst missionaries of worldwide reputation, and that such a powerful personality as Dr. Torrey does not visit Fredericton but once in a generation." The interest in the meetings increased daily, and on the final day of the campaign an estimated 5,500 were present for the last two services.[26]

Torrey's Saint John revival campaign of four weeks in November and December 1910 likewise generated major interest in the city of 42,500. Returning with Torrey were the Reverend W.S. Jacoby, Mary Moody Parker, Mary Anderson, and the Scotsman William McEwan, on hand to assist with the Gospel music. On most days there were three meetings and on a regular basis thousands went to the Queen's Rink to experience the "great soul-saving campaign." The meetings drew more people than had ever gathered at the rink, far exceeding even the "enormous gathering on the day of the late Dominion election." Newspaper reports indicated that the interest continued unabated to the last meeting, which could not hold all those who desired to hear Torrey.[27]

Torrey's three-week campaign in January 1911 at Windsor, Nova Scotia, a small centre, also attracted large crowds. Sponsored by the local Baptist, Methodist, and Presbyterian churches, Torrey, soloist William McEwan, and Mary Moody Parker held their main meetings at the Baptist church and other services at the Methodist and Presbyterian churches and the YMCA. The Halifax *Herald*, reporting the opening of the Windsor campaign, wrote that there was "no need of an introduction. The world knows Dr. Torrey ... The weeks to come are bound to be days and weeks of blessing to the people of Windsor and the county of Hants." As was the case in Fredericton, interest in the meetings increased daily, with many people arriving from outside points; crowds as large as 1,200 gathered to hear the famous evangelist.[28] After the Windsor meetings concluded, one Halifax citizen stated that, if a small centre such as Windsor could attract Dr Torrey, Halifax should invite the evangelist in order "to bring about a spiritual movement now in our city."[29] Even as late as 1910, newspaper reports presented "revival" as a powerfully laden symbol both for the growth of God's kingdom and for urban improvement.

Torrey's Canadian meetings were generally open to both women and men together, though at the larger cities he did have a number of separate gatherings. For example, he often filled the church with women only in the afternoons and with men only in the evenings. As had been the case for Moody, so, too, did Torrey and his sponsors make an attempt to reach workingmen; the objective was to make it easier for workers to secure seats or at least gain entrance to the evening meetings. This scheduling did not always work smoothly, though, as women attempted to gain access to men's meetings and vice versa. The Toronto *Daily Star* recorded the chaos of one meeting: "Ushers who were guarding the doors on the ground floor had a hard time to keep the women and their escorts from breaking through and getting into the reserved seats. But it was done, at the expense of some ruffled feelings, crushed hats, and torn dresses."[30] One female writer, hoping to enter the hall, approached a doorman and adopted the "various blandishments of cajolery, pleading, insistence – but all in vain."[31] The men's meetings in Ottawa attracted as many as 5,000. At the men's meetings, workingmen of all ages attended, with some clothed in little better than rags. At women's meetings, some brought children, "others came full of health and vigor, grand dames came with faltering steps, and cripples were wheeled in chairs. All were there."[32] In 1906 ladies of the Toronto YWCA discussed postponement of their meetings in January in order that members could attend the meetings.[33] Many revival attenders skipped dinner to guarantee a seat; overflow meetings gave others a second chance. There did not appear to be any significant differences between women-only and men-only meetings. Reflecting class trends, meetings held exclusively for businessmen tended to have the smallest attendance. Students and children also had their own designated meetings. Usually there were few seats to spare and Torrey often requested that individuals who attended a daytime meeting not to attend an evening meeting as well unless they brought an unconverted friend.

The meetings generally opened with a musical half-hour conducted by Charles Alexander, who made it a point to entice audience members, whether as soloist or groups, to sing. Using various techniques ranging from mock seriousness to open cajolery, Alexander rarely failed to have the audience singing for all its worth. The Toronto *Daily Star* stated that Alexander's pleasantries might initially appear shocking, but soon people recognized his skill as a singer and conductor and waved aside all prejudices.[34] Unquestionably, Alexander and his Gospel songs played a significant role in recapturing the spirit of an evangelical heritage that remained a core ingredient within the consciousness of many Canadians. In describing the Torrey-Alexander mission, a Toronto *Saturday Night* editor wrote, with keen insight, that revival-meeting songs "all carry recollections of the days when the listeners were younger and doubtless purer and more gentle. The prayers, the appeals, all carry hearers back either to the knee of the mother, to the little meeting-house to which they used to go, or to the church in which for many years they were youthful attendants."[35]

Alexander's methods and choice of simple Gospel tunes were expressions of a popular religion that rejected formality and advocated unceremonious worship of God. Providing listeners with a feeling of security, evangelistic popular music had a folk quality in which workers took comfort. As scholars point out, the "common people" easily learned and remembered Gospel songs. A line of division between those who appreciated and those who scorned the simple Gospel tunes "was drawn as cleanly as was the social line between the class which used it and the class which did not."[36] The bourgeoisie might reject this music, but ordinary working folk cared little that the tunes lacked sophistication.

Puzzled over the popularity of the "Glory Song" at the Toronto meetings, the *Mail and Empire* stated that the song's music and religious poetry were quite unspectacular.[37] One unidentified pastor, writing about the inspirational impact of the "Glory Song," testified that "when I hear that vast crowd singing those beautiful words my heart is filled with a great gladness. That one song must have brought thousands to Christ and saved a great army. It's a wonderful hymn and we shall never forget it. I feel uplifted by its very echoes."[38] This pastor and thousands of revival attenders, because they still undoubtedly embraced an evangelical heritage, were deeply moved by this popular Gospel song and its message of a loving saviour: "When all my labors and trials are o'er, And I am safe on that beautiful shore, Just to be near the dear Lord I adore, Will thro' the ages be glory for me."[39] Reporting on the impact that the revival music had on its listeners, the *News* declared that when the music concluded the audience had "pretty well 'forgotten' itself – forgotten the time and place, its neighbours and its clothes."[40] The impact of Gospel songs also went beyond the physical boundaries of revival sites. According to Sandra Sizer, "*Gospel Hymns* was in a sense a complete portable revival, containing all its forms and figures in melodies which could float upon the air... The community of feeling could be anywhere, at anytime, and could extend over any distance."[41]

Prayer, a collection for expenses, Scripture reading, announcements, and then Torrey's sermon followed the opening segment of heartfelt singing. Similar to his mentor, Dwight L. Moody, Torrey told the old story of sin and salvation with an emphasis on the Bible, the blood of Christ, the Holy Spirit, and the power of prayer. Condemning personal sins aggressively, Torrey spoke out against drinking, dancing, gambling, abortion, and mistreatment of the poor.[42] According to the Fredericton *Daily Gleaner*, Torrey was a "teaching evangelist" who maintained a high standard of biblical exposition; his addresses were masterpieces of logic and every argument was secured "with iron bolts of unanswerable gospel truths."[43] Referring to his blunt "condemnation of wrong," an Ottawa reporter recognized Torrey's aggressive and virile manner: "He is more likely, as a first impression[,] to arouse mental resentment, and it strikes one sometimes that he deliberately aims at that end, and then with the manly plea urges a right intellectual attitude and the facing of eternal problems in the light of future consequences and present duty."[44] Though he was not an eloquent man, the Toronto *Daily Star* claimed that Torrey spoke with power derived from intense earnestness: "He tells the story of the cross in simple language, such that the smallest child present could understand without difficulty."[45] Newspaper accounts portrayed him as an earnest evangelist who adopted a direct, no-nonsense, and masculine manner of preaching.

After his sermons, and with astute timing, Torrey invited those who wanted to accept Christ to rise from their seats. Next came a prayer from Torrey and more singing from the choir under the direction of his musical assistant. During this time, personal workers went among the audience to extend individual invitations to come to the front where penitents signed inquirer's cards and, as directed by Torrey, received encouragement to join a Bible-believing church. They were to avoid churches "where they tear the bible to pieces."[46] In contrast to most of Dwight L. Moody's meetings, there were no inquiry rooms established for those seeking to talk privately with revival workers about the state of their souls.[47] Torrey and Alexander placed more emphasis on personal testimonies in an open forum, and, unlike Jones and Small, Torrey stressed the importance of the atoning blood of Christ.

Throughout the campaign, revival participants requested prayers for specific men and women of various towns and cities. There were prayers for unidentified people such as "a nurse," "a lady," "a young woman," "a husband," "a brother," "a brilliant young man," "a distinguished military man," "two business men," "a wayward son," "an uncle," and numerous others.[48] Both the press and the evangelists realized the value of having individual testimonies and prayers heard and published in a pluralistic age when there was an increasing number of diversions competing with the churches for the attention of the masses.

One modern advertising strategy to win souls to Christ was the distribution of 200,000 cards at the Toronto meetings bearing the advice "Get Right with God." Speaking on the importance of reaching out to as many people as possible, one individual, in a letter to the editor, wrote: "We have been too conventional and timid in our methods of Christian work and these little touches of direct appeal are just what we need to stir the consciences of the unsaved."[49]

When it came to reaching the conscience of his listeners, Torrey was anything but timid. His fundamentalist-leaning attitude, for example, could be compressed into the three sentences preached to Christians in a Montreal audience: "Don't mind those who persecute you. If they kill you it will be only to send you to Heaven more quickly. Throw to the winds tonight your fear of man, that has snared you into a guilty compromise with the world."[50] The key components of Torrey's preaching were a literal interpretation of the whole Bible, the doctrine of atonement, the power of the Holy Spirit, and the doctrine of eternal punishment.

Though he once accepted the method of higher criticism in his early ministry, Torrey decided that such an approach was indeed false, and instead he relied on a literal reading and understanding of the entire Bible. Adopting an inductive method of biblical interpretation, he scrutinized a portion of the Bible and carefully synthesized the material in as exact terms as possible. He made the point that too many suspect theologians weaved "their theories out of their own inner consciousness without regard to facts."[51] He believed that society was anxious to hear the old-fashioned religion of the Bible, and he supported his propositions with numerous quotations of chapter and verse. For him, not only did the Bible and its accurate prophecies demonstrate its infallibility, but, from his experience, German scholarship placed souls in jeopardy.

Torrey warned that "a great many people would drop blood out of theology, but if they dropped all blood out of theology they would drop all blood out of their experience, and drop all access to God."[52] He preached that salvation and access to God could be obtained only through the atoning blood of Christ, and that the most serious sin was an individual's rejection of Christ. Regardless of the seriousness of people's sins, they could be saved immediately. To be accepted by God did not depend on good character; salvation occurred by receiving Christ as saviour.[53]

Edith Blumhofer notes that Torrey agreed with Moody in the latter's use of the phrase baptism in the Holy Spirit to describe an occasion when he experienced the intense love of God.[54] All could find rest and full happiness through the baptism of the Holy Spirit, an experience separate from conversion. First, one was to be "born again" by accepting Christ and then, by "opening one's heart" to the Holy Ghost, an even greater reality of blessedness would be achieved, signifying that the individual was ready to serve God. According to Torrey, "if one is born again he is saved, but he has not the fullness of the blessing there is for him, and he is not fitted for service."[55] Proponents of "higher life" such as Torrey held that the Holy Spirit empowered individuals to devote themselves to Christian service and to achieve victory over sin but was unlike Pentecostal or holiness teachings, which believed in the eradication of sin and the gaining of gifts through a Holy Spirit baptism.[56] According to Margaret Lamberts Bendroth, the 'higher life' message was appealing to masculine audiences.[57]

Torrey, like Jones and Small, presented an aggressive case for hell. But his message was more severe, without the humorous antics associated with Jones's sermons: "Forever and ever is the never-ceasing wail of that restless sea of fire. Such is hell, a place of bodily anguish, a place of agony of conscience, a place of insatiable torment and desire ..."[58] For Torrey, people in hell, with swollen and parched tongues, longed for a single drop of water. He knew that liberal Protestants questioned the doctrine, but he argued that the majority of scholarly ministers and clergymen believed "in the orthodox hell."[59] Even if there was not outright denial of the doctrine of eternal punishment, he judged that many clergymen were often too silent on the issue. According to Torrey, the "cruelest man on earth" was the clergyman who failed to warn others of an everlasting hell.[60] With grim determination, Torrey persevered because he believed that the stakes were very high; the unwelcome truth was that, "if even the dearest friend we have on earth persists in trampling this infinitely glorious

Christ under foot, he ought to be banished from the presence of God and to suffer forever and ever."[61]

Despite his propensity to preach fire and brimstone, Torrey repeatedly showed compassion for the working poor. When commenting on the evil in society, he singled out the sins of wealthy people more than those of the poor. To a Massey Hall audience, he declared: "There is not a man or a woman in this building to-night so low down in sin, whether it be the vice of the outcast, or the just as hateful sin of the upper classes living without God." Indeed, often "upper class sins are as cruel, mean, selfish, brutal in a refined way as those of the drunkard down in the slums who roasts his child in the oven in his drunken rage." It was the "cold-hearted, self-centered" upper class who "let the babes of the poor starve to death while they roll away in luxury."[62] Torrey vented his indignation at ladies living in "fashion, frivolity, and foolishment" and men who made gold their God, robbed workers, oppressed the poor, and promoted merciless competition in the business world.[63] At a revival meeting in Fredericton, he accused many of its citizens of worshipping "Plutus, the god of wealth."[64] Torrey was, at times, quite critical of the inequalities of industrial capitalism. At one Toronto meeting, the Toronto *Daily Star* recorded Torrey's condemnation of poverty: "This wretched Malthusian philosophy that the world doesn't bear enough to support all the inhabitants is false – a libel on God – and has been knocked higher than a kite by Henry George. Nobody need go hungry. The only trouble is that the wealth isn't properly distributed."[65] This is a remarkable statement coming from an American revivalist.

It is difficult to assess the extent of Torrey's acceptance and understanding of reform thought, since his revival message rarely probed deeply into social and economic issues. Nonetheless, it is striking that in the late nineteenth century he had helped organize the Convention of Christian Workers and also ceased to take a wage for his evangelistic labours, relying on God instead for all his needs.[66] Torrey appeared to fear that the bourgeoisie was in a much worse condition than the poor drunkards and outcasts of the city, for it was Satan who offered wealth, social position, and power.[67] Certainly, he seemed to have a better understanding than most other American evangelists of the shortcomings of the capitalist mode of production.

Torrey's concern for the working poor and his analyses of social conditions received little comment from the press and others.

Rather, it was his grim interpretation of hell that generated the most discussion during his visits to Canada, especially in Toronto. Writing that Torrey's ideas of eternal punishment had a strong medieval flavour, the Toronto *World* defined his literal hell as "The Torreyd Zone."[68] The *Mail and Empire*, more so than the other Toronto papers, published a number of letters that spoke out against him. One Toronto correspondent wrote: "Fancy Longfellow and Emerson having 'no access to God'... When one thinks of the vast numbers of the sweetest, grandest, noblest souls this old earth has ever known being in hell or on the road there, one feels more than indifferent about getting to Dr. Torrey's Heaven." Another writer, proclaiming to be a Methodist, stated that his early life "was darkened by the hellish presentation of the Gospel, and ... devilish lie of eternal torment." Only after apparently hearing the "Voice of God" speak to his soul did this Methodist know that an everlasting hell was "a devilish misinterpretation of the truth." Since that day, the more the writer heard of eternal fire the more he wondered "how any sane man can so libel God." Could the creator be "less loving than His creatures?" the writer asked.[69]

Other letters to Toronto newspapers passionately defended Torrey's position on hell. In the *News*, one correspondent responded to a Torrey critic with the advice that he should devote more time to reading the Bible and less to espousing the arguments of his favourite professor. This defender of Torrey argued that "the poor, suffering, sorrowing, sin-stricken wanderer" requires a saviour, not a higher criticism that denies the doctrine of eternal punishment. In his judgment, Torrey was "holding up Jesus Christ everyday, and, praise God, hundreds of sin-sick souls have found rest, and peace, and joy in Him."[70] In another letter, the Reverend Richard Hobbs asked how so many humanitarians could believe in the eternity of future blessedness and not in the eternity of future retribution, especially since "the greatest of all Teachers taught them both ...?" A Mr B.A. Kelly from Lynville rejoiced that, among Toronto clergymen, it was difficult to find one who disagreed with Torrey and tried to "lull poor sinners into eternity without any fear of punishment, [and] consequently no need of a Saviour."[71]

Others could not agree with these Torrey supporters. According to W.C. Good, few people with average intelligence believed in the infallibility of the Bible and the notion that Christ taught "the terrible and grotesquely materialistic flaming sword of eternal tor-

ment."[72] The Reverend C.W. Casson, an Ottawa Unitarian
clergyman, asserted that every sensible man had "long since discarded the idea of a hell of fire ... as unbelievable ... [and] a blas-
phemy against a God of love." Torrey's hell and brimstone, Casson
added, belonged "in the same category as a flat earth, a cheese
moon, and a last year's nightmare."[73]

   In the 23 January issue of the *Mail and Empire*, the editor
acknowledged that letters arrived daily concerning Torrey's theology. On that day, he published a few selections from the forty-seven
letters that had arrived. One particularly revealing letter noted that
the newspaper had informed its readers about three sermons
preached by Dr Jabez T. Sunderland, of the First Unitarian Church,
on the topic of Torrey's view of Unitarianism. The writer wanted to
know the impact of the sermons: "I was anxious to see the paper and
to know what the result would be. I have read it very carefully, but
your correspondent has omitted the number of converts there was at
that service, while on the same page is recorded 150 converts at Dr.
Torrey's meeting at Massey Hall." The letter writer asked: "Will you
kindly favor me by inserting these few lines asking for the number of
converts as a result of the preaching of Rev. Dr. Sunderland's sermon?" The *Mail and Empire* admitted that it was unable to grant
such a request.[74]

Torrey's conservative evangelical and populist message came
under attack from the well-educated elite but appeared to produce
results among others. From Toronto newspaper accounts, Unitarian
clergymen and other critics believed that their position was superior
since they appealed to the intellect rather than to emotion. But
Torrey did not have to defend his message and method because the
mass popularity of his meetings spoke volumes in his favour. Unfortunately for his critics, his words made a long-lasting impression.
True, Joseph T. Clark, editor of the Toronto *Saturday Night*, did not
appreciate that the city continued to debate the issue of eternal punishment even after the departure of the evangelists. This was a question, according to Clark, "that people in Toronto had, for the most
part, learned to forget, or were diligently trying to put out of their
thought."[75] But it is questionable whether Clark was speaking for
the many workers who heard Torrey. Implied in Torrey's message
was that no one could buy, with money or education, their way out
of hell. Hell could be seen as "a world of social reversal." The unjust
bourgeoisie who went to hell would pay for their social sins; as they

endured the eternal fire, gone would be their trappings of wealth and haughty attitude.[76] Perhaps, for workers, the powerful symbol of hell was a class leveller.

The debate on hell continued during Torrey's Ottawa campaign six months later in June 1906. While there was a small number of Unitarians – perhaps one hundred – in Ottawa, they made their voices heard. The Reverend C.W. Casson, a Unitarian who had criticized Torrey's Toronto campaign, accused him and other revivalists of using hell as the basis of their revival business; without the theme of hell, Torrey would be without theology and trade. Casson scoffed at the notion that the finest minds, such as Henry David Thoreau, Benjamin Franklin, and Thomas Jefferson, were in hell. Given that the elite offered superior company than the common masses, the choice for Casson was easy: "It would be better to suffer with the strong and sanely good, than to spend eternity with those whose highest aim is expressed in the sickly sentimentality of the 'Glory Song.'"[77] In reply to Casson, a correspondent signed "Believer" wrote that Casson was an "infidel," since anyone who had been privileged to hear Torrey's preaching of the Gospel could testify to the biblical soundness of his theology.[78] Torrey had his Canadian defenders, but the controversy concerning his hellfire preaching persisted. In a 1907 letter to the Montreal *Daily Star*, A.M. Edington asked: "Is not Rev. Dr. Torrey taking a little too much upon himself in condemning so many of his fellow creatures to the never-dying torment of hell?" Like other critics, Edington took exception to Torrey's opinion that "goodly" men were among the lost who was suffering "everlasting punishment in the flames of hell."[79]

Torrey's message, especially his condemnation of higher criticism and modern thought, received harsher treatment in large city newspapers than was the case for Sam Jones and Sam Small and Dwight L. Moody. The Toronto *World* not only published derogatory articles and letters to the editors concerning the Torrey-Alexander mission but also often maligned Torrey's theology in editorials. Professor Shailer Matthews of the University of Chicago, a Canadian, stated: "I have great sympathy with the evangelical movement. I don't believe, however, that to succeed in such a movement it is necessary to hold certain views maintained by Dr. Torrey. I maintain that men who believe in constructive higher criticism can save souls and do save souls."[80] Similarly, a *Globe* editorial warned of the potential dangers of Torrey's "undiscriminating and sometimes unscholarly slashes at theological teachers whose spirit is at least as reverent as his own." The editor took exception to his "vigorous disproving of theories exploded and abandoned a generation ago." Such "views would contribute little either to the religious life or to the official power of the churches." The old Gospel of sin and salvation, as Torrey defined it, needed to be broader to revitalize the church community.[81]

The most vocal critic of the Toronto campaign was a Unitarian who, in a lengthy Toronto *World* article, asked: Do the Torrey supporters understand the serious implications of having him "spend a month in a persistent effort to shake the confidence of the public in our best and highest Biblical scholarship and to awaken in the churches of all denominations distrust of the honoured men to whom we have committed the training of our ministry and the creation of our religious literature?"[82] The *World*, in its final editorial on the subject of Torrey, proclaimed it had a catholic mind, but it, nonetheless, was happy to state "we shall not see his like again."[83]

The *Evening Telegram* reported that some Torontonians thought Torrey's theology to be contrary to Christianity, science, and sense.[84] At the conclusion of the Toronto campaign, Canadian intellectual W.D. LeSueur wrote a letter to the editor stating it was dangerous to think that a genuine revival of religion could overcome all evils. A Comtean and Christian humanist, LeSueur argued that to make society better, man should depend first on man rather than God.[85]

During the 1907 Montreal campaign, one critic of Torrey, Norman Murray, described himself as a follower of the teachings of Robert Ingersoll the atheist. Torrey became so annoyed with Murray's interruptions that at one meeting he questioned Murray's moral character, upon which Murray took offence and had his lawyers issue a suit for defamation of character. Although Torrey claimed that Murray's suit against him was "absurd" and that he might counter with his own suit for damages, he later apologized in front of an overflowing church. Murray himself claimed that he was not an atheist and that he would support the principles taught by Dr Torrey "if that gentleman had better manners."[86]

In Toronto, controversy concerning Torrey spilled over from the newspapers into *Saturday Night*, a magazine that reflected bourgeois views more so than those of a populist nature. The publication also appeared to have some sympathy for Unitarianism since Unitarian sermons were in the magazine every week during the

Torrey-Alexander campaign. In its first report of the meetings, *Saturday Night*, while submitting a fairly positive appraisal, proposed that Torrey might have preached more about Christian virtues than the saving of souls.[87] In the following issue, the editor expressed considerable concern over Torrey's orthodox message: "It seems to me that less permanent good will be accomplished than might have been, by bringing from the cloisters of the past some of the harsher phases of theology of which many had hoped modern preaching had been divested." He deprecated Torrey's claim that one could be saved only through what the critic perceived as "a set and arbitrary way," adding that "all of this seems so terribly unnatural, un-God-like and unreasonable that one feels an aversion, not only to the doctrine, but to the preacher of it."[88]

The following week's issue of *Saturday Night* was even more disparaging of the revival meetings, which had become extremely popular among ordinary Torontonians. The editor suggested that the present revival phenomenon was an exercise in psychological suggestion which produced a magnetic force – one that almost changed the individual "into one of a great mass of uplifted human beings." Whether this message made any sense to readers, one can only speculate. An unmistakable point, however, was the editor's assertion that no one would claim that this revival occurrence "had even a suggestion of the supernatural in it, though in the old camp-meeting days it was called the influence of the Holy Spirit."[89] Here, the writer explicitly denied the essential spiritual element of the Torrey-Alexander revivals. In another lengthy editorial, the author proclaimed: "In their sensitized state individuals of an audience are apt to accept the theory that they are utterly depraved and are mere worms of the dust ..." This outcome was unacceptable and evangelists "must be held responsible for the proper use of the extraordinary conditions they create and the plasticity of the minds which they mould."[90] For this author, a Gospel of sin and salvation did not constitute a suggestion "on the highest plane." Adding to his scepticism was the viewpoint that revival attenders, because of the "plasticity" of their minds, could easily be moulded by Torrey and his message. In the same issue, an unidentified *Saturday Night* writer criticized the revival meetings for the "peculiarly narrow and backward-looking theological views" presented and Torrey's not so "gentle attacks upon about every form of progressive and reasonable religion in sight, including prominently that terrible destroyer of souls, the "higher criticism" of the Bible, and indeed rational views of the Bible generally."[91]

Torrey had his critics, then, yet many other Canadians approved his Gospel message; certainly, it was true that ordinary folk had been influenced by the Torrey-Alexander revivals. At the revival meetings, it was common to have petitions of prayer for workingmen such as "the workmen in the Firstbrook Box Factory."[92] But even more striking were the workingmen themselves who crowded into Massey Hall, coming "from the foundry, the factory, the workshop and the unfinished building."[93] Representatives of the working poor spoke of the pain and suffering in their lives. During a testimonial session at one meeting, a self-described drunkard declared: "I thank God this afternoon that I am here ... I love Him. I would sooner die for Jesus Christ than go back and serve the devil." Another man cried out: "I have just been released from Kingston penitentiary, where I have spent the last ten years for safe-blowing. I thank God for bringing you to Toronto, and that I have been saved through your agency."[94] This man and other males seemed all too conscious of the weight of their transgressions and were ready for transformation.[95] As Virginia Lieson Brereton explains, men were reluctant to begin the process of conversion and often pursued moral reform first and foremost, but once they made the decision to profess Christ they proceeded with less hesitation than women.[96]

The drama of other personal testimonies continued meeting after meeting and indicated the pervasiveness of an evangelical spirit within the city. In a letter to his wife, Alexander wrote that a reporter for the Toronto *Daily Star* led a Toronto *World* reporter to Christ. For the *Star* reporter, the other man's public confession of Christ gave him greater joy than any previous newspaper work.[97] A man brought his sister and her boyfriend to a meeting and both experienced conversion. One little boy who accepted Christ encouraged three other boys to give their hearts to Jesus. A young man related that "I brought my father who had done nothing else for thirty-four years but drink here, and he accepted Christ."[98] Several fathers rejoiced that their sons had been converted at meetings.

One sixteen-year-old boy who came forward to accept Christ was Oswald Smith. From his hometown of Odessa, Smith heard about the Torrey meetings from the newspapers and begged his mother to let him and his brother Ernie travel the ninety-four miles to Toronto, by train, to attend the meetings. At the final meeting, Smith sprang out of his seat and "with a sober face" took steps toward Torrey's grasping hand, whereupon he received counsel from a revival worker. Initially, Smith "saw no light" but then suddenly something happened: "I cannot explain it even today. I just bowed my head, put my face between my hands and in a moment the tears gushed through my fingers and fell on the chair, and there stole into my boyish heart the realisation of the fact that the great change had taken place. Christ had entered and I was a new creature. I was born again."[99] Smith would later become one of the most well-known Canadian pastors and evangelists of the twentieth century.

The conversion of Smith bears witness to the ability of Torrey to attract and motivate individuals to make a public decision for Christ. While few attenders were from the ruling class, there were many from the working class. Newspapers stated that there was a "manliness" about Torrey's revivals, thus making it clear to workingmen that their masculinity would not be questioned if they attended the meetings. Furthermore, Torrey's militancy might have appealed to men who saw most clergymen as weak. According to Betty DeBerg, clergymen at the start of the twentieth century were at risk since their identity was dependent on a profession that had been somewhat feminized.[100] The *Wesleyan* was also aware of this problem and it stressed that ministers "should study the ways of the world of men."[101] Attracting working-class men to the meetings did not appear to be difficult for Torrey.

Some who came had rough-and-tumble working-class backgrounds, such as Alfred Allen, the middleweight boxing champion of Canada. The rhetoric on revivalism and Allen provided fascinating reading for Canadians. Having made a small fortune from fighting and operating a saloon, Allen lived "the hardest, wickedest life" he knew how. After losing his saloon, Allen went on a two-year drunk which caused him to experience terrible hallucinations. He was sent to prison and upon his release he again fought for money, losing it immediately in drinking sprees. His life changed the Friday evening that he entered Dey's Arena in Ottawa: "I don't remember anything about the sermon. I remember that someone took me up front, and I promised to come again on Sunday night. To keep from drinking on Saturday I stayed in bed all day at my hotel." Allen then experienced a transformation. "Now my old life seems away off; I don't want to think of it. I don't want to go near a saloon again, and I'll never put another glove on." With great joy, he stated: "I never in all my life put in such a day as to-day. Yesterday was the happiest day of my life; but to-day is even happier than yesterday." He publicly accepted Jesus at the conclusion of Torrey's sermon "Heroes and Cowards," his face "radiant with the love of Christ." As the audience recognized that one of the men who came forward was Allen, "a thrill" ran through the building and many gathered around and grasped his hand, singing "Grace Enough for Me."[102] As was the case for many other males, Allen's public surrender was not an easy passage because conversions had a submissive and feminine character, the antithesis of a masculinity that upheld boldness and self-mastery. However, revivalism's focus "on victory and power turned this self-negating experience into a dynamic, self-authenticating one"; filled with the Holy Spirit, Allen became strong, wise, and effective.[103]

In newspaper reports on Allen's revival experience, class, masculinity, and revivalism intersected, representing "a new commercialism" with lasting implications for popular revivalism. Kathryn Teresa Long's study of American revivalism clarifies the impact of reports on well-known, masculine individuals. First, the press created a new category of "celebrity convert," providing a more interesting twist for readers than "ordinary" converts. Second, the merchandising of such revival stories as entertainment represented an estrangement of revivalism from its ecclesiastical roots, "a by-product of commmericialization that reflected changing patterns in the relationship of revivals to popular culture." Finally, such newspaper reports contributed to the image that revival represented "manly Christianity" and that a revival meeting could be a predominantly male-oriented event, an image that could attract and reassure working-class males. The narrative form of well-known notorious figures experiencing conversion received prominence in both secular and religious spheres, so much so that the evangelist J. Wilbur Chapman acknowledged that he knew "all the famous converts in America."[104]

If manly Allen could experience the revival fire, others could too. At one meeting, an Ottawa clergyman related how one man's son and wife experienced conversion, causing him to be the happiest man in Ottawa.[105] A mother rejoiced over the conversion of her two young sons; a housewife reported that three in her household found Christ; and a saved young boy desired "to bring his father to Christ." These were just a few examples of the many who gave similar personal testimonies.[106] Numerous testimonies were given of how revival attenders themselves were spreading the revival fire and bringing others "to the Saviour." For example, one newspaper reported that an elderly man from the west was asked by Torrey to "take the fire back to Alberta."[107] In a letter to the Ottawa *Citizen*, a Mr L. Foote believed that people were "tired of the barren husks of a world under judgement" and craved the living Christ that was being faithfully preached by Torrey.[108] Overall, criticisms of his proto-fundamentalism were certainly present throughout his campaigns in Canada, but newspaper stories like these, which could be multiplied many times, also indicate that his support among ordinary Canadians was wide and deep.

Canadian churches, for the most part, supported Torrey. Before the arrival of the Torrey and Alexander team in Toronto, the Baptist, Methodist, and Presbyterian churches, in numerous articles, predicted that great crowds would gather for the meetings.[109] Because of the formality of their church, most Anglicans failed to endorse the efforts of the revivalists. Still, it is noteworthy that the *Canadian Churchman*, the voice of high church Anglicans, did not criticize the work of Torrey and Alexander. The silent response of the *Churchman* indicates that the Anglican Church, perhaps compelled to acknowledge popular tastes, was careful not to antagonize some of its parishioners by criticizing the revival meetings. As John Webster Grant suggests, tensions within the Anglican Church concerning elite and popular religion in Ontario explains Anglican divisions over the adoption of the somewhat unceremonious format of special evangelistic services.[110] While maintaining that the Anglican Church was the true and divine agency established on earth for the conversion of individuals, the *Churchman* realized that visiting evangelists might be able to minister to the many engulfed by poverty who could not be reached by the Anglican Church.[111]

There were, however, Anglicans who wrote critical letters, including E. Soward, who not only labelled Torrey and Alexander "false teachers" but castigated other clergymen for "violating" their ordination vows. Their duty was to "banish and drive away all erroneous and strange doctrines ..."[112] One Anglican lamented, in a letter to the Toronto *World*, that many of the Anglican hierarchy were not supportive of the revivals. Anglican leaders failed to understand that perhaps thousands joined the congregations of other denominations because Anglican clergy did not encourage their people to attend the meetings. He continued: "Surely the church clergy must recognize, even if they only read the daily papers, that the gatherings of these enormous crowds to hear a plain, solid man, devoid of eloquence, but with intense conviction, proclaim the truths of the gospel, followed by open confession of sin and changed lives, must be of God and not man." Anglicans who did attend the meetings faced the indifference, the veiled opposition, and even the sneers of some Anglican leaders.[113]

Some Congregationalists were quite critical, even though Torrey was an ordained Congregationalist minister. Stating that he was the "literalist of the literalists," the *Canadian Congregationalist* questioned his unpleasantly narrow message, which ostracized "sincere, broad-minded, Christ-loving and man-loving men of liberal faith." Even more reprehensible were that Torrey's references to "Higher Critics" represented pandering to the prejudices of the masses, who were unfamiliar with the issues of higher criticism and Unitarianism.[114] The Reverend J.B. Silcox deplored Torrey's dogmatic preaching, his attacks on higher critics, and his emphasis on the "substitutionary" theory of the atonement (namely, that Jesus died in place of the Christian believer, thus paying the penalty for human sin). Silcox, moreover, claimed that many Toronto minsters disagreed with Torrey's attacks on the higher critics but were afraid to say so to the press. Another Congregationalist defended Torrey. Declaring that he was in a position to know the facts, the Reverend T.B. Hyde, secretary of the executive committee of the campaign, wrote that Baptist, Methodist, and Presbyterian ministers of Toronto passed resolutions heartily supporting Torrey's revivals. According to Hyde, "the power of God could be felt from day to day" at Massey Hall.[115] At least within Congregationalism, there was evidence of tension between the liberal and conservative wings of evangelicalism.

Recent studies that examine early-twentieth-century Canadian Presbyterianism do not mention the response of Presbyterian leaders to the Torrey-Alexander mission, even though there was extensive coverage by Presbyterian publications.[116] Appreciating that a revival spirit was active and flourishing in Toronto, the *Presbyterian* stated: "No other than the religious interest could have aroused and held the vast audiences which day by day and night by night for a whole month have packed Massey Hall."[117] Offering no criticism, the *Presbyterian* acknowledged that Torrey presented the "old fashioned

Gospel in the old fashioned way."[118] In another issue, the magazine published the impressions of four Presbyterian ministers regarding Torrey's work. One remarked on his "new emphasis upon the authority of the Bible," while all four recognized his controversial and dogmatic manner. But rather than being disturbed with his conservative theology, these ministers saw Torrey as an instrument of God.[119] After the conclusion of the Toronto campaign, the *Presbyterian* praised his dogmatic preaching, adding that "Jesus Christ was the great dogmatist." Torrey's words were often "unduly harsh," but the writer acknowledged that "the crowds continued to come and day by day and night by night large numbers rose to profess their purpose to consecrate their lives to Christ."[120] While one report in the *Westminster* wrote of the criticism concerning Torrey's orthodoxy, the publication's accounts of the Toronto campaign were mostly positive.[121]

Baptist clergymen throughout the Toronto revival sustained their initial endorsement of the Torrey-Alexander crusade. The *Canadian Baptist*, fully aware that others had criticized the revivalists, remained supportive of Torrey and Alexander's effective methods, which were attracting increasingly large crowds and demonstrating "a growing manifestation of power."[122] It devoted numerous pages of coverage to the meetings, including encouraging assessments written by many Toronto Baptist leaders. For example, a common observation was that Torrey and Alexander represented the old-fashioned Gospel and their approach of dealing with the "old truths" in the "old way" was done so in a fashion that glorified God.[123]

Baptists praised Torrey's ability to attract crowds of people and championed the harsh words that the revivalist used in attacking sinners. Using the analogy of a blacksmith, the Reverend Alex White claimed that Torrey wielded a "sledge hammer in his attacks on sin," breaking individuals rather than melting them. The masculinity of such fundamentalist-type rhetoric is undeniable. The Reverend J.D. Freeman used even more violent imagery to describe Torrey: as he delivers his propositions, "the naked sword of the Spirit gleams in his hand. It flashes forth incessantly as he thrusts it into those who now stand accused of high treason to Heaven's King. In his hand it seems to run réd with blood."[124] Although this description was unusual for its militancy, other Baptist leaders, such as the Reverends H.F. LaFlame, C.H. Schutt, and H. Francis Perry, all acknowledged the intensity of the revivalists in their attacks on sin. Laflamme wrote that Alexander was "the forge heating the meeting to a white heat" while Torrey was "the trip hammer pounding the mass into shape." Describing the revivalists' work and impact on Toronto, the Baptist Reverend C.W. King wrote: "They are fearless and unflinching in their loyalty to the truth. They have been severely criticized, of course. Such men will be. Doubt them when they are not. But the common people heard them gladly."[125]

Like the Baptists, the Methodists eagerly awaited the arrival of Torrey and Alexander to Canada, although Phyllis Airhart claims that early-twentieth-century Canadian Methodism had begun searching for a "new evangelism" which distanced itself from the "old paths" of an earlier revival tradition that preached a message of sin and salvation. As Airhart also points out, the Methodists still desired revival, but some of them protested that a purely other-worldly focus might temper enthusiasm for Christian service in the urban community.[126] Torrey's campaigns thus prove a good test for gauging the position of the Methodists on revivalistic methods in the first decade of the twentieth century.

The Methodist publications provided extensive and positive coverage and numerous Methodist clergymen of Toronto all spoke highly of the great work that the American revivalists were accomplishing in the city. In Toronto, the Reverend Marmaduke L. Pearson of Berkeley Street Methodist Church, grandfather of Lester Pearson, the future Canadian prime minister, wrote that the Torrey-Alexander campaign came "nearest to the good old protracted meetings to which Methodism owes so much." The Reverend T.E. Bartley of Elm Street Church joyfully recorded that men and women were anxious to be closer to Christ. The Reverend J.D. Fitzpatrick of the Fred Victor Mission summarized the impact of the campaign on the city: the decision to accept Christ was on the minds of many unconverted, clergymen were expecting to see larger numbers in their own services, and Christians had become more active in the personal work of telling others the importance of spiritual salvation. Concurring with Fitzpatrick, approximately twenty other Toronto Methodist clergymen made parallel observations in their appreciation of the enormous crowds and religious enthusiasm of the Torrey-Alexander campaign.[127]

The Methodist community, caught up in the evangelical-revival spirit, did not appear to be troubled with the method and message of the American revivalists. The *Christian Guardian* stated that there was "no clap-trap, no cheap sensationalism," Torrey spoke "with fearless and authoritative force," and his preaching was as "if Jesus Christ were at his elbow." In the same issue, the Reverend W.H. Adams did raise the issue of whether the message espoused by Torrey and Alexander was appropriate. Aware of the criticisms by liberal American Protestants of the Torrey-Alexander message, Adams entered Massey Hall on a fault-finding mission. According to Adams, it was not long into the service that he realized that the critics must have reached their conclusions from newspaper reports rather than from attending the meetings. The essentials of Torrey's message were sound and secure.[128]

The Methodist Dr John Potts, who had played a large role in bringing Sam Jones and Sam Small to Toronto in 1886, proclaimed that the Toronto campaign was "the greatest work of God I have ever known in Toronto."[129] Such glowing reports published in the *Christian Guardian* do suggest that an old-fashioned message of sin and salvation was not yet losing ground to a more liberal message. Concerning the public response, the *Canadian Methodist Magazine* seemed to speak for most Methodists when it reported that it could not be denied that "the marked simplicity of Dr. Torrey's sermons, and the great crowds that in every city throng to hear him, prove that after all it is the old gospel story that the hearts of men are craving."[130]

At the Montreal campaign, Methodists admitted that Torrey's views were controversial but Methodist clergymen were "second to none in their active cooperation."[131] In his report of the Montreal campaign, the Reverend Ernest Thomas made the point that Torrey's "unhesitating affirmations" were his strength. Like others, Thomas recognized the force of Torrey's conservative evangelical message and its ability to reach the conscience of the unchurched.[132]

In 1910 the *Christian Guardian* noted that Torrey – "the distinguished evangelist" – was about to begin his campaign in Fredericton. The *Wesleyan*, a Methodist magazine published in Halifax, wrote that his meetings in Fredericton and Windsor attracted large crowds and were a great blessing for many.[133] While evidence from periodicals about revival campaigns can never describe the complete picture, nonetheless it remains striking that there were so few Methodist objections to Torrey's activities in Canada. As late as 1910, Methodists in the Maritime provinces remained committed to

Torrey's revivalism, many Methodists preferred that revivalism in an "old-fashioned" form, and an admittedly growing interest in urban social service was not yet seen as an alternative to old-fashioned revivalism.

Like Sam Jones, Torrey was fearless in his attacks on sin. Yet Torrey had more in common with Dwight L. Moody since they both sustained a connection with ordinary working people. Torrey preached a message grounded in biblical exposition that the common individual could understand. Although he did not attack the ruling class with the passion of a Christian socialist, he did appear to be more sympathetic to the plight of the labouring poor than the American evangelists who came before him.

Ample impressionistic evidence suggests that the Gospel message, shorn of formality and situated in a popular-culture framework, had a special appeal to many of the working class in Toronto, Ottawa, Montreal, Fredericton, Saint John, and Windsor, Nova Scotia. Moreover, the large numbers and denominational breadth of Canadian evangelicals who lent their support to the evangelistic efforts of Torrey denote that, despite some signs of fracturing, Protestant ministers appreciated the place of conservative evangelicalism in Canadian Protestant circles. The church-union movement of these years, which embraced a spirit of unity and sought to find solutions for the economic and social crises of the urban centres, is often seen as a conciliatory movement. From this angle, Torrey's revival meetings, despite the religious enthusiasm they generated, might have been expected to be a source of potential conflict for evangelicals seeking to unite and Christianize Canadian society. But Torrey, for the most part, received support and cooperation from the evangelical churches.

An indication that Torrey's conservative evangelicalism did eventually show signs of falling out of favour in Canada was that, when he returned in 1910, it was to the Maritimes and not to the larger cities in central Canada. Evidence for this claim is lacking, but perhaps evangelical leaders in those larger urban areas, who seemed otherwise still eager for revivals, realized that Torrey's approach was moving beyond the boundaries of accommodation. Regardless of Torrey's success with the working class, the scathing comments from some Toronto journalists foreshadowed that revival constructed in terms of piety, power, and community would be harder to find in future press coverage. Torrey would have likely attracted large

crowds of working people in larger centres, but he needed the support of Protestant clergy and lay leaders. It is revealing that Torrey,
in a lengthy 1906 interview, stated that he did not think "that most
Churches take the interest they ought in the unchurched and especially in the poor."[134]

CHAPTER FIVE

Transition

Revivalism commanded the respect of most Protestants in Canada when J. Wilbur Chapman began plans to conduct a number of revival meetings in Winnipeg, the first of his many meetings to take place in nine Canadian cities between 1907 and 1911. By bringing with him a contingent of co-evangelists and workers to stage a series of simultaneous revival services, Chapman further enriched the Canadian revival experience. Like Torrey, Chapman believed in the premillennial second coming of Christ, the doctrines of human depravity and eternal punishment, and the inerrancy of Scripture.

Blending conservative evangelicalism with popular culture, Chapman's campaigns attracted large numbers of people, including more than 400,000 Canadians at the Toronto meetings. There were signs by 1911, however, that the appeal of revival meetings and conservative evangelicalism in general was beginning to wane among Protestant leaders. In the final days of the Toronto campaign, some Protestant clergymen were starting to question the effectiveness of professional revivalism in generating church-membership growth and keeping evangelicalism relevant and meaningful in Canadian society. Canadian Protestant leaders may have held unrealistic expectations of what visiting American evangelists could achieve, especially when the hosts themselves exerted paltry effort in reaching unchurched workers.[1]

The Reverend Charles W. Gordon, Presbyterian clergyman and noted Canadian author, was one of a number of clergymen who was instrumental in bringing Chapman and his assistants to Winnipeg in October and November 1907.[2] Winnipeg was the business and distributive centre for the prairies, and a growing number of immigrants and vast quantities of manufactured products and wheat continually poured through the city of approximately 100,000. Protestant leaders believed that, through the medium of professional revivalism, unchurched working people of the growing urban centre could be reached. In the past, representatives of Winnipeg churches had worked together for the Manitoba temperance program, but the Chapman campaign symbolized even greater harmony and unanimity among the churches as a large number of clergymen representing various denominations participated. Divided into six sections, the city experienced meetings in three Presbyterian churches, two Methodist churches, and one Congregationist church.[3] In addition to these six churches, there were a number of other churches that held at least one meeting with the help of one of the Chapman evangelists. Other revival sites included the YMCA auditorium, various factories, CPR "sheds," saloons, theatres, and community buildings.

Chapman's long list of associates represented a wide variety of backgrounds and experiences. Two of the more notable assistants were the wife-and-husband team of Virginia and William Asher, who had worked under the tutelage of Dwight L. Moody.[4] Asked by Chapman to join his band of evangelistic workers, the Ashers showed their ability to reach mainly working-class males.[5] Especially notable were their meetings in Canadian factories, saloons, and jails. Another of Chapman's evangelists at Winnipeg who sought to reach non-church attenders was "Conductor" James Burwick, former railroad man turned railway evangelist, who went among the railway men talking to those who were in trouble or sick. The *Manitoba Free Press* stated that Burwick's "membership in the O.R.C. and his practical experience in railroading enable[d] him to form large circles of acquaintanceship in a short time, and gaining [sic] them by his clear headedness and warm heartedness."[6]

The Reverend W.J. Dawson, from England, and soloist and choir leader A.B. Davidson held meetings at St Stephen's Presbyterian Church. The Reverend Thomas Needham, raised in the British Isles, and musical assistant John W. Reynolds concentrated their evangelistic work at Grace Methodist Church, which over the years had attracted a prosperous congregation.[7] One other non-American evangelist by birth, working with the Chapman campaign at Winnipeg, was the Reverend Henry Ostrom, assisted by soloist and chorus leader John P. Hillis and accompanist Mrs Edith Norton. The

Ostrom-Hillis-Norton team held most of their meetings at St Andrew's Presbyterian Church.

Another Winnipeg Presbyterian church that participated in the Chapman campaign was St Augustine's, where the Reverend Frank Granstaff and Owen F. Pugh, his musical assistant, held meetings. In north Winnipeg, the Reverend H.W. Stough was at McDougall Methodist Church with his assistant Charles E. Rykert. Chapman and three of his associates – soloist Paul J. Gilbert, chorus leader Charles F. Allen, and organist C.F. Marsh – held meetings in a few different churches but most of their meetings were at Central Congregational Church.[8] While Chapman's associates at Winnipeg had varied theological backgrounds, at least six of them had attended the Moody Bible Institute, which was to align itself with the fundamentalist movement in the First World War years and after.

As had been the case with Moody's successful Winnipeg campaign in 1897, the visiting evangelists and churches worked together effectively, generating religious enthusiasm and attracting the support of newspapers. The *Manitoba Free Press*, for example, provided extensive and positive coverage of the revivalists and their evangelistic work. Numerous photographs of the Chapman workers and daily reports of all the meetings in the various churches and other revival sites informed Manitobans of the campaign. Even the labour paper the *Voice* printed advertisements. Lasting almost three weeks, the Winnipeg campaign reportedly attracted between 4,000 and 5,000 people every night or about 80,000 in total. Confirming the success of the meetings was a letter from John Converse to Charles Gordon. Converse, chairman of the General Assembly's Committee on Evangelistic Work in Philadelphia, wrote that he valued Gordon's praise of the Chapman meetings in Winnipeg and expected that his testimony would "have important influence in bringing all denominations into line" for future campaigns in the United States.[9]

While the Winnipeg meetings were in progress, another part of the Chapman entourage was holding meetings at Portage la Prairie, a small city west of Winnipeg with a population of approximately 5,000 people. The Reverend D.S. Toy, who had also been associated with Dwight L. Moody, and singer Frank Dickson were in charge of the evangelistic services held at the Baptist and Presbyterian churches. Chapman paid a short visit and held two meetings. Like the *Manitoba Free Press*, Portage la Prairie's *Weekly Review*

acknowledged the revivals as worthwhile news and provided supportive coverage of the revivalists and their meetings.[10]

Chapman visited Winnipeg again in June 1908 to speak at the
General Assembly of the Presbyterian Church of Canada, but his
next revival campaigns in Canada occurred months later in the
fall.[11] These meetings lasted five weeks, from late September to early
November, and took place in the Ontario centres of Orillia, Barrie,
Toronto, Paris, and Brantford. Perhaps the most notable improvement for the Ontario campaign was the addition of Charles M. Alexander, the popular co-evangelist of the earlier Torrey meetings in
Toronto and Ottawa.

The drawing power of Chapman himself was evidently impressive, since the YMCA of Orillia, clergymen, and businessmen had
eagerly sought his assistance. Many other larger American urban
centres also requested his services, but, after two years of repeated
invitations and a feeling that God was calling him to Orillia, Chapman descended upon the city of approximately 6,000 people. The
long wait appeared to be worth it as the Reverend Canon Richard
Greene, the chairman of the general committee, claimed that for the
first time in Orillia's history the evangelical churches had united to
bring the Gospel message to the community.[12]

The committee that arranged for the visit spent several months
preparing for Chapman's arrival.[13] In the belief that prayer was
essential for the success of the revival campaign, "cottage prayer-
meetings" took place as early as two months in advance of Chapman's appearance. People gathered in various homes throughout
Orillia, as much as eight times a week, to pray that God would bless
the revival meetings.[14]

In addition to prayer, publicity and marketing for the campaign
were also extensive. Months before the meetings, a "publicity committee" had been formed in order to kindle the interest of the community for the coming revivals. One of its most important tasks was
to place advertisements, as early as a month before the meetings, in
the "choicest" spaces of various newspapers and to use newspaper
columns, stories, and photographs of the Chapman team to get the
word out. There were posters for stores, the front of "each church"
received signs, and large banners reading "The King's Business" and
"Chapman-Alexander, Sept. 30 to Oct. 13" adorned prominent
places above the major streets of the city. The publicity committee
believed it had "a good thing to offer the people and took every legit-

imate and lawful means, both in season and out of season, of letting them know about it."[15] Chapman himself recommended advertising and had asked the Reverend Charles Gordon, earlier in the year, to promote the team of Chapman and Alexander in the Canadian newspapers.[16] Even more so than during the campaigns of Moody, Jones, and Torrey, revival took on the shape of a commodity.

As the main revival site, able to accommodate 3,200 people, the new Palace Roller Rink received improvements including extra electric lights, three furnaces, and streamers. Meetings also took place in the afternoons at the Opera House, Salvation Army barracks, Baptist, Presbyterian, and Methodist churches, and other sites including factories, the Asylum, and county churches near Orillia. Other Chapman workers at Orillia were E.G. Chapman (brother of J. Wilbur and his business manager), Helen Alexander (Charles's wife), Ralph Norton (superintendent of personal work), Mr and Mrs Asher, soloist E.W. Naftzger, Robert Harkness (former Torrey pianist), Edwin H. Bookmeyer (secretary to Alexander), author George T.B. Davies, and G.W. Baker.

The meetings attracted people not only from the local area but also from the rural regions, some driving as far as forty miles. Others came by train from destinations such as Toronto, Newmarket, Bracebridge, Penetanguishene, Midland, Lindsay, Barrie, Coldwater, and Collingwood. The men's meetings at the Opera House attracted greater numbers than any previous political or religious event in the city. Night after night at the rink, crowds numbering between 2,000 and 3,500 heard Chapman and Alexander.[17] Both clergymen and lay people throughout the region viewed the revival as a major event.

As had been the case with the Manitoba press during the Winnipeg campaign, the Orillia newspapers provided extensive coverage of the campaign, with biographies, portraits of the evangelists, reports of audience turnout, and accounts of all meetings. An ardent supporter and image maker of revival, the Orillia *Times* made no apologies for devoting a vast amount of space to the campaign: "Nothing has transpired in recent years of more importance to the town or has stirred the community to such an extent as have the two weeks' meetings just closed."[18]

In the middle of the campaign, Chapman, Alexander, Harkness, and Naftzger also held a meeting in Barrie at the Opera House. Reporting on the Orillia meetings, the Barrie newspaper stated that clergymen of the Anglican, Presbyterian, Methodist, Baptist, and other churches united "in the most beautiful harmony."[19] Town businesses closed early and approximately 1,500 people crowded into the building.[20]

An enthusiastic Toronto welcomed Chapman's brief visit and revival meeting at an overflowing Massey Hall. Mrs Alexander almost stole the show when she spoke of her religious work. "I have always wanted to come to Toronto," she announced, "to thank you for the prayers which you made in my behalf when I was so ill. It is such a joy to be here with my dear husband. I have heard so much of you and the work here."[21] Commenting on the large crowd and the enthusiasm manifested, the *News* proclaimed that "it was quite evident that the interest and religious activity engendered by the Torrey-Alexander meeting in January 1906, have by no means died out."[22] Other major Toronto newspapers gave similar appraisals of Chapman's brief visit with references to the success of the Torrey meetings of 1906.

After their short visit to Toronto, Chapman and Alexander travelled to Chicago and then back to Brantford where members of their campaign team had been holding meetings. In Brantford, the preliminary work was done far in advance of the arrival of the evangelists, who had planned to hold meetings from 15 October to 3 November. Two weeks before the evangelists reached the city, the Brantford *Daily Expositor* declared that "as the days draw nearer for the opening of the campaign the interest and enthusiasm [are] deeper and the prospects in this city are very favourable for a successful evangelistic campaign."[23] In early October, sixty-five different locations throughout Brantford witnessed cottage prayer-meetings; these and other well-attended interdenominational meetings generated much excitement for the upcoming campaign.[24]

Participating in the three-week Brantford campaign were evangelists Ora S. Gray, Frank Granstaff, Thomas Needham, the Ashers, and children's evangelist C.T. Schaeffer. The main venues were First Baptist Church, Zion Presbyterian Church, and Colborne Street Methodist Church. Revival meetings also took place at other churches: three Methodist, three Baptist, two Presbyterian, and one Congregationist. Other revival sites included the Salvation Army Citadel, the YMCA gymnasium, the Opera House, the Wonderland Theatre, and a number of stores and factories such as Massey-Harris Company, Barber-Ellis Company, Schultz Brothers, the Waterous

Engine Company, Paterson Biscuit Company, and Buck Stove Works. Revival appeared to be everywhere, with men on the streets and in the shops telling others of the "Great Campaign" taking place in the city.[25] Both the *Courier* and the Brantford *Expositor* provided excellent and positive coverage of the revival meetings and their large crowds, even though Chapman and Alexander were only in the city for three of the many meetings that occurred.[26]

The *Star-Transcript* kept its citizens informed of the revival meetings held by the Reverend John H. Elliot, a Canadian-born Chapman co-evangelist, and soloist Everett Natzger in nearby Paris, a small town with a population less than 4,000. In his report of the Paris meetings, the Reverend R.G. MacBeth wrote in the local newspaper that special evangelistic services were necessary since it was vital that there be as much enthusiasm in religion as there was in baseball and hockey.[27] These years witnessed a proliferation of Canadian amateur sport at the local, provincial, and national levels and the greater number of leisure activities available in an increasingly modern society provided stiffer competition for churches seeking to win working people into their fold. MacBeth desired to see revivals generate an equal amount of excitement within the community, a wish fulfilled with the arrival of professional revivalism. In their one meeting at the Presbyterian church in Paris, for example, Chapman and Alexander, accompanied by Mrs Alexander, Robert Harkness, and George Davies, attracted 1,500 people. There were piety and power and, according to the *Star-Transcript*, the campaign had "deeply moved" the Paris community.[28]

Chapman returned to Canada from the United States in March 1909. Arriving in Winnipeg, Chapman, Alexander, and their fellow workers were on their way to Vancouver and then overseas. At Winnipeg, the Chapman team received a generous reception.[29] Their guest co-evangelist was Dr Wilfrid Grenfell, Arctic medical missionary and famous Canadian hero. Working together, but also holding services on their own, Grenfell, Chapman, and Alexander preached at three Presbyterian churches, and one Congregational church. At these churches and at Walker Theatre, many people failed to gain admission because of the crowds gathered for the services.[30] Leaving Winnipeg by night express, the Chapman-Alexander party arrived in Regina, the capital of Saskatchewan, where they held an impromptu meeting at the city square that drew between six hundred and eight hundred people.[31]

From Regina, the Chapman team went directly to Vancouver, where people came from every corner of the city long before the opening of the two-day campaign.[32] According to the *Daily Province*, the first meeting at the Wesley Methodist Church witnessed the greatest crowd in the history of the church, all of whom had gathered to experience the message of Chapman and the music of Alexander, Ernest Naftzger, and Robert Harkness.[33] At a meeting the next day, the city building inspector, a Mr Jarrett, forbade the opening of the service until those who were standing exited the building since there was the real danger that the overstrained gallery could collapse. A quickly arranged overflow meeting, led by Alexander, at the nearby Christ Church restored some order.

Robert Burkinshaw claims that Vancouver's Wesley Church and its minister, the Reverend Robert Milliken, were "a sounding board for liberalism and the social gospel" in the early twentieth century.[34] On the occasion of the Chapman meetings, however, the large revival crowds and Milliken's invitation to Chapman to use Wesley Church seem to reveal that there was acceptance for conservative evangelicalism in this "liberal" enclave.

As Chapman and Alexander began their work overseas, E.G. Chapman and a few of Chapman's associates stayed in Canada and assisted with a simultaneous campaign in the mining district of Kootenay, British Columbia.[35] A few of Chapman's workers also took part in a simultaneous campaign in Saint John, New Brunswick, in February 1910.[36] The final Chapman-Alexander revival meetings in Canada were at Toronto during the month of January 1911.

In Toronto, Massey Hall was the central site for the whole campaign and a large number of evangelists, their musical assistants, and approximately 3,000 personal workers were on hand to tackle the various sectors of the city of more than 375,000. Also, Australian evangelist Miss E. Stafford Miller led revival services for women at Metropolitan Methodist Church.[37] Highly organized and planned, the Chapman campaign saw the division of the city into a number of districts, with each evangelist assigned to a particular church.[38] Each of eleven districts had its own committee and the chairman of each district was a member of the central committee, whose offices were in the basement of Massey Hall. In addition to the services held at the chosen churches for the eleven designated districts, other meetings took place in approximately a dozen other churches. J.N. Shenstone, a leading Toronto businessman and chairman of the general committee, claimed that "140 churches were united in this movement."[39]

Besides churches, Virginia and William Asher and others held meetings at numerous factories and companies such as Taylor Safe Works, W. and J.G. Greey Foundry, Toronto Foundry Company, Cowan's Factory, Watson's Factory, Rawlinson's Factory, Canada Motor Cycle Company, Diamond Flint Glass Company, and the Grand Trunk sheds, to name only a few. Reports indicate that factory workers were receptive to the services, many participating in the singing and listening to a message of sin and salvation.[40]

The Toronto campaign was a notable media event. Major daily newspapers provided coverage of the revival services, each focusing on some aspect of the meetings to set itself apart from its competitors. The newspapers that had been critical of Torrey's interpretation of hell restored their construction of revival as a great spiritual happening. The Toronto *World* declared on 5 January that "today is the opening day of one of the greatest religious campaigns Toronto has ever seen or ever will see for many a day ..."[41] The *News* and the Toronto *Daily Star* gave particularly comprehensive coverage. The *News* spoke of the "Great Revival", the "Great Revivalists", and the "Sweeping Religious Revival," and it offered front-page coverage, large, bold headlines stretching across the width of the page, comprehensive accounts of Chapman's sermons, many photographs, and some sketches; in every issue, too, it included the lyrics and music of a Gospel hymn. The Toronto *Daily Star* also provided excellent coverage and had Professor Joseph L. Gilmour, Baptist minister, write daily special reports which supplemented the already full coverage by *Star* reporters of all the district meetings. More than 400,000 people were "conservatively estimated" by the newspapers to have attended the January campaign.[42]

Chapman's Canadian campaigns usually attracted a large number of people early in advance of the meetings' official opening. A song service was the first feature of a meeting and it played a vital role in preparing the audience to become responsive to the forthcoming Gospel message. Consistent with successful evangelistic teams since Moody and Sankey, a talented soloist was an essential component in a revival meeting. Soloists Paul J. Gilbert, at the 1907 Winnipeg campaign, and Ernest W. Naftzger, at all other campaigns, sang popular Gospel hymns to the delight of their listeners. As was the case with the Torrey-Alexander campaigns, Charles Alexander led the song services. Typical for Alexander, he might stop in the middle of a stanza of a hymn to tell the audience that too few people were singing and that if they did not want to sing they should leave the building since many more people were outside wanting to gain access. His warning always had the desired effect and the whole audience began participating with much renewed effort.[43]

On Alexander's mastery over audiences, one Vancouver reporter noted: they "laughed with him, they sang with him, and at times, when he played upon their heart strings of sympathy, momentarily they sorrowed with him."[44] He often asked for volunteers – solos or duos or groups – to sing a particular chorus and many who made brave attempts received praise and sometimes Bibles for their efforts. The song service, which usually lasted approximately thirty minutes, was followed by Scripture reading and prayer and then a solo song or two. There was a large selection of Chapman-Alexander hymns, but, regardless of the varying topics, all shared the central theme of Jesus as Lord and many were of a sentimental nature.

Prayer requests, mostly on the topic of families, were less common than at Torrey campaigns, but they did play an important role at some of the services. The Toronto *Daily Star* reported that, at one meeting, a Toronto woman asked: "Please pray for my daughter. She is only 16, and she has lost everything that a young girl can value in this life. She has killed her father, and she is killing me."[45] At another meeting, a man cried: "I am a redeemed drunkard. Will you pray for my wife and family. I have been separated from them for two years. Will you pray that we may be brought together once more?"[46] Following prayers was a forty minute sermon notable for quiet earnestness which generated fervent interest. According to one *Manitoba Free Press* headline, the keynote of the Chapman campaign was "Quiet and Reasonable Simplicity and Preaching of Gospel Truth."[47] Chapman was no Sam Jones when it came to theatrical ability, and he had neither the fatherly command of Moody nor the forceful presentation of Torrey, but the revival message that he delivered to Canadians often mesmerized his listeners. Struck by the power of revivalism, an Orillia observer stated that Chapman presented a message of sin and salvation "with a directness and simplicity, and a tenderness of voice which immediately arrests the attention and holds the interest of his hearers till the last word is spoken."[48] Chapman, recorded the Orillia *Times*, "has that subtle sympathy that finds a man's heart and lays a gentle finger upon its wound; but that same intuitive finger can point relentlessly at the sin that is lurking there as the preacher turns upon it the fierce of light of God's judgement."[49] When asked what he thought of the merits of Chapman as a public speaker, another man replied: "I don't know. In fact I didn't think about him at all; he made me think so much of the Man he was preaching about."[50] Chapman confidently preached a message of salvation through Christ in a quiet and earnest manner that suited early-twentieth-century Canadian Protestant clergymen who had been wary of the type of sensationalism common among evangelists like Sam Jones.

As a veteran revivalist, Chapman occasionally closed his sermon with a prayer while pianist Robert Harkness slowly and softly played a tune such as the tender notes of "Home, Sweet Home." At a Winnipeg meeting in 1907, the effect was striking, especially when, at the conclusion of the prayer, soloist Paul Gilbert began singing the touching song. In an era when many Canadians left home to work in the cities, it was no surprise that such hymns moved audiences. It was a packaged performance but there was no denying its ability to reach the hearts of its listeners, many of them weeping as they contemplated the nostalgic memories of home life in a simpler era.[51]

Often Chapman petitioned listeners who already professed Christianity to practise self-denial and promote Christian principles whereas new Christians were to profess their conversion. Reporting on a Massey Hall meeting of the 1911 Toronto campaign, a journalist recorded that "hundreds of men and women ... fled down the aisles toward the platform and confessed their faith." The scene itself was striking as "women with tear-stained faces sobbed aloud, and men knelt on the floor, while personal workers urged them to dedicate their lives to the Master's service."[52] Also at Toronto, Chapman occasionally invited revival attenders to an inquiry meeting in the basement of Massey Hall "to make a public profession of conversion." There were times, however, when he dismissed the audience without an appeal that they pledge to live a Christian life.[53] On these occasions he felt that the crowd was not ready and that conversion required more thoughtful contemplation. Both Moody and Chapman sought to save souls, but, whereas Moody almost always spoke of the "blood" and the "cross," Chapman might also speak of one's "pledge to live a Christian life."[54]

Chapman was not as confrontational as Torrey. In 1908 the Toronto *Daily Star* made some comparisons between the two, stating that Chapman was "much weaker in voice, less thorough in method, more theatrical in style, slower to seize psychological opportunities, and ... [his] sermon lacked somewhat in power and force as compared with Dr. Torrey's utterances."[55] While the severity and dogmatism of Torrey were missing, the theological message that Chapman brought to Canada was roughly the same as what Canadians had heard from Moody and Torrey. One Toronto reporter, in 1911, stated that Chapman was clearly a "conservative" who was unlikely to "trust the New Testament beyond, the endorsations [sic] of D.L. Moody."[56] Some of Chapman's most popular sermon subjects included: "The Unpardonable Sin," "Judgement," "Almost Persuaded," "Conversion," "The Christian's Relation to Amusements of the World," "They have Sown the Wind, and They Shall Reap the Whirlwind," "With Christ or without Christ," and "An Old Fashioned Home." For Chapman, paramount was one's acceptance of Jesus Christ as personal saviour: "I believe Jesus Christ to be the Son of God and the Saviour of the world. I believe in the Bible right through. I believe that men must be born again."[57] Occasionally, he did not mince words, such as when he declared that one is either for or against Christ. Like Moody and Torrey, Chapman held that it was vital for people to believe in a literal hell.[58] The task before him was to preach people "out of hell" but also to preach "hell out of" people.[59] Unlike Torrey, Chapman rarely used harsh descriptions to describe the fiery, eternal destination of the wicked.

As much as he cared for the social welfare of people, Chapman, like Jones, Small, Moody, and Torrey, was no social gospeller. Although he believed that Christians should assist those who were weighed down by the oppressiveness of the modern industrial state, his focus was predominantly on soul winning. Rather than promoting social activism and legislative remedies for economic problems, his idea of "social service" was for the church to rebuke "unchristianlike" behaviour: "This is the age of social service and it is the time when the church must be called upon to bear the burden of those who are oppressed. Selfishness, greed, avarice, and all kindred sins we rebuke without fear or favor ... But of course we insist upon the acceptance of Christ as personal Saviour."[60] As Chapman saw it, the solution to economic and social problems was Jesus.

A key objective of Chapman and his assistants was to stimulate the churches and encourage them to engage in evangelism on their own.[61] When visiting evangelists departed from a city, it was vital that local Christians continued the work of Christianizing the community. For some meetings, workers distributed "covenant" cards that professed one's willingness to assist pastors and to pledge to do Christian service.[62] At the 1911 Toronto campaign, regularly appointed Christian helpers, who consisted of women, college students, and day labourers, dispensed cards that read: "MY COVENANT – To pray daily for the evangelistic work now in progress in the city. For J. Wilbur Chapman, Charles M. Alexander, and members of their party, and for the unsaved of the city. I will respond as far as possible to the public appeals which may be made for special prayer services."[63] Instead of an atmosphere of partisanship and parochialism, a spirit of harmony prevailed at most of his campaigns. Chapman was able to tap into the churches' awareness that, despite theological differences, they all sought to build the Kingdom of God.

Chapman and his associates cast their net wide to reach those who were less likely to attend a church service. His co-evangelists, especially, made a concerted effort to reach the working class. At the 1907 Winnipeg campaign, Conductor James Burwick preached at the CPR shops, which were a beehive of activity because of expansion. At these meetings he told railroad labourers not to be ashamed of Christ. He realized that some of the men present had little use for churches but he explained that, until something better appeared, they were the "best things we have got"; his advice was, "Let us stick to them."[64] Burwick understood that one method to reach his audience was to narrate his experiences as a railroad man who had experienced conversion to Christ. With his forehead bearing the scars of a tough life, he presented a powerful testimony to his working-class audience.[65]

Virginia and William Asher likewise made their mark among workers, in addition to some of the so-called "riff-raff" of society. For example, the largest number ever seen in the gallery of Winnipeg's Stony Mountain Penitentiary gathered to hear their message in 1907.[66] The Ashers also targeted male working-class space such as drinking establishments, where they gained access by obtaining the consent of the proprietor. Although the Ashers did not discuss the ethics of the saloon business and preached only salvation through Christ, it was striking that Winnipeg bar owners would allow the couple to hold evangelistic meetings in their taverns.[67] It is also indicative of workers' tolerance of conservative evangelicalism. At one meeting in the Queen's Hotel, almost "500 people jammed into the bar" to experience the spirit of the meeting, where William Asher preached of God's love. Despite the rowdy setting, the bar audience listened respectfully and was quick to participate in the singing of hymns, and even those who could not sing enthusiastically whistled the Gospel tunes.[68]

The Ashers also made their mark on Orillia, holding meetings in various factories, the Asylum, and country churches near Orillia. A report in the Orillia *Times* recounted the Ashers' impact on a tavern audience in another city when William told the story of the prodigal son in the vernacular while Virginia sang a song and prayed for the patrons "as a mother or sister might." Readers learned that "the whole crowd of hardened, crime-stained, drink-sodden men sank to their knees." This revival story closed with a powerful conclusion. William singled out the tavern owner and dared him to give up his old life and accept Jesus Christ as a personal saviour. Recalling his depraved and violent history, the man "hesitated, flushed and then turned pale, but in a moment he squared his shoulders, looked the little preacher square in the face, and said 'I will.'"[69]

It mattered little that this story was melodramatic; males responded to the conservative evangelicalism offered outside the boundaries of mainstream churches. The press described the conquering of vice and how the message of Christ reclaimed "debauched" individuals. One working-class conversion included "the worst man in a large manufactutory." Signifying his transformation, he presented William Asher with a cigarette box, tobacco, clay pipe, and a cocaine bottle, stating, "I surrendered all to Jesus and will take Him for my life."[70] In Brantford at the Kerby House, men clasped a "tankard of beer" with one hand and a "gospel hymn leaflet" with the other, gradually pushed their beers away, discarded their cigarettes, cigars, and pipes, and listened intently and silently to the Ashers as they spoke of Jesus Christ. In the Commercial Hotel bar-room, a large Brantford crowd demonstrated "order and devotional interest" in the Ashers' biblical message and hymn singing. At one meeting in Kelly's pool hall, few were present and yet the Ashers' service was "very heartily entered into."[71] In press reports, revival became an extraordinary and uplifting event with a lasting impact. For example, an Orillia journalist commented that the Ashers' work

"will long be remembered here, particularly for their kindly minis-
tration to the poor and the neglected."[72]

According to newspaper reports, the Ashers experienced success in
reaching out to Toronto working-class men interested in the services
and in the message of sin and salvation. The Toronto *Daily Star*
observed that the Ashers's efforts were "rewarded by a hushing of the
crude life."[73] In respect for the evangelists, Toronto working men
were on their best behaviour. More than one hundred Taylor Safe
Works's workers "blackened from their morning's toil ... [and] seated
on workbenches, sections of vaults, and large steel frames" heard
William relate "the old, old story."[74] At the Grand Trunk freight
sheds, "a fair number of the railway-men turned up to listen to some
good Gospel and good singing" presented by William Asher and
W.W. Weaver, another Chapman evangelist.[75] While attendance at
noon-hour services in Toronto varied because some employees went
elsewhere for lunch, workers were receptive to a conservative evangelical message of personal sin and redemption through Christ.[76]

Besides hearing the Ashers in saloons and factories, working men
attended other services conducted by Chapman evangelists. During
the Chapman campaigns there were meetings held in churches in
most districts of the cities, including some in and around working-class neighbourhoods. Moreover, there were "men only" meetings at neutral sites, such as the Orillia Palace Roller Rink, Toronto's
Massey Hall, and Winnipeg's Walker Theatre.[77] These sites attracted
male workers who might have found "respectable" mainstream city
churches threatening. At one Massey Hall service, there were "some
considerably aged unshaven workingmen in rough clothes and the
immaculately attired. A leading Toronto physician mounted the
platform and told the meeting of his change of heart, while the broken English of an Italian was heard with others in earnest prayer."[78]

Nancy Christie and Michael Gauvreau argue that there was a rich
vein of evangelicalism among working-class people that was waiting
to be mined by astute clergymen hoping to revitalize their
churches.[79] William Asher was effective in gaining the respect of
working people since he had the ability to communicate successfully
in the vernacular. "It is a wonderful thing to watch the faces of the
men [in saloons]," wrote an Orillia *Times* reporter, "as he shows
that he is as familiar with their 'lingo' as they are themselves. They
know that if he understands their talk, he understands them."[80] At a
number of Toronto factories, working people heard the Ashers' ser-

mons, the message of which was, for some, likely to be familiar. Managers of the Christie Brown Company, for example, had promoted gospel lunch-hour meetings for female and male employees for more than twenty years. At one Toronto foundry, owners W. and J.G. Greey had constructed a little chapel on the job site and, for the previous sixteen years, had conducted daily meetings between 7:00 and 7:30 in the morning.[81] It is difficult to say whether these managers were practising social control.[82] Whatever the case, employers' evangelical services suggest that evangelicalism was alive and well among working-class families.

Meetings held by the co-evangelists were almost always a mixture of both women and men.[83] However, Chapman and Alexander occasionally held men-only gatherings because men, on account of conflicting work hours, were often denied seats at day meetings. Like Moody and Torrey, Chapman aspired to win men to Christ, believing that the conversion of men had an important and far-reaching impact on the community. In her study of the 1909 Boston revival campaign, Margaret Lamberts Bendroth argues that Chapman's urban revivalism was effective in "remasculinizing" Protestantism by presenting "men with a vigorous masculine ideal, challenging them to higher standards of moral character at home and in the workplace." Chapman himself represented aggressive virility and physical strength: "he was no sissy" and, according to one press report, his "broad, heavy jaw" gave "his face a look of force and determination almost brutal."[84]

The men-only assembly made it easier for Chapman to reach a "man's intellect and feelings." On the surface, men-only meetings did not appear unique in format, but Chapman no doubt subtly adjusted his message to make it more applicable to the lives and sin of men. For example, he told Toronto men that, for every fallen woman on Toronto streets, one would not have to go too far to find a fallen man. This was true even though "society doesn't say so."[85] Chapman's sermon for men only could be persuasive, an example being his closing words to Toronto men: "Stand upon it [the Bible] and all the devils in hell cannot upset you. You are safe if you have made fast your feet upon the Rock of Ages. For the sake of your wife and children, come. For the sake of your manhood, come. I plead with you to come. There has been a strange sense of the Spirit of God in this meeting. He is waiting to be gracious. Take Him! Take Him!"[86] Here, men were to be courageous, to become saved, and to

have their manhood upheld.[87] In an age of more saloons and sporting and leisure activities, his revival meetings offered a product that
successfully competed for the attention of workingmen, a fact
proven by the large attendance figures.

Another impressive component of the Chapman campaigns was
the work of women evangelists. Besides Virginia Asher's achievements, there was the evangelistic work of Miss E. Stafford Miller at
the 1911 Toronto campaign. Miller was in charge of the
women-only meetings on weekday afternoons at Metropolitan
Methodist Church. The format of the meetings was identical to that
of other revival meetings, the only difference being that the women
were in charge – from the female evangelist to the young lady ushers.[88] The YWCA might have assumed charge of the arrangements for
the women's meetings, but the president decided that the work was
more than it could undertake. Nevertheless, women from the YWCA
did sing in the choir at Massey Hall and acted as ushers at the meetings for women.[89] At the Metropolitan Methodist services, sermons
were on weighty biblical topics; Miller's first discourse was on the
study of the Bible.[90] As the campaign progressed, the Metropolitan
women's meetings became increasingly popular and each meeting
usually attracted hundreds.

Miller rarely preached to anyone but women, and there were also
some limitations placed upon Virginia Asher. The Toronto *World*
wrote of the "Lady Evangelists" gathering together with some local
Toronto women at tea rooms,[91] but the term "evangelist" was used
cautiously in regard to women. As a number of studies demonstrate,
restrictions on women became more common as gender distinctions
heightened within an increasingly urban and industrialized society.[92]
In Canada, there was only so much freedom given to women when it
came to "preaching" the Gospel.[93] In the context of revivals, Virginia Asher had freedom to preach, yet her talks were "addresses"
and the majority of these were at women-only meetings. At this
time, ordination of women was possible among holiness and Pentecostal groups but mainstream Protestant denominations in Canada
refused to ordain women.[94] Although the primary focus of the Chapman campaigns was workingmen, reaching women was also
important.

Not all Protestant churches provided support. The Anglican
Church, as had been the case with the revivals of Moody, Jones,
Small, and Torrey, was aloof from the campaigns. In a letter to the

Canadian Churchman, a J.J. Rooney asked why the Anglican Church failed to join other Protestant churches that supported the 1907 Chapman campaign in Winnipeg. Stating that other Winnipeg Anglicans were asking the same question, Rooney added, "I am quite certain the sympathy of a number of our people will be alienated from our Church by attendance at these services. To my way of thinking it seems the Church in this city has lost a golden opportunity."[95] The few involved Anglicans, such as an Archdeacon Phair and the Rev. J.J. Roy, rector of St George's Church and chairman of the north-central district for the Winnipeg campaign, received praise from the *Presbyterian* but not from an Anglican publication.[96] At Orillia, Canon Richard Greene was a prominent Anglican who played a large role in the promotion of the Chapman-Alexander campaign; however, the *Canadian Churchman* provided no coverage of this campaign or other Chapman campaigns between 1907 and 1911. The position of the Anglican Church on evangelicalism in general, and revivals in particular, was usually unsympathetic. The so-called high church party placed much emphasis on reverence, as they perceived it, and often frowned on the "fanaticism" and "emotionalism" of revival meetings. As in earlier campaigns, especially the Toronto meetings of Moody and Torrey, there were Anglicans who fully supported American revivalists in the hope that their church would not, indeed, miss a golden opportunity, but these Anglicans were few and far between.[97]

Unlike the Anglicans, Canadian Baptist clergymen demonstrated solid support for the Chapman meetings. In *Canadian Baptist* reports on the Orillia campaign, W.F. Roadhouse rejoiced in the methods and ideals of the revival meetings, stating that no one could experience Chapman's earnest and passionate message and not be awakened: "His messages burn ... He never apologizes, but pointedly, courageously he smites the sins of the home life as well as of the individual."[98] In Roadhouse's estimation, the revival meetings, "undoubtedly of God," had transformed the whole city, with citizens on the streets talking primarily of spiritual matters.[99]

The *Canadian Congregationalist* also gave positive coverage to the Orillia meetings, including a full-page photo of Charles Alexander on the front cover of one issue and other photos and information on the campaign. A message by the editor stated that the Orillia meetings garnered ample space "because we believe in Dr. Chapman's work, because we believe in revival effort and because our readers are deeply interested in this work."[100] In the issue printed one week later, the paper spoke of the even "greater things" which took place. Recording that people were singing in the streets and greeting and speaking to each other throughout the city, the *Congregationalist* declared, "The whole town seems to have been caught up into a higher condition of spiritual life. Nothing like it ... has ever been experienced in this place."[101]

A number of studies claim that Canadian Methodists – the most consistent supporters of nineteenth-century revivalism – were by the early twentieth century losing faith in mass-revival meetings as a means to Christianize society. Historian Phyllis Airhart argues that Canadian Methodism, in this period, showed far less enthusiasm for the Methodist revival tradition of the past. The old Methodist type of revival faded in the midst of a greater leaning towards "progressivism" and social gospel thought.[102] Yet, given the high participation of Methodist ministers in the campaigns by American evangelists, Airhart's argument requires modification. Some Methodists were indeed showing less enthusiasm for revivalism, but the participation of many Methodist churches and clergymen in Chapman's campaigns suggests that Methodist leaders were willing to give major revival campaigns at least one more chance to demonstrate their effectiveness in reaching the unchurched.

The *Christian Guardian's* initial report of the 1907 Winnipeg revival meetings spoke well of the evangelistic work of Chapman, Dr Henry Ostrom, and the Reverend W.J. Dawson, claiming that the simultaneous campaigns appeared to be an outstanding success. While the account did acknowledge that a revival campaign held at one central site would be more spectacular, it stated that Chapman's approach might have more permanent results.[103] At this time, there was hardly any questioning of revivalism and conservative evangelicalism. On the topic of class meetings and revivals, a November 1907 *Christian Guardian* article stressed the need for revival and, especially, class meetings where lay leadership could conduct "aggressive evangelism." What was required was "less pulpit effort and more gatling-gun, rapid-fire testimony in revival meetings."[104] Behind the masculine and military metaphor was the central message that Methodists should share their religious experiences with others in the community. In an assessment of the 1907 Winnipeg campaign, "A.S." stated that the age of revivals was not past, especially since preaching the "great fundamental truths of the Gospel" attracted the most attention. To reach the masses, it was better to appeal to the heart and conscience rather than engage in preaching "which aims at the general and gradual development of the social and ethical instincts of the people."[105] The conclusion was inescapable: to influence the masses, the preaching of sin and salvation was crucial. During the 1908 Chapman campaigns in Ontario, the *Christian Guardian* acknowledged that, through evangelism, hundreds gathered "in the old-fashioned way."[106]

While some Presbyterians questioned particulars of professional revivalism, the Presbyterian Church in Canada had modelled its own evangelism programs on those of Chapman, a Presbyterian himself.[107] The *Presbyterian*, published in Toronto, provided positive coverage of Chapman's campaigns in the United States, Portage la Prairie, Winnipeg, Orillia, Toronto, Paris, and Brantford. In its report of the 1907 Winnipeg meetings, the *Presbyterian* expected great results because of Chapman's past accomplishments and his avoidance of sensationalism, exaggerated statements, and extreme emotionalism. According to David Marshall, Canadian Presbyterian clergymen were wary of urban revivalism and the possibility that such services might lack reverence for God.[108] Some Presbyterians remained cautious, vigilant towards "unnatural excitement" and unwisely conducted meetings, but the Presbyterians had little to fear with Chapman. According to the *Presbyterian*, the Winnipeg campaign was notable for its absence of excessive emotionalism, its capacity to move the whole city, and its ability to unite churches, all characteristics that prompted even greater support for the meetings.[109]

On the success of the Orillia campaign, D.C. MacGregor reported in the *Presbyterian* that the secret of Chapman's power to stir the whole town was prayer and that he preached a simple message about sin and its consequences. "Is it any wonder," MacGregor asked, "we had great manifestation of the Spirit's presence and power?"[110] Despite the competing excitement over the 1908 federal election, the revival crowds were large.[111] Assessing the impact of the revival in Paris, the Reverend R.G. MacBeth wrote how the community was "deeply moved ... beyond the power of human computation" and how clergymen and their parishioners found inspiration to continue evangelism and personal work in their community.[112] A *Presbyterian* article entitled "Evangelism" stated that "it can be said confidently that evangelism, wisely conducted, has justified itself by its results. This is true of many 'revival' services held in Methodist and Baptist Churches, as well as in Presbyterian Churches, and of the 'missions' held in Anglican and Roman Catholic Churches."[113]

Initially, the denominational press's commentary on the Toronto campaign of 1911 indicated that church acceptance for modern revivalism constructed to popular tastes would continue. Reports in the *War Cry* – the official organ of the Salvation Army in Canada – demonstrated that even Salvationists were appreciative of the campaigns of Chapman and his workers. Chapman communicated with the Salvation Army's chief secretary on the phone, expressing his delight that the army was taking an active part in the upcoming campaign. He believed that the Salvation Army, among all the churches, had the greatest potential to reach the unsaved.[114] One issue of the *War Cry* printed a Chapman sermon on saving souls and added: "You can become that which Dr. Chapman desired to be above all things. You can become a winner of souls, and spend your days in straightening crooked lives, in brightening miserable homes, and preparing people for Heaven. Will you do so?"[115]

Lynne Marks claims that the Ontario Salvation Army had experienced a loss of evangelical fervour by the 1890s as it increasingly embraced social-rescue work, an argument supported by S.D. Clark's important study published in the late 1940s.[116] While Marks's assessment is probably correct, the army's greater concern for social work did not stifle all of its enthusiasm for revivalistic meetings. A special night set aside by Chapman near the conclusion of the Toronto campaign brought Salvationists and Chapman's staff together for a large meeting at Massey Hall. Because of the immense crowds and spiritual results, so-called "Army Night" was "a great success."[117] Commenting on the role the Salvation Army played on Army Night, Baptist clergyman Dr Joseph L. Gilmour declared that the Salvationists' emphasis on soul winning made them fit in easily into the whole spirit of the Chapman revival.[118]

The *Canadian Baptist* gave good press to the 1911 Toronto revival meetings largely because it believed that the "flame" kindled in past Toronto revival campaigns continued to burn.[119] The Baptists held that their churches would reap results providing they played an active role in making the meetings successful.[120] Yet, although the *Canadian Baptist* reported near the end of the campaign that the "continuous impact of the Gospel of Christ in song and story" blessed many Torontonians,[121] a few weeks later the magazine was sensitive that the meetings had not generated the same magnitude of enthusiasm as past campaigns. Putting on a brave front, the *Canadian Baptist* wrote that, even if mass revivalism had reached fewer people than expected, it was still crucial that the church continue to follow the example of the evangelists and be "a soul winning church."[122]

Other denominational publications such as the *Canadian Congregationalist* found it difficult to be as sanguine. Before the 1911 Toronto campaign had begun, the *Canadian Congregationalist* claimed that great good was done at the previous Torrey-Alexander campaign and "much interest will be taken in these meetings throughout the whole Dominion and the reading public will eagerly devour what is written."[123] The *Canadian Congregationalist* offered other reports, yet the most revealing account was its overall assessment of the January campaign published in early March, admitting that "the city was not moved as was hoped and expected. The flotsam and jetsam of the city remained absolutely untouched." At best, the campaign brought Christians a little closer to Christ, but the city as a whole mostly continued "as though nothing had happened." The Congregationalist paper suggested that Toronto leaders were at fault: "We were unprepared ... we gave little time or thought to the serious business of winning men to Christ." Rather than relying on prayer and fasting, Toronto had banked on the commercialization of revivalism – "great bill-board posters, large choirs and bands of evangelists."[124] This Congregationalist newspaper saw the popular-culture strategies, but not the piety.

Like the Congregationalist press, the contrast in the Methodist coverage before and after the January 1911 Toronto campaign was telling. In an article on the upcoming Toronto meetings, G.A. Warburton spoke of Chapman's winning personality and absence of dogmatism.[125] Other early reports of the Toronto campaign were all affirmative.[126] As the Toronto campaign was in progress, the *Christian Guardian* stated that Chapman's personality was warmer than Torrey's. Yet, without making any connection to the different styles of the evangelists, the publication also acknowledged that Torrey's campaign had generated more widespread religious enthusiasm.[127] Before the conclusion of the campaign, the *Christian Guardian* began taking a more middle course on American revivalism and conservative evangelicalism. One Methodist argued that there should be room for both "ethical teaching" and the old-fashioned method of appealing to individuals to be reconciled to God. Although the writer did not clarify what he meant by ethical teaching, he appeared to be suggesting that soul winning, which Chapman promoted, and greater church involvement in social issues, which social gospellers advocated, should go hand and hand.[128] The work of Phyllis Airhart on Ontario Methodists' search for and acceptance of a new, progressive evangelism supports this interpretation.[129] The *Christian Guardian*'s report on the close of the Chapman-Alexander campaign acknowledged that the simultaneous meetings were less spectacular than previous campaigns and that the number of conversions was lower than expected. A particular difficulty that one Methodist writer had with the campaign was the introduction, on a few occasions, of premillennial ideas at Bible readings by Ford Ottman, a Chapman worker. The references to premillennialism, the writer argued, hindered the spirit of harmony so essential in revival campaigns.[130]

Soon after Chapman and Alexander departed from the city, the Reverend C.E. Bland suggested that every evangelistic effort should include a definite social program.[131] If the goal of social service were absent, evangelism would prove itself inadequate. As Airhart argues, it was an age when the worth of religion depended on its achievements; Methodists demanded a religion that took action against the social ills of the community and the nation. Of course, Methodists had always applied religion to everyday life but now there was a louder call for personal service rather than personal regeneration. It was a step closer to the social gospel.[132]

Responding to social gospel-type strategies, "An Old Evangelizer" wryly pointed to some Methodist leaders' bewilderment on the issue of evangelism and protested that they stressed "the need of living a moral life" without any reference to the evil of sin, the unquenchable fire, and necessity of repentance.[133] Two visions were at work among Methodists: some Methodists stressed the conservative evangelicalism favoured by American evangelists, while an increasing number of Methodist leaders after January 1911 were advocating greater attention to social service.

Many Toronto Methodist ministers also favoured doing their own evangelizing instead of using professional revivalists. Reporting the results of a questionnaire on the Chapman-Alexander campaign in Toronto, W.B. Creighton, editor of the *Christian Guardian*, noted that more than 30 per cent of Toronto Methodist clergymen gave less than enthusiastic opinions of the effectiveness of the campaign in increasing church membership and reaching the unsaved.[134] Creighton himself became sceptical of revivalism and, as Airhart argues, the *Christian Guardian* adopted a "new anti-revival" tone during this time.[135] This movement among Toronto Methodists foreshadowed the Methodist Church's declining emphasis on conservative evangelicalism and perhaps its growing openness to the secularizing forces identified by Ramsay Cook and David Marshall.[136] While it has been argued that the "real leadership" of the Methodist Church continued to uphold old Wesleyan doctrines,[137] the less than brimming support for professional revivalism suggests that by 1911 fewer Methodist leaders were looking backwards to the evangelicalism of the past.

The Presbyterian press showed a similar tendency. Before the start of the January 1911 campaign by Chapman and Alexander, the *Presbyterian* declared that the simultaneous evangelistic model adopted by the Presbyterian Church in Canada had produced encouraging results in various regions of Canada over the past few years. In both small and large urban centres of the early-twentieth-century period, many Canadian Presbyterians glorified the old Gospel message that brought many people of various denominations together. One *Presbyterian* commentator, on 5 January 1911, claimed that a revival campaign was simply the "persistent presentation of fundamental religious truth, with the endeavour to secure the personal acceptance of it by individuals. Such work needs no apology or commendation." There might be differences expressed concerning the methods but none on "the necessity for telling men the truth about God and duty, about sin and death and redemption through Jesus Christ."[138]

But, later, a report by F.A. Robinson noted that there were few unsaved who came to the meetings.[139] Some Presbyterian ministers believed that the campaign had brought "lasting good," whereas others were ambivalent. The Reverend J. McP. Scott, for example, remarked on the awakening of some Christians and the conversion of others, but he also commented that the expected "deep, far-reaching movement of God" did not transpire. The Reverend W.G. Wallace and the Reverend A. Logan Geggie, two Presbyterian clergymen closely involved with the campaign, agreed that the harvest was not as extensive as many had expected. Rather than placing the responsibility upon Chapman's shoulders, the Reverend Jason

Murray considered Toronto Protestant leaders culpable: "The fact is that we were not ready for this campaign. 'The hunger was not on us'; a few years hence and such a movement would have shaken Toronto as it never has been shaken."[140] In an address on 30 January 1911 at Metropolitan Methodist Church, Chapman declared: "I will never go to another city again until I have the evangelical ministers pledged to help me ... We have done the best possible under the circumstances in this city, but if we had done better I would be exceedingly happy this morning."[141]

Of course, the campaign was far from a failure. Chapman himself admitted that, if he were a Toronto pastor, he might "in the next three months have the greatest spiritual harvest he had ever had."[142] That more than 400,000 people did attend the Toronto meetings remains impressive.[143] There was still a significant measure of enthusiasm for revival meetings and conservative evangelicalism even if fewer Protestant leaders concurred. One Congregationalist writer made a strong case for revival meetings: "They are needed oftener than we think. It is worth a great deal to a city and community to have the great truths of the gospel kept clearly before them night and day for a month. It is the only way to make a real impression."[144] Old ways linger long.

The Methodists were the most receptive to the social gospel of all the major denominations in Canada,[145] but they, too, were slow to embrace a social Christianity that placed less emphasis on individual conversion. The positive reception of Chapman by those involved in the social gospel movement in Canada was in large part because the early Canadian social gospellers remained closer to evangelical Protestant traditions than was the case in the United States.[146] The Reverend Frank Granstaff, a Chapman co-evangelist, himself stated: "The church is the communism, the socialism, the confraternity of Jesus Christ. It is a people for God's own possession. God owns, fills, controls us. This is a definition of the church in action."[147]

But Granstaff also stressed that he "was an old fashioned preacher and, instead of being ashamed of it, glorified in it."[148] A conservative evangelical message was the central focus of the campaigns, but equally important was that the application of this message was done in a manner that apparently did not initially cause a negative reaction. In both the secular and the denominational press, there appeared to be a consensus of positive support for the theological message that Chapman promulgated in many English-Canadian cities. The Chapman evangelistic campaigns attracted several hundreds of thousands of participants.

Of the unchurched who attended the Chapman campaigns, many likely represented the working class. There were not enough people from bourgeois circles to fill the rinks, churches, and other revival sites to overflowing proportions. Unlike the formal atmosphere of Sunday services, daily revival meetings in neutral sites such as halls and roller rinks offered a more attractive setting for workers. Class-related issues such as elaborate churches, pew rents, and bourgeois ideals of social respectability and status alienated many industrial workers. The Reverend Hiram Hull of Winnipeg stated that men stayed away from church because they thought it was "a class institution." A recent study argues that early-twentieth-century Presbyterian leaders, applying modern business methods to the church, preached more on the suppression of social vice that threatened bourgeois ideals than on the compelling love and grace of God.[149]

There were workers suspicious of the alliance between the clergy and business leaders.[150] For some, the relationship between revivals and capitalists was too close. As the Winnipeg revival campaign was in progress, the *Voice*, a working-class paper, reported that the birth of the Chapman evangelistic movement was dependent on some of the wealthiest men of Philadelphia, including those who were notoriously anti-union.[151] The main Canadian sponsors of the meetings were well-known and respected clergymen such as T.B. Kilpatrick and J.G. Shearer, who had direct connections with men of business, and Charles W. Gordon, wealthy from his books and real estate investments, and successful businessmen such as Winnipeg's J.A.M. Aikens, G.F. Stephens, and Sir Daniel McMillan, Orillia's J.J. Thompson, and Toronto's J.N. Shenstone, to name only a few. Leading capitalists supported the Chapman campaigns and, thus it is not surprising that the Winnipeg meetings received the favour of people such as William Whyte, vice-president of Winnipeg Electric Railway Company – the company that attempted to eliminate union activity the year before the arrival of the Chapman evangelists.[152]

It would be too simplistic to link all workers' spiritual yearnings with labour politics. Still, Protestant denominations built and equipped huge churches, gathered large, influential, and wealthy congregations, and raised vast sums of money for religious purposes but failed to attract large numbers of Canadian workers into church

membership, even with the assistance of popular American evangelists, including the Ashers, who preached primarily in working-class
space (industrial work and leisure sites).[153]

The Chapman simultaneous-revival format may be partly answer-
able for the lack of worker interest and the beginnings of a more critical attitude towards modern revivalism. On the one hand, the
Chapman campaign held meetings in working-class space such as
factories and taverns, on the other hand, the failure to attract more
workers, may have been, in part, due to most of the meetings being
held in city churches rather than in one public revival venue. For
obvious reasons, the well-built and distinctively defined denominational churches had less egalitarian appeal for workers wanting to
experience earthy, emotional revival. Moreover, with the simultaneous-revival format, the press had a harder job in packaging the
services as a big media event: journalists could not cover revival
activity occurring in a dozen or so different sites at one time. One
expects that the revival excitement itself was diffuse and weaker
than that of the campaigns led by Moody, Jones and Small, and
Torrey.

Chapman did generate much excitement and spiritual renewal
among church members and churchgoers who attended the meetings.[154] But the Chapman campaigns could not easily achieve both
renewal and substantial church growth. Not only was there the issue
of class, but Protestant leaders did not provide the support that
Chapman required for his last and most ambitious Canadian campaign. In a biography of Chapman, John Ramsay argued that
Toronto churches had committed their complete cooperation and
backing for the January campaign but, nonetheless, became
involved with supporting activities such as secular concerts and lectures.[155] If unchurched revival attenders were reluctant to join mainstream churches in large numbers, Canadian Protestant leaders were
mostly to blame, not short-term visitors. The year 1911 marked a
transition point for revivalism in large Canadian cities. Although the
secular press showed no signs of curbing its coverage of revivals,
widespread church support for American revivalism had come and
gone.

CHAPTER SIX

Results

In the late nineteenth and early twentieth centuries, masses of people from rural areas and from other countries descended on Canadian cities seeking work and a better life. In the midst of this, Protestant leaders mainly focused on the issue of the city's Christian and moral character rather than on working-class grievance and need or the shortcomings of capitalism. As many Protestants saw it, the city needed revival and there were great expectations among Canadian Protestant clergy and lay leaders that visiting American evangelists would play a major role in the revitalization of Canadian Protestantism and the "re-moralization" of civic space.[1] Certainly, American evangelists consistently drew enormous crowds that surpassed other public attractions and events throughout Canada. But, in an era when many workers experienced alienating work and dispiriting living conditions, how effective was revivalism in regenerating Protestantism and resisting secularizing forces?

More than 1.5 million unchurched and regular church members attended the campaigns of four American revival teams from 1884 to 1911. Church members experienced a revival of their faith, but many of the unchurched and non-members who gathered at the meetings avoided taking the additional step to local church membership. When the 1911 Toronto meetings fell short of the expectations of Canadian clergymen, the fleeting support for American modern revivalism became more apparent.

The praise from many city newspapers, the strong interdenominational support, and the high attendance and conversion figures in American cities attracted the attention of Canadian clergy and lay leaders to the work of popular American evangelists. If these evangelists could become a media sensation and have such apparent success in America, where there was a great movement of people from the rural areas to the cities, the expectation of equal and perhaps greater success in Canada seemed reasonable.

Numerous comments published in Canadian newspapers testify to the impressive star-status bestowed on high-profile American evangelists during their campaigns in Canada. Moody, Jones and Small, Torrey, and Chapman all received accolades from the editors of newspapers and denominational publications. For example, a *Manitoba Free Press* reporter wrote: "The name Moody has a magnetism about it that would stir the hearts of nine-tenths of the people of Canada ..." As a man who spent "his life for the good of others, and for the uplifting of mankind," he was worthy of the highest respect.[2] Predicting that some Torontonians would condemn Sam Jones, the *Globe* pointed out, before his arrival in Canada in 1886, that the greatest evangelists throughout history suffered abuse from their contemporaries.[3] A Mr John W. Garvin claimed that Jones "is the greatest man that ever came to this country in that work."[4] Torrey, Chapman, and those who assisted them benefited from similar supportive comments from newspapers throughout Canada. Positing that Alexander was the greatest Gospel evangelist in the world at the time, the *News* reported, in 1906, that his impact on Toronto was obvious since the streets were alive with the singing of his Gospel songs.[5] Canadian editors' construct of "revival" promised an alluring commodity for mass consumption, but it should be stressed that the product they were selling had to be tenable. Without substance, modern revivalism could not thrive meeting after meeting, day after day, week after week, and year after year.

Popular revivalism was one of the earliest institutionalized responses of the Canadian evangelical churches to the growing number of unsaved.[6] According to an 1886 *Globe* article entitled "Church Going and Working Men," the only sure way to attract workingmen was to preach the old Gospel rather than "lifeless essays."[7] This message could be found in the press from coast to coast. At Moody's 1884 campaign, one man in the gallery stated, "He had been a tavern-keeper, selling whisky and driving people to hell, but he had found conversion. He thanked God for the Salvation Army, for though a Church of England man he knew the work the Army was doing."[8] Protestant leaders who might have admired the evangelistic work of the Salvation Army in Canadian cities, but who were wary of the more sensational methods of the Salvationists, found the Gospel message and the evangelistic zeal of the American evangelists to be appealing.[9] As one Methodist leader claimed, "there were a great many laboring men in the town whom, he understood, had a desire to hear Sam Jones."[10]

In American revival historiography, which rarely examines occupational data, there is the misconception that the overwhelming majority of revival attenders were "middle-class." In fact, however, the few studies that closely investigate revivalism and class status show a high level of working-class attendance.[11] Although newspaper reports discussed the mass appeal of the evangelists and hinted that a large number of the proletariat gathered to hear the revivalists, they rarely gave anything close to precise information on those who attended. Many reports stated that "all classes and conditions of the people were there" and some reports claimed a version of the following: the "rich merchant" sat side by side with the labourer or the labourer sat alongside the banker.[12] Such reports may have represented the press's desire to manufacture "community." Certainly, it would take great imagination to believe there was an equal number of bankers/rich merchants and labourers at meetings.

"The object of these meetings," Moody stated, "is principally to reach the non-church goer." Those who gave testimonies or called for prayers appeared to be mainly working class, such as "one poor old woman" who asked Moody to pray "for her son, who was wild with drink."[13] Capturing the drama of working-class participation, one journalist related how an old derelict-like man sat beside him at a Moody meeting in Toronto in 1894. The man was dirty, his hair stood straight up, and his face "was purple and bulbous, his lashes had been obliterated on his eyelids, and his eyes peered out from swollen and disgusting red lines." His clothes were old and did not fit well. He carried a stick that he pounded upon the floor, a floor that was the recipient of his regular spitting, and he recognized many of those whom he saw at the meeting (perhaps people of similar circumstances). When the service began, the journalist recounted, "I watched the old man at my side. He had ceased to chuckle ... I thought, 'that is a tear wandering down the man's cheek,' and when I looked again I beheld another. He was quiet now, save for his heavy breathing. This wretched creature was doubtless echoing the petition that he heard." At this particular meeting, "6,000 people assembled in the evening, most of them being workingmen."[14]

Presenting specific class information, one Toronto *Daily Star* report stated that, for a Torrey meeting, the "first gallery was occupied entirely by young ladies from stores, offices, and factories of the city."[15] A Mr Thomas Woodhouse, like other individuals who assessed American revivalism, claimed that most revival attenders "do not go to any church."[16] One Toronto commentator expressed the view that men converted at the Jones campaign "were, to my personal knowledge, wrecks of intemperance and depravity, whose homes were wretched and whose lives were miserable in the extreme."[17] When one defines the working class as consisting of those who sold their labour power, it becomes obvious that there were far more workers than merchants and professionals at revival meetings.[18] The evangelists' apparent ability to attract both down-and-out and "respectable" working-class people went a long way in gaining the support of many Canadian Protestants.

Dwight L. Moody, described by a John W. Campbell as having a "fearless, manly and open face," provided the foundation of modern revivalism in Canada and his campaigns, which received outstanding and wide support, ranged from Montreal to Victoria.[19] The popularity of Moody's meetings in the United States may have levelled off by 1880, but in Canada his popularity showed no signs of abating even in the 1890s.[20] A variety of organizations and associations representing most Protestant denominations sponsored his visits to Canada. Usually both the YMCA and other evangelical organizations jointly supported his Canadian revival efforts. The YMCA's interest in evangelism corresponded with its goal to attract all young men to its movement and guide the moral development of the city.

At the Toronto campaign of November 1894, the ten-man executive committee consisted of six denominations: the Reverend John Potts, the Reverend George Bishop, and the Reverend Albert Crews (Methodism); the Reverend Dr Sims (Congregationalism); the Reverend Elmore Harris (Baptist); Hilyard Cameron Dixon (Anglican); and four laymen (Baptist Hamilton Cassels, Anglican S.H. Blake, Presbyterian Robert Kilgour, and Elias Rogers). While not on the committee, H.A. Massey had written to Moody inviting him to preach in the new hall he built.[21]

A number of clergy and laity who were beginning to show some concern over the teachings of higher biblical criticism especially welcomed Moody. For example, the Reverend Harris was a strong Moody supporter, a major figure in the late-nineteenth-century proto-fundamentalist movement (forerunners of early-twentieth-century fundamentalism) in Ontario, and founder of the Toronto Bible Training School, created in May 1894, six months before the arrival of Moody in Toronto. The creation of the Bible school received the full support of Moody, whose own Bible Institute in Chicago was showing promise.[22]

Another prominent figure in bringing Moody to Toronto in 1894 was Samuel Hume Blake, respected lawyer and an Anglican involved with the late-nineteenth-century Niagara Prophecy Conferences (concerned with the promotion of premillennialism) and Toronto's proto-fundamentalist movement. When it became obvious that Moody's Toronto meetings showed no signs of losing popular support among the working masses, it was Blake who asked Moody to stay one extra week.[23] A Presbyterian, well-known manufacturer, and participant in the Niagara Prophecy Conference committee, Robert Kilgour, was a member of the executive committee of the Moody meetings. The other prominent businessman and "proto-fundamentalist" who sat on the committee was Elias Rogers. Involved with the Quakers and the Christian Alliance, Rogers was also a supporter of the Toronto Bible Training School. Well-known Torontonians who assisted Moody but were not on the committee included Anglican lawyer Henry O'Brien and Presbyterian businessman John J. Gartshore, both of whom had ties to proto-fundamentalism.[24]

Although prominent capitalists (particularly the Toronto proto-fundamentalists) did assist Moody in Canada, many others did not participate in the meetings. For example, all the noon meetings established for businessmen during the 1887 campaign had meagre attendance, an unusual occurrence for American revivalism.[25] For the 1894 Toronto campaign, there were well-known Methodist businessmen who did not appear to be involved in American revivalism. Toronto millionaire Methodist church members such as Joseph Flavelle, George Cox, A.E. Kemp, and H.H. Fudger, who attended and took active roles in the Sherbourne Street Church, were missing in the daily press accounts covering the American revival meetings. As a biographer of business tycoon Joseph Flavelle notes, "revivalism and respectability did not mix well." For some well-established Methodist congregations, there was little enthusiasm for either the puritanism of "old-fashioned Methodism" or the fire-and-brimstone message of revival meetings.[26]

At least in the case of Toronto, the small number of the bourgeoisie who did support Moody appeared to have adopted premillennialism and conservative evangelicalism. The issue of respectability
probably was not as important to these supporters since their adher-
ence to proto-fundamentalism likely isolated them somewhat from
capitalists such as Joseph Flavelle. Overall, the Canadian ruling
class did not appear to provide Moody and other American evangelists the wide and consistent support that they received from the
bourgeoisie in the United States. The lack of information in newspapers on those who financially supported American revivalism in
Canada also suggests American and Canadian differences, a topic
that, it is to be hoped, will receive attention in future studies.

The sensibilities of the working class were more in line with revivalism and an orthodox message than was the case for those in bourgeois
circles. Certainly, at Moody's revival meetings, many workers gathered. Yet how many actually entered the church fold? The value of
church memberships for measuring the effects of revivalism is far from
exact. David Marshall warns that "statistics depend on the churches'
definitions of membership, which have never been precise or constant;
and also how zealously they have been in collecting accurate
records."[27] Moreover, the movement of people and clergy, the various
stages of church development, and other factors make statistical comparisons questionable. Nonetheless, abundant quantitative data on
church membership does offer reasonably helpful conclusions.

Although some of Moody's revival meetings in the 1894 Toronto
campaign were at the Metropolitan Methodist Church, that church
did not experience growth. In fact, unlike Walmer Baptist and
Cooke's Presbyterian, Metropolitan lost members in the year after
the campaign. As Methodists discussed the merits of professional
revivalism, such disappointing results likely fuelled some criticism of
evangelical outsiders who not only preached a proto-fundamentalist
message but apparently failed to entice workers to seek church membership. Three Toronto clergymen, the Reverends' H.M. Parson, W.
Frizzell, and Mutch (first name unknown), all identified as
proto-fundamentalists, did attend and support the meetings, but
even their churches did not experience a significant change in the
pattern of membership growth.[28] The meetings did not stop the
decline of new memberships which the Reverend H. Parson's
church, Knox Presbyterian, had been experiencing since at least two
years before the arrival of Moody.

There is, however, more to the story. The growth of membership in the Presbytery of Toronto was impressive, growing by 1,145 in the year of Moody's campaign, after having shrunk the year before. The Toronto district total for the Methodists followed a similar pattern. The Methodists showed a decrease in membership of 404 in 1893 but made steady gains in the three years after the campaign. The overall gains are consistent with one Toronto newspaper report which claimed that "1,500 souls were converted" at the revival campaign.[29] The late-nineteenth-century Moody revivals appeared to have had at least a modest impact on increasing church memberships.[30]

Church growth and revivalism had a long history, particularly within Methodism. Historians have traced the development of Canadian Methodism from its early-nineteenth-century sectarian beginnings to its late-nineteenth-century status as a respectable church with its own colleges, missions, religious organizations, and members who represented some of the leading businessmen and families of communities throughout Canada. A driving force behind these evangelical activities was revivalism.[31] Phyllis Airhart, as we have seen, argues that revivalism and the commitment to a basic evangelical message not only helped define Methodism but also sparked its remarkable growth, making it the largest Protestant denomination of the second half of the nineteenth century.[32] In 1886 the *Canadian Methodist Magazine* proudly proclaimed that Methodism was an evangelistic church and revival was its vital air. Methodists believed that, to have revival, there must be preaching that prompted an unconverted individual to seek a personal relationship with Christ. But revival did not just represent an isolated event – it was to have an enduring impact.[33] The Jones and Small revival meetings in Toronto, for example, could be expected to raise the moral tone throughout Ontario and lift the hearts of brethren labouring in the mission and educational fields at home and abroad.[34]

Representing the old guard of Methodism, the two key clergymen who brought Jones and Small to Canada in 1886 were the Reverend Hugh Johnston and the Reverend John Potts. Of Irish heritage and known for his ability to identify with the masses, Potts had been in the ministry since 1857, had supported Moody's Toronto meetings, and was a minister to Elm Street Methodist during Jones's visit. Following Pott's suggestion, Jones published a volume of his Toronto revival sermons in remembrance of the city's "wonderful awakening" in 1886. In the introduction to Jones's collection of sermons, entitled *Sam Jones and Sam Small in Toronto*, Potts wrote: "Never in the history of this city was there a more fearless denunciation of sin – of sin in its public and wide-spread manifestations – than by the simple, unostentatious, but heroic soldier of the Lord Jesus Christ."[35] Clergyman to Carlton Street Methodist Church, the Reverend Hugh Johnston had been in the ministry since 1859. Born in 1840, Johnston was a successful minister who held desirable city appointments including Centenary Methodist in Hamilton, St James Street Methodist in Montreal, and Metropolitan Methodist in Toronto. He travelled with Jones to Georgia in 1887 and in 1893 moved permanently to the United States, where he joined the Methodist Episcopal Church. Both Potts and Johnston showed no signs of lessening their support for Jones and Small. As the chairman of the revival committee, Dr Potts stated that the Jones and Small campaign was far more successful than he had anticipated, a conclusion with which many other Methodist ministers agreed.[36]

Information on specific numbers of conversions was often missing in the newspapers, but some reports indicated that a good number of people proclaimed their desire to become Christians at the Jones-Small campaign. Ten days into the Toronto meetings of October 1886, approximately six hundred conversions had taken place and from this total almost three hundred revival cards had been forwarded to the Reverend Hugh Johnston, secretary of the Jones-Small committee, to be sent to the proper churches. The revival cards provided clergy with basic information:

"THE SAM JONES REVIVAL CARD"
Name ...
Business Address ...
Residence Address ...
Spiritual Condition ...
Church Preferred ...
Minister's Name ...

Of the denominations indicated, 74 per cent of the cards were sent to the Methodists, 8 per cent to the Anglicans, 7 per cent to the Presbyterians, 4 per cent to the Congregationalists, 3 per cent to the Baptists, and 1 per cent both to the Salvation Army and to the Society of Friends.[37] While it cannot be proven, one newspaper journalist made the observation that Presbyterians and staid Methodists attended Small's meetings whereas "regular Methodist" and Salvation Army followers appeared at Jones's meetings.[38] On the last week of the campaign, the Toronto *World* reported that "there seems to be no limit to the 'great awakening,' which the Georgia evangelists have enlisted in the ranks of Toronto sinners."[39]

Published conversion numbers usually ranged from thirty to fifty for each meeting. However, the totals are ambiguous since some penitents failed to keep their commitment and consequently fell away before attending and joining a church. Also, a number of people who came forward were already Christians, seeking to reconsecrate their lives to Jesus. Because Moody had held a short campaign at Toronto less than two years before the Toronto revival of Jones and Small, and because the city's population was growing steadily, membership figures must be interpreted cautiously. Nonetheless, keeping this in mind, certain observations can be made on the Jones and Small campaign of 1886.

Of twelve Methodist churches, all but one had a rise in membership between June 1886 and June 1887. Sherbourne Methodist, church to a number of wealthy Methodists and known as the "millionaire's church," only added two members, whereas Agnes Methodist Church, located in the slum-ridden St John's Ward, added 152 members, the largest increase for a single Toronto Methodist church. The membership figures for the Toronto district suggest that Jones and Small might have attracted new members into the churches. Whereas membership rose by 858 in the year before their meetings, it increased by 1,155 in the following year. From 1887 to 1888, membership increased by 996, thus levelling off some.[40] Furthermore, these figures may underestimate the number of working-class conversions because many who attend religious services do not necessarily become official church members. Another issue that needs to be investigated concerns the nominal working-class Catholics who participated in the revival meetings but were unlikely ever to join the fold of a Protestant church. Overall, the membership numbers indicate that Toronto newspapers and Methodists had good reason, at least for the 1886 Toronto campaign, to give the efforts of Jones the benefit of the doubt. This was the high point, however; other meetings were far less effective, in part, because of the southern evangelists' ill-chosen comments about the working class and trade unions.

The enthusiasm generated during Jones's short engagements in 1887 was fleeting. In its story on a Jones meeting in March 1887, the

Montreal *Gazette* reported that "there was neither the rush nor the crush which characterized Moody's revival meetings in Montreal."[41] Jones represented an important voice for many Methodists anxious about the sin in society, but there were Canadian Protestants who wondered if he could have a positive and enduring impact on the community. It was a sign of Jones's inability, and Small's as well, to attract broader support from the Protestant community that the fall 1887 visit to Canada by a lesser known American and proto-fundamentalist evangelist, Dr Leander W. Munhall of Philadelphia, who did emphasize traditional evangelical theology, received strong support from the laity, clergy, and journalists of Toronto.[42]

Of course, Jones did influence ordinary Canadians. In a seven-page letter to Jones, a man who called himself "One Anxious to become a Christian" told how he attended, out of curiosity, one of Jones's Toronto meetings. Having never been in a place of worship for ten years, the correspondent did not initially expect much: "Little did I think that your sermon on Conscience would have such an effect on me. Your words struck deep into my hard heart, and after you had concluded I stood up before the Almighty, and that vast audience, as one who wished to lead a better life." Although this correspondent did not claim to have experienced salvation, he sought to become a Christian. With great excitement, the correspondent looked forward to attending another meeting, this time hoping "to get nearer to the blessed Truth."[43] If more records existed, there would be many other similar stories revealing Jones's impact.

Of Sam Jones, the popular journalist and caricaturist J.W. Bengough stated in 1886 that "it may be true that his expressions frequently sound irreverent to our Canadian ears, but nobody believes that the irreverence is intentional."[44] Only a few years later, well-known Canadian commentator C.S. Clark wrote that Jones's drawing cards were his "vulgarity," "slangy style of oratory," and "continental notoriety."[45] His earthy and masculine manner and language assured him the notice of many working-class people during a time when there was a groundswell of conservative evangelicalism at the grass-roots level and when a large number of American and Canadian evangelists were holding revival meetings in cities, towns, and villages across the country.

But what was the revival experience for Canadian Protestants in the early twentieth century? Reuben Torrey's campaigns in Toronto, Ottawa, Montreal, Fredericton, Saint John, and Windsor, Nova Scotia, resulted in large numbers of revival attenders. For the Toronto campaign, more than 220,000 people gathered to hear Torrey and Alexander in January 1906. Some of the key Torontonians involved with the campaign included conservative evangelicals: the Reverend T.B. Hyde (Congregationalist), the Reverend McTavish (Presbyterian), the Reverend Thomas (Baptist), the Reverend W.F. Wilson (Methodist), and Baptist layman J.N. Shenstone, who was the treasurer of the committee.[46] Unlike the newspaper coverage of Jones and Moody, there is no information on the clergymen who might have been on the platform with Torrey; even their names are unknown. One cannot be certain but it is possible that a number of clergymen chose not to show their endorsement for the sometimes controversial Torrey. Of those who supported the meetings, the Reverend Hyde took on the most responsibility. A minister of the Congregationist Church, Hyde had been a student and supporter of the Moody Bible Institute.[47]

Torrey's proto-fundamentalist message and the negative criticism he received throughout the campaign did not stop large masses of people from converging at the meetings. More than two weeks into the campaign, the Toronto *World* editor, who had earlier suggested that the humbler classes were the most impressionable, wrote that "hundreds of honest souls have turned their courses into better channels. So long as that is accomplished, The *World* does not want to quarrel with the evangelist, however great the temptation."[48] According to the Toronto *Daily Star*, more than 4,400 individuals came forward to accept Christ publicly during the month of the Torrey and Alexander campaign.[49] Of all the Toronto newspapers, the *Daily Star* did the most impressive work in promoting the revival themes of piety, power, and community. Still, a number of Canadian clergymen were less sure of the evangelists' ability to strengthen Protestant life and some found the declared number of converts suspect. The Reverend J.B. Kennedy, a Baptist, declared that he had names of penitents sent to him but few of these individuals actually proved to be "really regenerated." Moreover, Kennedy argued that the crowds came to the meetings because of the high degree of organization and advertisement, not because of Torrey himself.[50] Such an assessment, however, was rare and many Canadian evangelical ministers valued the impact that Torrey had on the popular mass mind.

The Torrey-Alexander meetings in Toronto in January 1906 did appear initially to have a positive impact on the growth of churches directly involved with the meetings. From December 1905 to December 1906, the membership of Cooke's Presbyterian increased by 177, a significant increase compared to the preceding years. The Metropolitan Methodist Church grew by 141 from June 1905 to June 1906. Jarvis Street Baptist, which did not directly participate in the meetings, had a modest increase of 38. Perhaps better indicators of church growth was the total membership of the Presbytery of Toronto, which showed an increase of 2,228, and for the Methodist district of Toronto, whose increase was 1,739. For the Presbyterians, the increase was especially significant: the rise of membership for 1906 was much higher than that for the previous and following years.[51]

The excitement generated at the Toronto campaign likely had a positive effect on the Ottawa meetings held in June 1906. Indeed, the impact was far-ranging since, during the Ottawa meetings, Torrey had met with Montreal revival planners such as J. Ritchie Bell of the Sailors' Institute, C.K. Calhoun of the YMCA, the Reverend Dr Gordon, and the businessman W.H. Goodwin to discuss the proposed mission in that city.[52] All those connected with the Ottawa campaign were enthusiastic over the results; the executive committee included the Reverend P.W. Anderson (Presbyterian) and four laymen who represented other denominations. Alderman Charles Hopewell, for example, was a contractor/politician and Methodist. The Reverend W.S. Jacoby, an American who was in charge of personal workers and who had told of his conversion experience at one meeting, claimed that, for its population, Ottawa was the most successful campaign that Torrey and Alexander had on their world tour.[53] Torrey's co-evangelist Charles Alexander wrote that the Ottawa experience was highly successful.[54] According to George Davis, who travelled with the evangelists, the children's meeting was one of the largest ever addressed by Torrey, perhaps only London and Liverpool having a larger meeting of its kind.[55]

At one of the last meetings, the Reverend H.I. Horsey, a local clergyman, asked the audience to raise their hands if they had been blessed by the revival and the Ottawa *Evening Journal* captured the response with vivid words: "In every part of the building hands were held up. In the auditorium and on the platform. Hands, hands, hands, everywhere. The strong hand of the man, the gentle hand of the woman, the little, confiding hand of the child, the withered hand of the aged, the soft, well-cared- for, bejewelled hand of the rich, the hard, toil-worn and toil-stained hand of the poor – all were held up." According to the journalist, the response was "a silent, but very striking and eloquent testimony" to the impact and "suitability of the message preached and sung by the evangelists to all sorts and conditions of men, the rich, the poor, the young, the old."[56] There was no breakdown on how many of the respondents were of the working class, but the sheer numbers present at the meeting meant that the number of workers must have been substantial.

As for church-membership patterns, consistent with other years of growth, membership numbers for the Presbytery of Ottawa saw an increase of 400. The Methodist churches did better. For the Methodist district of Ottawa, an increase of 248 represented a significant rise in comparison to previous and later years.[57]

More striking figures are those relating to Torrey's 1910 revival campaign in Fredericton, New Brunswick, sponsored by the Reverends W.H. Smith, J.W. McConnell, J.H. McDonald, and A.A. Rideout, representing a Presbyterian, a Methodist, and two Baptist churches. Torrey received a copious amount of press in the *Daily Gleaner*, Fredericton's major newspaper, including a report estimating that approximately eight hundred conversions had resulted from the meetings. In a pastoral address at a Methodist conference in the Maritimes, Methodists reported that, at the Torrey campaign in Fredericton, "the Holy Ghost has spoken through the lips of these mighty evangelists, bringing to the souls of hundreds a more devoted and aggressive discipleship, winning many hundreds from the power of sin, and impressing the entire community with a deeper respect and reverence for revealed religion."[58]

Given the rise of memberships during Torrey's visit in May and June, the newspaper and both the Methodist and Presbyterian churches had good reason to be enraptured with the results. From June 1909 to June 1910, the Methodist Church in Fredericton grew by 125, reversing a previous decline. Likewise, the Fredericton district of the Methodist Church for this period had an increase, in contrast to a decline the year before. St Paul's of Fredericton witnessed an increase of 83 in its membership, a substantial rise from earlier and later years. Far more impressive was the change in membership of the Presbytery of Saint John, which encompassed both the Saint John and Fredericton regions. The increase of 448 corresponded to the revival in Fredericton and also the simultaneous campaign in Saint John, where some of Chapman's helpers assisted.[59]

The Torrey campaign, particularly, consisted of a strong working-class flavour. For example, of the twenty-nine ushers listed, four were business owners, two were educators, and the rest represented an assortment of trades such as painter, carpenter, teamster, book-keeper, clerk, and mason.[60] A quartet that sang included a painter and blacksmith. On the matter of converts, class identification is more difficult. Many of the converts, however, were young people. Of the sixty-four who were entered in the communion registrar of the St Paul's Presbyterian Church in the aftermath of the Torrey Campaign, thirty were young females (identified as "Miss") and approximately the same number were males.[61]

The impact of Torrey was significant elsewhere, too. The Reverend R.P. McKim, chair of the Saint John campaign, exulted over the numbers who experienced Torrey's meetings at the Queen's Rink in the port city, where in total approximately 100,000 assembled to hear Torrey and his assistants.[62] The number of converts during the main meetings is unknown, but at one meeting, held at the Ludlow Baptist Church, Torrey assistant Mary Moody Parker encouraged 38 young people to accept Christ, and later in the day, under the direction of Torrey co-helper Dr Jacoby, another 152 people agreed to commit themselves to Christ at the Portland Street Methodist Church.[63] In a report on the Torrey meetings in Windsor, Nova Scotia, the *Maritime Baptist* reported that 325 professed faith in Christ.[64]

As already explained, J. Wilbur Chapman, unlike Torrey, adopted a campaign format in which at least several evangelists preached at different sites throughout the cities they visited. Among Canadian Protestant clergymen, there was also the notion that Chapman's meetings tended to be less dogmatic and more open to progressive views concerning the role Protestantism played in moral reform. Some who promoted Chapman, such as Presbyterian clergymen C.W. Gordon, T.B. Kilpatrick, and J.G. Shearer, have been identified as leaders of progressivism[65]; and some were conservative evangelicals, such as the Reverend T.B. Hyde, who had supported Torrey. Chapman was able to tap into the churches' awareness that, despite theological differences, they all sought to "re-moralize" public space. At all their Canadian campaigns, people and ministers representing most Protestant denominations came together to support Chapman's brand of American revivalism.

Perhaps the key to this support was the perception that Chapman and his co-workers were reaching those who had rarely if ever attended church. Many press reports suggested that working men and women could find something appealing about the campaigns. For the Winnipeg campaign, the *Manitoba Free Press* described the "Union Church Parade," which saw the Chapman evangelists and the Salvation Army band lead a massive procession of Winnipeg citizens representing all the Protestant churches. Marching up and down the main streets of Winnipeg, the parade and the "scouts," who handed out evangelical literature as they marched, demonstrated the exuberant religious enthusiasm which could easily arise from Canadian urban revival meetings and which appealed to working people.[66]

However, ministers interested in the social gospel movement might have been disappointed that the Chapman campaigns – including Virginia and William Ashers's efforts among the working poor – represented conservative rather than social-reform thought. Others found the Chapman revivals too businesslike. The *Voice*, a Winnipeg labour paper, described the Winnipeg campaign as "a modern, up-to-date, business-like affair" managed by "polished gentlemen" with the "old revival seance beaten about as far as the new electric cars have it on the old Red River cart."[67] If other working people shared this sentiment, the task of enticing revival participants to join a church must have been difficult. Indeed, one working-class commentator concluded that the meetings had failed to attract workers to church life.[68] Winnipeg church membership figures support this assessment. Although Augustine's Presbyterian Church showed a marked increase, St Stephen's Presbyterian Church had only a modest increase and St Andrew's Presbyterian Church lost members.[69]

Church-membership numbers at the time of the Toronto campaign also reveal modest growth. The *Presbyterian* had commented that the meetings held by Chapman and Alexander attracted mostly church-attending people, rather than those on the periphery.[70] Because the 1911 Toronto campaign occurred in January, the most important numbers to compare are the membership rolls of 1910 and 1911. Of the eleven participating city churches, two congregations lost members, three made modest gains, and six showed a significant increase. The Methodists had the worst record since only one of their four participating churches had a marked increase. Another variable to consider is the visit of British evangelist Gypsy Smith, who held a campaign at Massey Hall, Toronto, during the month of May 1909. The Gypsy Smith meetings, however, do not appear to have produced much of an impact. The overall pattern of growth of the Baptist and Presbyterian churches remained fairly consistent, with a little rise in numbers as a result of the Chapman-Alexander campaign.[71]

An examination of the Presbyterian and Methodist membership rolls in the Toronto area indicates that the Chapman meetings might have had an impact on church growth. For the Presbyterians, the years 1910 to 1913 represented good gains; however for the Methodists, the numbers show that the best years were 1912 to 1914, indicating that the Chapman campaign had no immediate impact on church memberships.[72]

There were conversions in Toronto, but were there enough? In 1911, of a city workforce of 170,000, two-thirds were blue-collar workers and the remaining one third were white-collar workers, included a large number of sales workers and clerks.[73] At this time, there was also a large number of unemployed transient people living on the streets.[74] The commentary among some Protestant clergymen after the Chapman campaign underscored that the meetings did not have an impact on the working poor of society. Of course, unlike the Torrey experience, the Chapman campaign held far more meetings in churches and fewer in neutral public space. Spread over many sites, the simultaneous-meeting format was likely less effective in generating religious excitement than the utilization of one major revival venue. Being more institutional, revival lost part of its popular-culture edge. There was also the impossible task of the press in providing adequate coverage of the meetings, with the result that the presentation of the themes of piety, power, and community in revival rhetoric became more difficult. For a variety of reasons, the membership figures for the years before and after the visits of the Chapman evangelists in 1911 reflected only modest growth, probably not enough to induce some liberal and wealthy evangelicals to provide the regular sponsorship of professional revivalists.

In 1906 the *Wesleyan* reported that it did not agree with all the methods of Torrey and Alexander, but "it is enough, if sinners are being led to Christ and men and women are being soundly converted."[75] Yet the enthusiasm for American conservative evangelicalism was waning for an increasing number of Canadian clergymen. This is not to say that Torrey and Chapman did not have a long list of supporters. They did. Evangelists such as Chapman were much sought after, unsuccessfully in the case of Halifax, which invited Chapman to hold meetings at the port city in May 1911.[76] Still, American revivalism was losing support. Why? Ramsay Cook, David Marshall, and others point to the secularization of Protestant society and church life. Phyllis Airhart claims that Methodists found the evangelical message from the United States to be too dogmatic to suit their tastes. Michael Gauvreau makes the argument that Canadian evangelicalism experienced a fracture in the early twentieth century.[77] All these interpretations help to explain the change that occurred within the Canadian Protestant experience, including the place of American revivalism, and, they are, in various ways, complementary to the argument presented in this study. The story of American revivalism in Canada indicates that a secularization process was unfolding, that an increasing number of Methodist leaders questioned evangelical orthodoxy, and that the rhetorical tone of Canadian evangelicalism demonstrated a fracturing of a real or imagined consensus.

In 1906 the Toronto *World*, in a statement concerning Torrey's proto-fundamentalist message, hinted of a division in the evangelical community: "It is difficult to urge that the bounds of grace, wisdom and understanding may be wider than those delimited by Dr. Torrey in Massey Hall, without the hypersensitive old-time religionists getting the idea that you are hostile to Dr. Torrey's message and method."[78] Revivalistic piety faced countervailing trends that increasingly viewed conservative evangelicalism almost as a relic of the older order. Religion prospered institutionally but the sway of biblical principles, as interpreted by American evangelists, was waning in various circles.[79]

In another affair, the Reverend Charles Gordon and Reuben Torrey corresponded with each other on the possibility of Torrey holding a revival campaign in Winnipeg in January 1907. Torrey even postponed a revival campaign at an American city to be open for a Winnipeg date, but, for some reason, the Winnipeg meetings did not take place. If there was a reluctance to have Torrey visit, it might have been due to his assertive and intolerant demeanor.[80] Or perhaps some Winnipeg ministers were uncomfortable with inviting the proto-fundamentalist. By December 1906, it was Chapman who had received an invitation from Gordon to hold a campaign in Winnipeg; unlike Torrey, Chapman had not been identified as a dogmatic and militant preacher. Similar sentiments were manifest in smaller centres such as Saint John, where clergy debated accepting Torrey's revivalism.[81]

Canadian ministers such as C.W. Gordon were quite particular on which evangelists they worked with. In 1908 E.G. Chapman and Gordon exchanged some sharp letters and telegrams on the issue of which evangelists would be available for the Kootenay, British Columbia, campaign of 1909. J. Wilbur Chapman had selected the workers for the meetings in British Columbia, but Gordon notified E.G. Chapman that he was unhappy with the choice of evangelists. Gordon and other Presbyterian ministers wanted the Ashers, the saloon evangelists, James Burwick, the railway evangelist, and, most important, Chapman and Alexander. This, however, was impossible since Chapman, Alexander, and the Ashers were to be in Australia.[82] One evangelist whom the Canadian Presbyterians accepted was Scotchman John Thompson, "a man of the type of Burwick" who, like Burwick, had "been down and out" before becoming an evangelist.[83] Gordon and other Presbyterians appeared to want more than just any evangelist who preached sin and salvation. For the meetings at the lumber and mining centres, they desired to reach the unchurched and the evangelist had to be suitable for this task. Gordon's notion of revivalism also hinted at greater concern for social reform than what had been accepted in the past. As for the Baptists, John S. Moir acknowledges that the Canadian Baptist publication, which had avoided commentary viewed as theologically liberal, began in 1913 to show editorial interest in the social gospel movement.[84]

There was talk among some Canadian ministers of having Billy Sunday, the most famous American evangelist during the war years, visit Canada. But, except for a short engagement in Vancouver, in 1916, when he visited as a spokesman for temperance, a major Sunday campaign did not occur.[85] The likelihood of Canadian Protestants uniting together to sponsor a fundamentalist-type evangelist such as Billy Sunday was minimal. By this period, "fundamentalists obviously had little in common with Methodist progressives." In 1912, only one year after the Chapman campaign in Toronto, the *Christian Guardian* defended Washington Gladden after Sunday had reproached the well-known social gospeller.[86]

Described as a Sam Jones clone, Sunday was even more militant than Jones and was not likely to be endorsed by most mainline Canadian Protestant clergymen. The fundamentalist Sunday had little patience for "wishy-washy, sissified" Christianity, as the following prayer makes clear: "Lord save us from off-handed, flabby-cheeked, brittle-boned, weak-kneed, thin-skinned, pliable, plastic, spineless, effeminate, ossified three-karet Christianity."[87] In a *Christian Guardian* report on Sunday's New York campaign of 1917, Edgar William Dynes disclosed Sunday's sensational language. Sunday explained: "I use words, some of which were so long that they would make the jaws of a Greek professor squeak for a week, but I made no impression; so one day I said, 'God, I have doped it out wrong,' and I loaded up my gospel with rock salt, ipecac, cayenne, barbed wire, tobacco and kethchup, and the feathers have been falling ever since. I tell you, friends, you can't fight a skunk with cologne. A religious sensation is better than religious damnation." According to Dynes, no evangelist had ever "preached hell fire and damnation with more fervor" than Sunday; he epitomized "extreme orthodoxy."[88]

For Canadian Protestant clergymen, theology did appear to play a role in the decline of enthusiasm for American professional evangelists. Strong support for the evangelists wavered even among those who had played an integral role in bringing the Americans to Canada. The Reverend C.W. Gordon, for example, became "a conservative proponent of the Social Gospel." In his fictional account *The Arm of Gold*, Ralph Connors (C.W. Gordon) mentions Reuben Torrey and his literal interpretation of the Bible. But "Mr. Torrey" is no hero in Connor's novel. Rather, a saintly Presbyterian theologian who embraces higher criticism rides into a town and saves the local congregation from dividing on the issue of the infallibility of Scripture.[89] Connor was a good storyteller and his fictional account of how a higher critic saved a Torreyite from biblical "error" reveals much about the change that had occurred in some Protestant circles.

But were people at the grass-roots level concerned about theology? Did working-class Protestants take issue with revivalistic piety, evangelical orthodoxy, and the inerrancy of the Bible? There cannot be any conclusive answer to this question because of the scarcity of memoirs and records of workers who experienced American revivalism. Nonetheless, in newspaper accounts there is ample impressionistic evidence supporting the position that the working class favoured rather than challenged an evangelical message. This corresponds with recent scholarship on the interaction of religion and the working class which demonstrates working-class support for revivalism and evangelism. If Lynne Marks's recent plea for greater integration of religion in Canadian labour history finds acceptance, more scholarship on the evangelical beliefs of workers will be forthcoming.[90] Even the respected Marxist historian Bryan Palmer states: "Many workers indeed negotiated some kind of relation to generalized Christian belief, a point with which there can be no disagreement."[91]

As for commentary in working-class publications on the topic of religion, the main focus was not on theological concerns but rather on the issue of churches representing a class institution. There were working-class intellectuals such as Colin McKay who questioned old-time religion, but many other working-class commentators, reflecting the voice of grass-roots workers, exhibited no trepidation over conservative theology.[92] Socialist intellectuals who generally spurned most aspects of Christianity were few and they faced the challenges of other socialists who had not rejected Christ. The issue generated numerous letters to the editor of the Western Clarion in 1909 and again in 1911, a fact acknowledged by a "Mrs W.D.": "There has been so much in the Clarion of late about religion one would almost think that the Socialist party had turned into a camp meeting."[93] Responding to anti-Christian sentiments, Spencer Percival, a self-professed "Socialist," wrote: "I believe that He will come again to this earth and set up a righteous government and put down with a strong hand wickedness, greed, and tyranny. Probably when He comes, what Socialists advocate will be put in force."[94] While working-class intellectuals were on solid ground when they exposed bourgeois aspects of church life, they were in a much more precarious position, even among their comrades, when they dismissed Christianity completely. From coast to coast, moderate and radical working-class publications presented the arguments of those who supported Christianity.[95] As one commentator wrote: "It is not necessary to make a man an atheist to make him a revolutionary Socialist. Some people's religious convictions are very strong ... You might as well try to drive back the incoming tide of the ocean as to destroy the faith of a man, who in religious matters, can say, 'I know.'"[96]

Working-class people participated in revival meetings in large numbers; there is no other explanation given the sheer numbers who gathered at the meetings to hear an old Gospel message. As a late-nineteenth-century Methodist minister counselled, people are most religious when they experience powerlessness, uncertainty, and material insecurity.[97] Revivals articulated new freedoms that were difficult to find in churches catering to bourgeois sensibilities, and, consequently, workers embraced American revivalism but did not take the next step and become church members.

There were clergymen who advocated a social gospel message, yet most churches represented bourgeois ideals. Discussing the issue of churchless people in the city and how ministers had lost touch with the working class, the *Wesleyan* stated: "If he [a clergyman] too feels the pressure of the crass materialism of the day, and, consciously or unconsciously modifies his message to meet the views of the rich men who pay most of his salary and who consequently must be deferred to, it is small wonder."[98] Another clergyman asked: "How many capitalists in the church in their relations with their men, act on the principles of justice and human brotherhood?"[99] Fearing the worse, as early as 1888, the Victoria *Daily Colonist* declared: "Our churches like our theatre and big hotels will become places into which men and women with empty purses and poor clothes will not think of entering."[100] In a similar vein, Methodist clergyman James Henderson stated: "We have millionaires in our Churches, but what do they care for the most part for the hungry and unwashed multitudes." According to Henderson, people in the future "will look on the pinched features and impoverished homes of the proletariat of to-day as we look on the brutal serf who was worse off than his master's hounds."[101] Ironically, the social gospel clergy who understood working-class grievance and need were the very ones who were likely to water down the evangelical message that workers welcomed.

In some cases, Canadian Protestant leaders were reluctant to assist American evangelists with revival activities aimed at working-class people. For example, the proposed three-week Chapman-Alexander campaign at Hamilton, an industrial city, had been arranged to take place immediately after the Orillia meetings in 1908, but the Hamilton committee failed both to secure a large meeting place (the armoury) and to make adequate preparations for the campaign.[102] A recent study on religion and wealth in turn-of-the-century urban Canada indicates that Presbyterians and Methodists placed first and second in a wealth/status index, ranking higher than Anglicans, Irish Catholics, and Baptists.[103] More work remains to be done on patterns of bourgeois religiosity, but perhaps the achievement of wealth weakened Methodist and Presbyterian support for conservative evangelicalism and working-class issues. Studies do show a connection between religious enthusiasm and social status – the working class preferring "fire and vigour" and the wealthier favouring "well-ordered ritual."[104] In order for American revivalism to survive in Canada, the approval of Methodism and Presbyterianism – the two largest evangelical denominations – was imperative. If the Methodists and Presbyterians were not supportive, who would pay the bills?

Even though the evangelists received no stipulated amount for their services, a revivalism that embraced consumer strategies was costly.[105] Expenses included renovations to revival sites, rent, advertising and printing, electric light and gas, choir expenses, hotel expenses, and telegrams. The cost for renovations and rent of the rink for Moody's Victoria campaign, for example, was $585.[106] At the Crystal Rink in Montreal, Moody announced the need for collections because of extra expenses totalling more than $1,000.[107] Several times throughout the 1894 Toronto campaign, Treasurer J.M. Treble reported in the press that the meetings were in danger of running "a large deficit."[108] According to the Hamilton *Spectator*, Moody received $1,800 for his Toronto meetings.[109] The Reverend Hugh Johnston defended the high expenses of the Jones campaign (Jones and Small received $2,500) by stating that the "Musical Festival" held in the rink cost $15,000 – a much higher figure than that of the revival meetings.[110] Days before the final meeting of Torrey's 1906 Toronto campaign, the committee reported that collections "barely covered [the] expenses" of the meetings.[111] The campaign cost a total of $7,000, of which $2,000 went to the evangelists.[112] For the Ottawa campaign, the evangelists received $1,400.[113] The expenses for Chapman's Winnipeg meetings totalled $5,000 of which the local churches had to provide $3,000.[114] "SHORT OF CASH IN EVANGELISM," read the headline of the Toronto *Daily Star* at the conclusion of the 1911 Chapman Toronto campaign. The bold subheading, "The Committee in Need of Money to Pay Balance of the Expenses," conveyed sharply that "the work" resulted in "a considerable deficit."[115] Major revival campaigns were costly affairs, but, working together, the Protestant churches and lay supporters could meet the demands. There was considerable volunteer work and members of the committees themselves offered their services for free.[116] Still, considering the expenses involved, the survival of major revival campaigns was in jeopardy if the churches and lay leaders could not go beyond working at the practical level to fashion a common vision of revivalism. And it was precisely this common vision that was so noticeably lacking.

In the early nineteenth century, Charles Grandison Finney's revival in Rochester, New York, left a legacy of a united bourgeoisie and a divided working class.[117] In Canada, by contrast, revivalism in the early-twentieth-century period may have caused more of a fragmentation of the bourgeoisie. Additional sources will need to be uncovered, but available evidence suggests that much of the bourgeoisie chose not to support professional revivalism and a theological message moving in a distinct fundamentalist direction. Overall, Canadian church-attending capitalists likely remained supportive of their own churches, but they were distancing themselves from the working class and were not as visible at the revival campaigns as was the case in the United States.

In fusing revival Protestantism and popular culture, American evangelists were successful initially in reaching Canadians who confronted the new mass culture, industrialism, and consumerism of the modern city. But, by the second decade of the twentieth century, Canadian Protestants showed greater reluctance to offer theological and financial support for American revivalism. This tendency hampered outreach to the working class and was connected to the secularization of Canadian Protestantism. Recently, George Emery has briefly discussed the debate between secularization or "declension" theorists, who see a decline in evangelicalism in Canadian society, and the "evolutionist" theorists, who hold that change rather than decline takes place in the Canadian Protestant experience.[118] For those who adhere to the former interpretation, in one aspect or another, revolutionary ideas on science and religion, higher criticism of the Bible, Victorian optimism about progress, religious relativism, the social gospel, and the triumph of consumerism and modernity played a role in undermining the place of conservative evangelical beliefs in public life.[119] Focusing on the issue of whether conservative evangelical beliefs declined in Canadian Protestant society, this study of American revivalism in Canada complements the declension story, with certain revisions.

David Marshall's argument that revivalism's accommodation with popular culture resulted in secularization requires qualification when the focus is on visiting American evangelists. Moody and others did adopt the forms of secular mass culture in order to compete in an increasingly consumer-oriented society, but their strategies did not change their orthodox beliefs. For example, while twentieth-century fundamentalists expressed ambivalence about embracing popular culture, their adaptation to mass culture rewarded them with successful evangelism without compromising an orthodox message.[120]

In contrast, a major indicator of the secularization of Canadian Protestantism was, in Marshall's words, the "softening of orthodox evangelical doctrine."[121] With secularization unfolding, an increasing number of Protestant leaders questioned the conservative theology promoted by American evangelists. Perhaps potential Canadian supporters feared the cultural irrelevance of proto-fundamentalism. Whatever the reasons, it was clear that their lack of support spelled alienation for those workers who embraced American revivalism. Workingmen attracted to American evangelists and their old-time religion message would never again experience mass evangelism of the magnitude witnessed from 1884 to 1911. Some Canadian Protestant leaders continued to express concern about the need to reach the common people, but the leadership as a whole had eliminated the assistance of major American revival campaigns. While popular culture presented both opportunities and threats to evangelistic work, evangelists focused on the opportunities whereas an increasing number of Canadian Protestant leaders focused on the threats.[122] Revival was still a prized event with most of the daily press, but campaigns constructed to popular-culture tastes were complex events that required widespread sponsorship.

With the old, tried, and true method of revivalism adapted to consumer culture and superbly promoted in press coverage, many Canadian evangelicals hoped that they could win the working masses and spark a moral and spiritual uplift within their communities. But, in the early twentieth century, it was apparent that modern revivals in the cities were not having a large enough impact on the working class to justify, in the minds of Canadian Protestant leaders, the time, organization, and financial expense involved. Nor did it help that a number of these same leaders were cool to the orthodox message of the Americans, one that they saw as unsuited to an increasingly secular society.

Conclusion

The drama of revivalism, so amply recorded in newspaper and magazine accounts, is undeniable. One example is the Montreal *Daily Star* account of one of Moody's departures: "Then there was a last farewell from the crowd, which was partly drowned by the puffing and panting of the iron horse, and the train which carried the man who had kept thousands and thousands spellbound for a fortnight and had shown them the road to a higher, a better life, disappeared into the darkness."[1] A myriad of revival stories in the popular press voiced the themes of piety, power, and community. In public space, pietistic revival represented power that brought working people together in community fashion, a fact that Methodist, Presbyterian, Baptist, Congregationalist, evangelical Anglican, and other churches had become aware of by the early 1880s.

At first, impressed with the successful endeavours of famous evangelists in the United States, Protestant clergy and lay leaders welcomed modern revivalism to Canada with enthusiasm and optimism. In a period when urban centres were experiencing dramatic demographic and social change, evangelical leaders and American evangelists shared a common goal to "re-moralize" civic space. Yet, in the second decade of the twentieth century, the faith that Canadian clergymen placed in American evangelists began to unravel, as did the allegiance of many workers to the churches themselves.

There were American evangelists who had held meetings in Canada in earlier years and there were others who visited Canada afterwards, but no other period in Canadian history can match that of 1884 to 1911, when Dwight L. Moody, Sam Jones and Sam Small,

Reuben Torrey, and J. Wilbur Chapman – the most well-known and popular evangelists of the day – repeatedly came to Canada and drew unprecedented attention from the Canadian secular and denominational press. And why not? Thousands and thousands of working men and women filled the rinks, halls, churches, theatres, and even taverns to hear the evangelists. Not only does a large compilation of newspaper fragments provide evidence of working-class attendance, but church records and occupational data indicate that workers participated in revival meetings.

Dwight L. Moody, probably the greatest evangelist of the nineteenth century, attracted masses of ordinary men and women in central and western Canada from 1884 to 1898. The popularity of his Canadian meetings assured Canadian Protestant leaders that their faith and support for modern revivalism made perfect sense. His work provided confirmation that an old-fashioned Gospel message, packaged in an urban-revival format and constructed to popular-culture tastes, remained relevant. The ready acceptance of his message, based as it was on biblical principles, points to the continued existence of a conservative religiosity within Canadian Protestantism during these years. It was no coincidence that, after his first Canadian revival campaign in 1884, the number of evangelistic teams that imitated his urban-revival format increased. Ministers who may have been previously wary of professional revivalism could not deny the impact that Moody had on the popular mass mind. Privately he did embrace the ideals of American individualism and free-enterprise capitalism, but his revival message and focus were on Christ and he did not antagonize people with insensitive comments regarding class relations.

Flamboyant Methodist Sam Jones from Georgia, joined by fellow American Sam Small, brought a populist brand of evangelicalism to Ontario. The revival team of Jones and Small received its fair share of accolades from the secular press, but, unlike Moody's lasting support, their welcome to Canada had limitations. While Canadian Protestants embraced American revivalism, they preferred a Moody-type revival that focused on a biblical message of sin and salvation. Jones and Small fell short on this issue and they also undermined their popularity with the daily press by attacking labour-union activity.

In the early twentieth century, Canada was more consumer-oriented and popular mass evangelism faced difficult challenges in effectively reaching the unchurched. To be sure, the large crowds of working people who attended Reuben Torrey's meetings indicate that he presented a revival message which many Canadian Protestants wanted to hear. In his revival campaigns in Toronto, Ottawa, Montreal, Fredericton, Saint John, and Windsor, a significant number of Canadian evangelical leaders provided support, demonstrating that most Protestant ministers favoured an old-fashioned Gospel message as a way to revitalize Christians and alleviate some of the problems of community life. Unlike most evangelists, as well, Torrey spoke out against capitalism on a number of occasions. Yet, for all his appeal, he generated controversy for his dogmatic theology. Beginning to take on the role of a fierce defender of orthodox Protestantism, Torrey relied heavily on a proto-fundamentalist understanding of Protestantism to denounce the "error" of others. An indication that his work was beginning to be challenged by Canadian Protestants was that his last visits were to smaller urban centres in the Maritimes as opposed to larger cities in central Canada.

As had been the case for Moody and Torrey, Chapman received broad support from Protestant ministers. From 1907 to 1911, he introduced Canadians to the format of simultaneous evangelistic meetings, held by a contingent of co-evangelists and workers in the various districts of a city. Representing an innovative approach, the Chapman campaign tried to reach unchurched workers in factories, saloons, theatres, and community buildings. The Chapman revival attendance – in excess of 600,000 during these years – demonstrates that revivalism continued to have significant appeal. However, while widespread support indicates the existence of a broad evangelical consensus on revivalism, this consensus was dependent on the success of revivalism in meeting popular-culture desires. When the Toronto campaign in January 1911 failed to meet the expectations of a number of ministers, the suitability of professional revivalism as a tool to Christianize the nation became questionable. Also, the lack of support in Toronto was indicative of a larger problem: in an increasingly secular climate, both professional revivalism and conservative evangelicalism were undergoing greater scrutiny by a growing number of Protestant leaders who sensed the inevitability of modern forces.

American revivalism was not necessarily a failure. Offering comprehensive reports of mass revivalism, the press played a key role in manufacturing "revival" as an extraordinary public event that moved cities. In fact, unlike the Protestant leadership, press interest and support for American revivalism did not level off. On the topic of whether popular revivals had an enduring impact, one man shouted at a 1906 Torrey meeting: "Nineteen years ago I was converted on Chestnut street, as a result of the Sam Jones and Sam Small revival, and Christ has kept me by His power ever since."[2] Such statements leave no doubt that, for many, revivalism had brought about real results.

Still, something was lost in the immediate years after the 1911 Chapman campaign at Toronto. Challenged by an increasingly modern and secular society, many Canadian Protestants were developing new strategies to solve the problems they confronted in growing urban centres. Even dressed in masculine, modern, and popular-culture attire, the old-fashioned Gospel, and especially the proto-fundamentalist message that American evangelists promoted, represented an outdated expression of Christianity for those influenced by progressive thought. Canadian Protestant leaders found no fault in the economic conservatism that was implicit in parts of the evangelists' message, but, in the second decade of the twentieth century, fewer accepted the theological conservatism of evangelists and the costs of modern revivalism.

Canadian Protestant leaders' support for direct working-class outreach was also waning. Examples of Canadian mainstream evangelical leaders entering and focusing primarily on working-class culture are rare. The efforts of J.S. Woodsworth among Winnipeg workers are noteworthy, but Woodsworth was no evangelical. The examples that Nancy Christie and Michael Gauvreau provide of early-twentieth-century evangelism in working-class space are all the more striking in that they appear to have represented the exception rather than the rule.[3] On no consistent basis did Protestant clergymen initiate direct working-class evangelism in Canadian urban centres. Commenting on the issue of reaching Canadian workers, the Presbyterian clergyman E.I. Hart declared: "We must cease to despise the Gospel waggon, the Gospel tent, and the street preacher."[4] As one who knew well what he was talking about, William Asher, of the Chapman campaigns, warned at the conclusion of the Toronto campaign that saloon evangelism – "an undeveloped field" – could not continue to be overlooked.[5] But it was, as was revivalism.

Spurred by a number of forces, including enticing press rhetoric, the working masses found their way to the rinks, halls, and churches in order to experience revivalism. There was a combination of press hype and genuine revival in the city, but, by 1911, fewer Canadian clergymen and other Protestant leaders were willing to support the American brand of revivalism. Despite the secularizing of faith, Canadian Protestantism would support revivals in the future. However, gone was the era of regular, widely backed, major campaigns. Revival in the city and the full force of American revivalism were limited to a specific period, and a relatively brief one at that.

Notes

INTRODUCTION

1 Multiplying the approximate number of meetings (800) by an average of 2,000 participants per meeting, yielded the total given here. It should be noted that many of the meetings had over 2,500 attenders and a sizeable number attracted more than 4,000. Of course, it is impossible to know the exact number who attended since some individuals attended more than one meeting.

2 On sorrow, humility, and redemption, see Blumhofer and Balmer, *Modern Christian Revivals*, xii. For a definition of evangelicalism, see Noll, *Evangelicalism*, 6.

3 Pierard, *The Unequal Yoke*, 28–30.

4 For the 1775 to 1812 period, George Rawlyk offers another interpretation, arguing that Canadian evangelicalism was then more populist and democratic than the American variety. See Rawlyk, *The Canada Fire*, xvi. Rawlyk also notes America's civic humanism and republicanism. For an astute assessment of George Rawlyk's scholarship, see Noll, "George Rawlyk's Vision from the Periphery and the Study of American History," 29–51. For the American experience, see Hatch, *The Democratization of American Christianity*.

5 Quoted in Evensen, "'It Is a Marvel to Many People,'" 259.

6 Lumsden, *Close the 49th Parallel etc.*

7 Historians who distance Canadian Protestants from the American experience include George Rawlyk, Michael Gauvreau, and Nancy Christie, to name only a few. On the similarities and differences between American and Canadian evangelicals in the late twentieth

century, see Reimer, "A More Irenic Canadian Evangelicalism?"
153–79, and, Reimer, "A Generic Evangelicalism?" 228–42.

8　Forbes and Mahan, *Religion and Popular Culture in America*, 2–5.

9　This understanding of popular religion is put forward by M. Meslin,
cited in Maldonado, "Popular Religion," 6.

10　Williams, *Popular Religion in America*, 17–19.

11　I use the terminology in Clarke, "Religion and Public Space in
Protestant Toronto, 1880–1900," 69–70.

12　Minnix, *Laughter in the Amen Corner,* ix. Jones was considered by
some to be the most widely quoted American in the nineteenth century. Unfortunately, Minnix's study makes no mention of Jones's for-
ays into Canada.

13　According to William McLoughlin, Chapman was in Montreal with
his assistant Billy Sunday in the 1893–95 period. McLoughlin, *Modern Revivalism*, 378. Lyle Dorsett indicates that Chapman and
Sunday were in "Gault," Ontario, in the same period. Dorsett, *Billy
Sunday and the* Redemption *of Urban America*, 53. I have yet to find
any reference to these visits in the Canadian press.

14　Toronto *Daily Star (TDS)*, 28 January 1911. The *News*, on 31 January
1911, stated that over 600,000 people had attended the January
meetings. The formula for arriving at this figure was not revealed and
thus the total is suspect.

15　Long, *The Revival of 1857–58*, 26–45. In Canada, the press knew
that "Christianity was even a better draw" than leisure and sporting
activities. See Kee, "Revivalism," 75.

16　On revival and the mass media in the American experience, see
Evensen, "'It Is a Marvel to Many People,'" 252.

17　For more on "orientational metaphors," see Lakoff and Johnson,
Metaphors We Live By, 14–21.

18　An especially helpful introduction to the study of language is Johnstone, *Discourse Analysis*, 1–28.

19　For more on the impact of language and emotion in history, see
Costigliola, "The Creation of Memory and Myth," 38–54.

20　Rutherford, *A Victorian Authority*, 197–202. Kee, "Revivalism," 75.

21　For example, see Evensen, "'Expecting a Blessing of Unusual Magnitude,'" 26–36.

22　Moore, *Selling God*, 6–11, 184–6.

23　Weisberger, *They Gathered at the River*, 176–7, 271.

24　Heinrich, "The Last Great Awakening," 355; Douglas, *The
Feminization of American Culture*; DeBerg, *Ungodly Women*, 18–21.

The best recent work on masculinity and American revivalism is Margaret Lamberts Bendroth's "Men, Masculinity, and Urban Revivalism," 235–46.

25 Long, *The Revival of 1857–58*, 90.

26 Helpful historiographical works on this scholarship include: McKillop, "Culture, Intellect, and Context," 7–31; Reimer, "Religion and Culture in Nineteenth-Century English Canada," 192–203; Owram, "Writing about Ideas," 47–70; Gauvreau, "Beyond the Half-Way House," 158–77; and Opp, "Revivals and Religion," 183–193.

27 Marshall, *Secularizing the Faith*, 86–98. For a study critical of secularization theories, see Stark and Finke, *Acts of Faith*, 57–79.

28 Airhart, *Serving the Present Age*, 71–2, 85, 93. For more on Methodism, see Semple, *The Lord's Dominion*.

29 Christie and Gauvreau, *A Full-Orbed Christianity*, 43, 59–65.

30 Marks, *Revivals and Roller Rinks*.

31 Denning, *The Cultural Front*, xvii.

32 Hogg and Abrams, *Social Identifications*; Kiesler and Kiesler, *Conformity*.

33 Sizer, *Gospel Hymns and Social Religion*, 52. What requires exploration is how long this community, in regard to workers, lasted. Emphasis in original.

34 Rawlyk, *The Canada Fire*, xvii. Also, on the difficulty of "piecing together fragments" of working-class culture, see Palmer, *A Conflict of Culture*, xi–xii.

35 On class, see Veltmeyer, *The Canadian Class Structure*.

36 Two early, influential studies concerning the "middle class" are Weisberger, *They Gathered at the River,* and McLoughlin, *Modern Revivalism*.

37 See Ellis, "Gilboa to Ichabod," 24. The percentage numbers are: white collar, 26.83; blue collar 11.89; industrial workers, 5.18; and labourers 6.40 – for a total of 50.3. Others who sold their labour power were in the category of managerial, sales, and semi-professionals (17.68).

38 For example, there was middle-class leadership of Calgary Methodist churches and evangelistic meetings during and after the visits of the American evangelists H.L. Gale and J.W. Hatch. See Crouse, "'The Great Revival,'" 18–23.

39 Emery, *The Methodist Church on the Prairies, 1896–1914*, 29–33. Of course, I may fall in this same trap by using a broader definition of

the working class, but the risk is worthwhile when the final result seems more accurate.

40 Beckert, *The Monied Metropolis*, 6.
41 Thomas, *Revivalism and Cultural Change*, 2.
42 On scholarship and religious faith, see McCarraher, *Christian Critics*, 4.
43 See Palmer, "Historiographic Hassles," especially 128–44; Marks, "Heroes and Hallelujahs," 169–86. Marks attributes such a "blind spot" to the "resolutely secular world view" of Canadian labour historians (171).
44 On the high cost of revival campaigns, see Hambrick-Stowe, "'Sanctified Business,'" 81–103.

CHAPTER ONE

1 "Moody and Sankey," New York *Times (NYT)*, 25 October 1875.
2 "Moody and Sankey," *Nation*, 9 May 1876.
3 On revival crowds, see "Sam Jones Defines Love," "Men's Vices Condemned," and "A Crowd at the Rink," Baltimore *American*, 17 and 29 May 1886.
4 Chicago *Tribune (CT)*, 5 April 1886.
5 McLoughlin, *Modern Revivalism*; Caldwell, "Women, Men, and Revival."
6 McLoughlin, *Modern Revivalism*, 167.
7 Frank, *Less Than Conquerors*, 36.
8 Evensen, "It Is a Marvel to Many People," 251.
9 On group forces, see Hogg and Abrams, *Social Identifications*, and Kiesler and Kiesler, *Conformity*.
10 Weisberger, *They Gathered at the River*, 91.
11 Finney, *Memoirs*, 16.
12 Finney, *Lectures on Revivals of Religion*, 203.
13 Bruce, "Born Again," 109.
14 McLoughlin, *Modern Revivalism*, 13.
15 For the impact of reformers on the city, see Boyer, *Urban Masses in America, 1820–1920*.
16 W.R. Moody, *The Life of Dwight L. Moody*, 33–4, 39–41.
17 Morrow, *Best Thoughts and Discourses of D.L. Moody*, 10.
18 Moody and Sankey Folder, article by George Mansfield, MBIA.
19 Weisberger, *They Gathered at the River*, 185.
20 Moody, *The Life of Dwight L. Moody*, 132–5.

21 Ibid., 225, 227. According to Sankey, the meeting at Agriculture Hall, London, drew 17,000 people. Moody and Sankey Folder, MBIA. Various letters written by Henry Drummond, who assisted Moody, provide an inside account of Moody's 1873–75 meetings. See Smith, *The Life of Henry Drummond*, chapter 4.

22 *NYT*, 5 October 1875, 12.

23 *Canada Christian Advocate*, 27 October 1875.

24 Richard L. Dufus, quoted in Dorsett, *A Passion for Souls*, 21.

25 Jones, *The Life and Sayings of Sam P. Jones*, 45–7, 53.

26 Marsden, *Fundamentalism and American Culture*; Szasz, *The Divided Mind of Protestant America, 1880–1930*; Brereton, *Training God's Army*.

27 Jones, *The Life and Sayings of Sam P. Jones*, 68.

28 See Crouse, "Methodist Encounters," 163.

29 J.H. Bryson to Jones, 6 October 1886, Sam Jones Papers, box 6, folder 1, UGL. On the eve of Jones's 1886 Toronto campaign, Bryson wrote: "I have just learned that your health is seriously impaired and that you may have to give up your labor as an evangelist."

30 Minnix, *Laughter in the Amen Corner*, 221–2.

31 *Globe*, 15 October 1886. This issue provides, by far, the best Canadian newspaper account of Small's transformation from drunkard to evangelist. Also, see Jones, *Sam Jones and Sam Small in Toronto*, 125.

32 Toronto *World (TW)*, 12 October 1886. Two days later, the newspaper reported that the two Sams promised "to do some heavy execution against the powers and patronage of Satan ..."

33 McLouglin, *Modern Revivalism*, 330–1, 344.

34 "Dr. Torrey's Conversion," drawer 51, MBIA. Torrey wrote: "'Ecce Homo' especially made it clear to me (though it is not by any means an orthodox book) that I ought to come out and make a public confession of Christ. As I had been known in college as anything but a Christian I felt that I ought to make my public confession of Christ then and there..." *Ecce Homo*, an extended essay that gave little attention to the crucifixion, was originally published anonymously in 1865 and drew comment from many leading British periodicals of the day. See Pals, *The Victorian "Lives" of Jesus*, 39–50.

35 "Dr. Torrey's Conversion."

36 Davis, *Torrey and Alexander*, 21–32.

37 Staggers, "Reuben A. Torrey," 53–7, argues that Torrey decided to study at Germany specifically in order to learn arguments confirming the validity of the Bible.

38 Ibid., 77.

39 Chapman to Torrey, 25 June 1903, J. Wilbur Chapman, drawer 36, MBIA.

40 Davis, *Torrey and Alexander*, 45, 248–9.

41 Charles Alexander to A.P.F.H., 17 June 1905, Charles Alexander, drawer 34, MBIA.

42 Davies, *Torrey and Alexander*, 46–50.

43 McLoughlin, *Modern Revivalism*, 374–5. McLoughlin mentions only Kittrell, stating that Alexander remained with him for "a short stint."

44 Ottman, *J. Wilbur Chapman*, 16–32.

45 J. Wilbur Chapman, Biographical Drawer 36, MBIA. Ottman, *J. Wilbur Chapman*, 41. His marriage to Irene was short since she died in 1886, less than one month after delivering their first child, a daughter. In late 1888 Chapman married Agnes Pruyn Strain, a gifted Bible teacher, and they had three sons and one daughter.

46 McLoughlin, *Modern Revivalism*, 377–8. For more on the Chapman-Sunday team, see Dorsett, *Billy Sunday and the Redemption of Urban America*, 51–8. Dorsett also records that Chapman and Sunday held a campaign in "Gault," Ontario (53).

47 John Wilbur Chapman Papers, Guide to Collection 77, BGCA.

48 For this period, see Freeman, *Who Built America?*; Beckert, *The Monied Metropolis*; and Rottenberg, *The Man Who Made Wall Street*.

49 Beckert, *The Monied Metropolis*, 4.

50 Chicago *Interior*, quoted in *Manitoba Free Press* (MFP), 9 July 1894.

51 Ibid. In the Montreal *Daily Star* (MDS), 28 November 1894, Moody made a similar observation.

52 Smith, *The Search for Social Salvation*, 102.

53 See Kealey, *Toronto Workers Respond to Industrial Capitalism, 1867–1892*; Kealey and Palmer, *Dreaming of What Might Be*.

54 McLoughlin, *Revivals, Awakenings, and Reform*, 145–6, 149. McLoughlin designates the years 1890 to 1920 as the third great awakening, when revivals were supported by rural-born, middle-class Protestants seeking comfort and encouragement during an age when social and scientific thought challenged their beliefs, values, and institutions.

55 Boone, *The Bible Tells Them So*, 11.

56 This pervasive argument is found in much of the scholarly literature on Moody and other like-minded evangelists. For example, see McLoughlin, *Modern Revivalism*; Weisberger, *They Gathered at the River*; Findlay, *Dwight L. Moody*; and, more recently, Gilbert, *Perfect Cities*, chapter 6. See also Moore, *Selling God*.

57 Abrams, *Selling Old-Time Religion*, 2–3, 23–4.

58 Weisberger, *They Gathered at the River*, 162, 173, 206, 229.

59 Findlay, *Dwight L. Moody*, 286–7; Gilbert, *Perfect Cities*, 177.

60 For reasons why the term "bourgeoisie" is more suitable than "elites," "aristocracy," "plutocracy," or "ruling class," see Beckert, *The Monied Metropolis*, 6.

61 Hambrick-Stowe, "'Sanctified Business,'" 81–2, 88, 92.

62 Beckert, *The Monied Class*, 199–202; Hambrick-Stowe, "'Sanctified Business,'" 89, 91–2; Gilbert, *Perfect Cities*, 182; Hall, "Moving Targets," 145. MDS, 8 February 1898, described Moody as belonging to "the type of men who have made America a great industrial and material empire – the great captains of industry..." The Vancouver *Daily News-Advertiser* (DNA), 28 October 1888, wrote that if Moody had not been the "greatest evangelist in the world, he would be one of its business kings or merchant princes." For more on John Wanamaker and the relationship of religion and business, see Schmidt, *Consumer Rites*, 162–9, and Smith, *The Search for Social Salvation*, 245–58.

63 Hambrick-Stowe, "'Sanctified Business,'" 93.

64 Minnix, *Laughter in the Amen Corner*, 106; Hambrick-Stowe, "'Sanctified Business,'" 94.

65 McLoughlin, *Modern Revivalism*, 369.

66 Hambrick-Stowe, "'Sanctified Business,'" 93. Also, see Smith, "Evangelicals Confront Corporate Capitalism," 77, 79.

67 Michael Zuckerman states that "capitalists could not capture Christianity unequivocally, and because they could not, their reliance on religion for legitimation was doomed to be displaced by more dependable defenses of their privileges and power." See Zuckermann, "Holy Wars, Civil Wars," 224.

68 McLoughlin, *Modern Revivalism*, 300, 327. For an assessment of a Jones campaign in the United States, see Johnston, "Sam Jones' Union Meetings," *Globe*, 24 September 1887. At these meetings, Jones appeared to have widespread denominational support.

69 Helpful studies on this issue include: Marsden, *Fundamentalism and American Culture*; Szasz, *The Divided Mind of American Fundamentalism*; Sandeen, *The Roots of Fundamentalism*; Hutchison, *The Modernist Impulse in American Protestantism*.

70 As was the case in September 1908 at Orillia, Ontario, Chapman received positive coverage at his Vermont campaign in November 1908. On the results of a typical meeting, the Burlington *Free Press and Times*, 12 November 1908, stated: "Many Christians arose to

reconsecrate their lives to God, while numerous others rose to accept Christ or to confess Him as their personal Saviour" (J. Wilbur Chapman Papers, BGCA). In a letter to the *Canadian Baptist* (CB), 22 December 1910, J.F. Vichert described the success of Chapman's campaign at Fort Wayne, Indiana, and stated that no Toronto church cooperating with Chapman would be disappointed.

71 McLoughlin, *Modern Revivalism*, 379. Also, see Conrad, *Boston's Awakening*, 24–47, 73–80. Also, see "Chapman- Alexander Campaign Held in Boston," The *Canadian Congregationalist* (CC), 19 January 1911.

72 McLoughlin, *Modern Revivalism*, 263, 265; Findlay, *Dwight L. Moody*, 269.

73 McLoughlin, *Modern Revivalism*, 287.

74 Ibid., 305. Minnix, *Laughter in the Amen Corner*, 71.

75 McLoughlin, *Modern Revivalism*, 367, 370.

76 Ibid., 379–80, 387–8. See also a report on the Philadelphia campaign in CB, 30 April 1908.

77 "The Good Work of the Two Sams," CT, 6 April 1886.

78 Quoted in Nelson, "Revival and Upheaval," 238.

79 McLoughlin, *Modern Revivalism*, 526.

CHAPTER TWO

1 *Week*, 11 December 1884.

2 Rawlyk, *The Canadian Protestant Experience*, 102–3.

3 Exceptions to this were the better-known evangelists James Caughey and Phoebe and Walter Palmer. See Bush, "James Caughey, Phoebe and Walter Palmer and the Methodist Revival Experience in Canada West, 1850–1858."

4 On improvements to newspapers, see Phillips, *Mass Media*, 12–13.

5 French, "The Evangelical Creed in Canada," 22–3.

6 Long, *The Revival of 1857–58*, 37.

7 TW, 5 December 1884. On 6 November 1899, the *Mail and Empire* (ME) stated that Sankey had been in Toronto twenty-one years ago. Possibly, Moody was also there in 1878.

8 Toronto *Evening News* (TEN), 4 December 1884

9 In its report of the Montreal campaign, CB, on 14 January 1886, noted that Moody had been in Montreal "a year ago."

10 On this tragic episode, see Bliss, *Plague*.

11 *Presbyterian Record* (PR), February 1886, 45–50.

12 MDS, 1 October 1887.

13 *PR*, February 1886, 45–50.

14 "No Standing Room, Over 7,000 People Present," *MDS*, 15 October 1887.

15 Victoria *Daily Colonist (VDC)*, 17 October 1888.

16 *DNA*, 3 November 1888.

17 Ibid., 7 November 1888. In the 9 November issue, it was reported that Moody "had very successful meetings in New Westminster."

18 "Sin and Satan," *Daily Free Press (DFP)*, 6 January 1890.

19 "Unabated Interest," London *Advertiser (LA)*, 9 January 1890.

20 See the reports in *LA* from 11 to 21 January. According to Kevin Kee, Crossley and Hunter "incorporated many of the strategies of theatre, including humour, melodramatic stories, and entertaining music." See Kee, "Revivalism," 21.

21 *TW*, 5 November 1894; *TEN*, 5 November 1894; Toronto *Mail (TM)*, 5 November 1894.

22 *TEN*, 19 November 1894.

23 Hamilton *Spectator (HS)*, 28 November 1894.

24 *MDS*, 28–29 November 1894.

25 Ibid., 12 October 1897

26 Ottawa *Daily Free Press (ODFP)*, 15 October 1897.

27 *Evening Journal (EJ)*, 15 October 1897.

28 Ibid., 18 October 1897.

29 *Daily Whig (DW)*, 19 October 1897.

30 *Daily Examiner*, 21–22 October 1897.

31 Brantford *Courier (BC)*, 23 October 1897.

32 Brantford *Expositor*, 28 October 1897.

33 *Globe*, 23 October 1897.

34 *Daily Mail and Empire (DME)*, 28 October 1897.

35 *Globe*, 28 October 1897. Also, "Mr. Moody Talks to Ten Thousand," *DME*, 28 October 1897.

36 "A Great Gathering," *MFP*, 5 November 1897.

37 *MFP*, 6 November 1897.

38 "Moody's Plain Talks," ibid., 8 November 1897.

39 *Western Sun*, 18 November 1897.

40 For an example of supportive coverage, see *MDS*, 7 February 1898.

41 Moore, *Selling God*, 185.

42 Putney, *Muscular Christianity*, 2. Making fun of Moody, the *Sunday Times* of Boston labelled him a "muscular Christian" (23).

43 Bendroth, *Fundamentalism & Gender, 1875 to the Present*, 17–18. Also, "on the crisis of American masculinity," see Martin, "Billy Sunday and Christian Manliness," 812.

44 *Evening News (EN)*, 7 November 1894. For examples of denominational approval of men-only meetings, see the *Evangelical Churchman
(EC)*, 15 November 1894, and CB, 16 January 1890.

45 Douglas, *The Feminization of American Culture*, 97–8.

46 Marshall, *Secularizing the Faith*, 91–3. In a brief analysis of a volume
of Gospel tunes, Marshall notes that within the songs pious religious
feeling was stressed. On the "common people" learning Gospel songs
easily, see Reynolds and Price, *A Survey of Christian Hymnody*, 102.
In *Gospel Hymns and Social Religion*, 176, Sandra Sizer records that
one source estimated that Ira D. Sankey's *Sacred Songs and Solos:
Twelve Hundred Hymns* sold fifty million copies.

47 *Canadian Methodist Magazine (CMM)*, vol 21, January 1885, 76.

48 Bradford, *D.L. Moody*, 31–2.

49 TW, 3 December 1884.

50 Ibid., 8 November 1894.

51 "Mr. Moody in Toronto," EC, 11 December 1884.

52 "Moody," MDS, 7 October 1887.

53 TM, 5 December 1884.

54 *Globe*, 22 November 1894.

55 Boone, *The Bible Tells Them So*, 11, 19.

56 Marshall, *Secularizing the Faith*, 76–81.

57 DNA, Oct. 31, 1888. Also see *Globe*, 4 December 1884, and ODFP, 18
October 1897.

58 Peterborough *Daily Examiner*, 22 October 1897; DW, 20 October
1897.

59 MFP, 9 November 1897.

60 VDC, 27 October 1888. In his early years as an evangelist, Moody
made a special effort to preach hell after one man told him that the
evangelist's sermons were enjoyable because he preached so little on
damnation. Daniels, *Moody*, 457–67.

61 LA, 9,11 January 1890.

62 MDS, 6 January 1886.

63 TW, 24 November 1894.

64 Boone, *The Bible Tells Them So*, 99.

65 TW, 16 November 1894.

66 See Kee, "Revivalism," 44.

67 MDS, 17 October 1887.

68 Cook, *"Through Sunshine and Shadow,"* 7, demonstrates that at the
local level the Woman's Christian Temperance Union upheld traditional evangelicalism in the late nineteenth century.

69 *Globe*, 22 November 1894.

70 Van Die, *An Evangelical Mind*, 19–25. Also, see McDannell, *The Christian Home in Victorian America, 1840–1900*, 104.

71 *Globe*, 4 December 1884. Sutherland, *Children in English-Canadian Society*, 18–19.

72 Pedersen, "'Keeping Our Good Girls Good,'" 20–4.

73 *BC*, 25 October 1897.

74 McLoughlin, *Modern Revivalism*, 527.

75 Quoted in Dorsett, *A Passion for Souls*, 407–8. As Dorsett states, Moody promoted a religious solution rather than a political one.

76 *MDS*, 7 February 1898.

77 *TW*, 17 November 1894; *TM*, 4 December 1884; *DW*, 20 October 1897; *MDS*, 12 October 1897.

78 *TW*, 8 November 1894.

79 *MDS*, 12 October 1897.

80 Ibid., 19 October 1887; "The World Growing Worse," *TW*, 20 November 1894; "A Premillennialist", *Globe*, 20 November 1894.

81 For a discussion of millennialism, see Westfall, *Two Worlds*, 182–9. Post-millennialism, an optimistic view of history, holds that a Kingdom of God on earth can be established before the second coming of Christ, an interpretation that made sense to many Protestants since it holds that God allows humans to play an important role in the unfolding of a divine plan.

82 *MDS*, 19 October 1887. Also, *TEN*, 20 November 1894.

83 *Globe*, 3 December 1884. Also, *MDS*, 6 October 1887, and the *Globe*, 15 November 1894.

84 Rutherford, *A Victorian Authority*, 200.

85 Evensen, "'It Is a Marvel to Many People,'" 260.

86 *MDS*, 4 October 1887.

87 Ibid., 5 October 1887.

88 Ibid., 12 October 1887.

89 Ottawa *Free Press (OFP)*, 15 October 1897.

90 *DW*, 19 October 1897.

91 *DNA*, 7 November 1888.

92 *VDC*, 14 October 1888.

93 Ibid., 30 October 1888.

94 Findlay, *Dwight L. Moody*, 300–1.

95 *TW*, 5 December 1884.

96 "He Will Stay till Monday," *TW*, 23 November 1894.

97 "The Evangelists," *VDC*, 14 October 1888.

98 Weisberger, *They Gathered at the River*, 12.

99 Thomas, *Revivalism and Cultural Change*, 1–2.

100 Laon, "Messrs. Moody and Sankey and Revivalism," 510–13. For a rebuttal, see George Grant, *Canadian Monthly* (September 1875), 250–5.

101 Ronald Sawatsky, "Looking for That Blessed Hope," 103–12.

102 Clark, *Of Toronto the Good: A Social Study*, 165.

103 *TM*, 20 November 1894.

104 "Toronto 'Moodified,'" *Canadian Churchman (CCM)*, 15 November 1894. Also, see "Moodyism an Exposure," ibid., 18 October 1894.

105 "'Reverends' and Others," ibid., 22 November 1894.

106 "'Converted' – to What," ibid., 6 December 1894. In contrast, P. Toque's letter, ibid., 20 December 1894, agreed with Moody that there was "no such thing as being half-converted."

107 "Mr. Moody and His Methods," ibid., 6 December 1894; "Mr. Moody and His Methods," ibid., 13 December 1894.

108 See Baskerville, "Did Religion Matter?" 90.

109 "A Pious Fraud," *Palladium of Labor (PL)*, 13 December 1884.

110 Allen, *The Social Passion*, 3–17; Grant, *The Church in the Canadian Era*, 75; Fraser, *The Social Uplifters*, 33, 44; Masters, "The Anglican Evangelicals in Toronto, 1870–1900," 61; Johnston, *McMaster University: Volume 1*, 94.

111 Allen, "Salem Bland: The Young Preacher," 78.

112 Rawlyk, "A.L. McCrimmon, H.P. Whidden, T.T. Shields, Christian Higher Education, and McMaster University," 38–9.

113 *CMM*, January 1885.

114 "Mr. Moody at Massey Hall," *Westminster*, 30 October 1897.

115 Marks, *Revivals and Roller Rinks*.

116 Magney, "The Methodist Church and the National Gospel, 1884–1914."

117 Hague, "Moody." An editorial, *EC*, 18 November 1897, noted that "Moody has been stating with great force some plain truths." Also, see ibid., 11 November 1894.

118 "The Moody Evangelistic Meetings," The *Christian Guardian (CG)*, 14 November 1894.

119 *PR*, November 1897, 282.

120 On the American experience, see Evensen, "'It Is a Marvel to Many People,'" 261.

121 "Minutes of the Hamilton Methodist Conference, 1896, 70, UCA. Similar opinions were expressed in the minutes of other conferences

during the 1890s. For example, Minutes of the Montreal Annual Conference, 1892, 65, and Minutes of the London Annual Conference, 1895, 71.

122 *CG*, 9 December 1896; "Professional Convert Manufacturers," ibid., 8 December 1897; Decrease of Increase," ibid., 10 August 1898.

123 "Mr. Moody and His Work," ibid., 21 November 1894.

124 Clark, *Church and Sect*, 381. Moyles, *The Blood and Fire in Canada*, 11–12.

125 *BC*, 25 October 1897.

126 *TM*, 5 November 1894.

127 Rev. R.G. MacBeth, "Moody in Winnipeg," *Westminster*, 13 November 1897.

128 Salem Bland Papers, box 5, file 377, UCA.

129 Particularly helpful in understanding Moody's spiritual impact is a recent biography of the evangelist: Dorsett, *A Passion for Souls*, 387–401.

CHAPTER THREE

1 Kingston *Daily News (DN)*, 15 March 1887. According to this paper, Jones's name was "fast becoming a household word both in Canada and the United States" and his writings were sold "on almost every train that rushes through our country."

2 Minnix indicates that the evangelists, on several occasions, held meetings in the same city in the same year but did not join forces (*Laughter in the Amen Corner*, 98–9). They did, however, work together for at least one meeting. See "Sam Jones with Moody" newspaper article, Sam Jones Biographical File, MBIA.

3 *Globe*, 6 October 1886.

4 *TW*, 12 October 1886.

5 *Sam Jones and Sam Small in Toronto*.

6 Minnix, *Laughter in the Amen Corner*, 94.

7 *TEN*, 11 October 1886.

8 *Globe*, 11 October 1886.

9 Ibid., 25 October 1886.

10 Ibid., 27 October 1886.

11 Ibid., 28 October 1886.

12 *TEN*, 13 December 1886; *TW*, 13 December 1886.

13 *Globe*, 13 December 1886.

14 *TW*, 14 December 1886; *Globe*, 15–16 December 1886. Joining Jones on the lecture platform were the Methodist clergymen Hugh

Johnston, E.A. Stafford, Dr Briggs, and Dr Williams. At this time, one individual wrote: "Would you give a lecture in Cobourg in the Presbyterian Church or Concert Hall in our town…" Letter dated 14 December 1886, Sam Jones Papers, box 6, folder 3, UGL.

15 Ibid., Letter from Iroquois to Jones, 8 March 1887, box 6, folder 7, UGL.

16 TEN, 7 March 1887. Also see TW, 7 March 1887, and Globe, 7 March 1887.

17 "Sam Jones in Hamilton," HDS, 8 March 1887, "Sam Jones Preaches," ibid., 10 March 1887.

18 LA, 8–12 March 1887.

19 Galt Reporter (GR), 18 March 1887. The first night he presented a lecture and the following morning he preached a sermon.

20 Montreal Gazette, 14–15 March 1887. Jones was still big news and even a Stratford newspaper, a city four hundred miles from Montreal, provided coverage of this meeting. See the Stratford Beacon, 19 March 1887.

21 MDS, 14–15 March 1887.

22 DN, 15 March 1887; Kingston British Whig (BW), 16–17 March 1887.

23 Globe, 22 August 1887, reported that preparations were made at the summer resort for the arrival of Sam Jones and Sam Small. In its August 25 issue, the Globe noted that immense audiences gathered to hear Sam Small preach and that Jones was to arrive the following day, but it gave no coverage of Jones's meetings. For excellent coverage of Jones in action at Grimsby, see the Toronto News (TN), 26 August 1887. HS, 29 August, stated that Jones visited Hamilton, for a few hours, before returning to Grimsby. There is no mention of Sam Jones's visit(s) to Grimsby Park in Youman, Grimsby Park. Youman does, however, mention the visits of American evangelists Dr Palmer and Mrs Palmer (22).

24 David Marshall, Secularizing the Faith, 130–1.

25 Globe, 21 September 1887.

26 DFP, 22–24 September 1887; LA, 22–24 September 1887.

27 For more on Crossley and Hunter's distinctive revivalist style, see Kee, "The Heavenly Railroad."

28 "Rev. Sam P. Jones," TM, 8 October 1886.

29 Toronto Evening Telegram (ET), 8 October 1886.

30 Globe, 11 October 1886.

31 William Magney, "The Methodist Church and the National Gospel," 9–26.

32 *TEN*, 8 October 1886. "An Old-Time Revival," *Globe*, 26 October 1886.

33 "Rev. Sam Jones Opens up," *TW*, 8 October 1886. On Jones's quick drawl, see the *Globe*, 7 October 1886.

34 *ET*, 9 October 1886.

35 *Globe*, 12 October 1886.

36 The interview was printed in a Kingston daily, *BW*, 16 March 1887.

37 *Globe*, 11 October 1886. As an "actor-preacher" and "consummate performer" himself, Jones shared some characteristics with Harry Stout's George Whitefield (Stout, *The Divine Dramatist*, xix–xxvi).

38 "Six Hundred Souls," *Globe*, 20 October 1886.

39 Ibid., 14 October 1886.

40 *DFP*, 11 March 1887.

41 Occasionally, some inspiring Gospel songs were included at the lectures, such as "All Hail the Power of Jesus' Name," "Jesus, Lover of My Soul," and "At the Cross."

42 *LA*, 10 March 1887.

43 *MDS*, 15 March 1887.

44 "Sam Jones in Galt," *GR*, 18 March 1887.

45 Minnix, *Laughter in the Amen Corner*, 32, 81.

46 Brereton, *From Sin to Salvation: Stories of Women's Conversions, 1800 to the Present*, 38.

47 *ET*, 11 October 1886. When Sam Small also revealed a trace of anti-intellectualism in a sermon which criticized colleges, the editor of the *Week* – a Toronto intellectual journal – responded with some sarcastic remarks (*Week*, 16 December 1886).

48 Minnix, *Laughter in the Amen Corner*, 122–7.

49 *TM*, 11 October 1886.

50 *Globe*, 11–12, 16 October 1886.

51 Ibid., 18 October 1886.

52 Marks, *Revivals and Roller Rinks*, 162.

53 DeBerg, *Ungodly Women*.

54 Quoted from Minnix, *Laughter in the Amen Corner*, 41.

55 *Globe*, 20 October 1886.

56 Marshall, *Secularizing the Faith*, 41–8.

57 "The Outside Sinners," *Globe*, 13 October 1886. Also, "Sam Jones' Creed: Believes in Eternal Hell and the Literal Reading of the Bible," *MDS*, 15 March 1887.

58 "The Outside Sinners," *Globe*, 13 October 1886.

59 Ibid., 21 October 1886; *TM*, 20 October 1886.

60 "The Two Sams," *TEN*, 27 October 1886.

61 *Globe*, 27 October 1886.

62 *ET*, 27 October 1886. In a letter dated October 1886, the Reverend Manly Benson, a Methodist clergyman, wrote that Jones's "too short stay in Toronto has made our hearts warm to you ... (Benson to Jones, Sam Jones Papers, box 6, folder 1, UGL).

63 *TEN*, 13 October 1886.

64 Ibid.

65 *TW*, 19 October 1886. Even "Woman's World" offered a positive assessment of Jones, though, as a man, he was liable to err when he preached to "the better half of creation." See the *Globe*, 23 October 1886.

66 *Globe*, 22–28 October, 1 November 1886. In the 16 October issue, the *Globe* reported that it had a staff of stenographers at each meeting and was the only newspaper that had "full, complete, and graphic reports." Such industry did have a price given the *Globe's* claim that its "reports are being systematically stolen by the *Evening Telegram* and reproduced without acknowledgement" (editorial, 12 October 1886).

67 *Globe*, 22 October 1886.

68 Ibid., 26 October 1886. The headline above this letter to the editor was entitled "An Old-Time Revival."

69 W. Calvert to Jones, 9 October 1886, Sam Jones Papers, box 6, folder 1, UGL. Calvert was especially delighted with Jones's "fearless" denunciation of the whisky business.

70 See "Bro. Jones Discussed in a Barber Shop," *TW*, 16 October 1886.

71 Ibid., 14 October 1886.

72 *Globe*, 16 October 1886. A similar argument is made in "The Georgia Revivalists," *TEN*, 22 October 1886.

73 *Globe*, 30 October 1886.

74 *ET*, 23 October 1886.

75 Ibid, 19 October 1886. Though expressed with different words, this same message was printed in *ET* editorials throughout the weeks of the first campaign.

76 Airhart, *Serving the Present Age*, 4.

77 "The Southern Revivalists," *CMM*, November 1886.

78 *CG*, 20 October 1886.

79 "Sam Jones in Toronto," ibid., 13 October 1886; "The Revival in Toronto," ibid., 20 October 1886. In the letter issue, see the paper's strong reply to the Reverend Worrell's argument that the Toronto *Mail* should not publish Jones's sermons.

80 "The Revival: Shall It Go On?" CG, 27 October 1886.

81 For the list of churches, see *Globe*, 27 October 1886.

82 "Sam Jones in Toronto," CG, 15 December 1886.

83 EC, 21 October 1886. On a related topic written by an evangelical Anglican, see the Reverend Dyson Hague, "Whose Fault Is It? – A Plea for Hearty Services," *Dominion Churchman (DC)*, 18 November 1886.

84 *Canadian Independent*, 15 November 1886. In the same issue, almost three pages were filled with Jones's sermon literature. The 1 December issue, however, was critical of Jones's use of tobacco.

85 "The Revival in Toronto," CG, 27 October 1886.

86 "Religion in the Gutter," DC, 21 October 1886.

87 "Presbyterians on Revivals," ibid., 18 October 1887. This piece reported the criticism by the Reverend Parsons, a Presbyterian, of "miscalled revivals."

88 TM, 13 October 1886.

89 Ibid., 14 October 1886.

90 TW, 15 October 1886. For another letter in support of Jones, see "Defending the Revivalists", ibid., 19 October 1886.

91 TM, 16 October 1886.

92 Ibid., 18 October 1886. Dillon wrote that he had recently settled in Canada "and consequently – and happily – have never heard of Sam Jones and his hysterical performances in the name of religion."

93 MDS, 18 March 1887.

94 *Week*, 21 October, 4 November 1886.

95 TM, 16 October 1886.

96 Rudy, "Unmaking Manly Smokes," 101.

97 Cook, "Evangelical Moral Reform," 178.

98 *Globe*, 18 October 1886.

99 TW, 27 October 1886.

100 Ibid., 29 October 1886.

101 Ibid., 23, 26 October 1886.

102 *Mail*, 13 December 1886. Also, see "Tobacco an Evil," the *War Cry*, 24 September 1887. This was published during the week of Jones's lectures in London, Ontario.

103 Nellie Smith to Jones, 9 March 1887, Sam Jones Papers, box 1, folder 7, UGL. Smith added: "Should it be necessary to use this little incident I trust you will not disclose names unless for God's glory."

104 *Grip*, 6 November 1886.

105 *Irish Canadian*, 4 November 1886.

106 *PL*, 13 November 1886.

107 *TW*, 28 October 1886.

108 *ET*, 27 October 1886; *TW*, 28 October 1886.

109 For examples of paid lectures by clergymen, see "Scrapbook–Lecture Broadsides," Richmond Hill Public Library, Local History Room, Richmond Hill, Ontario.

110 Hamilton *Daily Spectator* (*HDS*), 9 March 1887. Jones also defended himself at his London lectures (*LA*, 11 March 1887).

111 When a report in the Montreal *Witness* gave the impression that he was in Montreal for a money-making venture, an *MDS* reporter came to his defence, clarifying that all but $200 of his lecture earnings was allegedly going towards the Methodist Theological College (*MDS*, 15 March 1887).

112 *DFP*, 24 September 1887.

113 In 1906 Jones claimed that he had made more than $750,000 over the years as "the best-paid preacher in the United States." Hambrick-Stowe, "'Sanctified Business,'" 94–6.

114 *Globe*, 16 October 1886.

115 *TW*, 28 October 1886.

116 Quoted in McLoughlin, *Modern Revivalism*, 312.

117 "Sam Small to Working Girls," *Globe*, 25 October 1886. According to the *Globe*, "it was the largest gathering of women ever held in the city."

118 *EN*, 21 September 1887.

119 Ibid.; *Globe*, 21 September; *TW*, 21 September 1887; *EN*, 22 September 1887.

120 *EN*, 23–24 September 1887; "Sam Small's Attack," *TW*, 24 September 1887.

121 Kealey and Palmer, *Dreaming of What Might Be*, passim.

122 "The Churches and the Masses," *Globe*, 30 September 1887.

123 *TN*, 26 September 1887.

124 "Work for a Revival," *CG*, 10 November 1886.

125 Ibid., 27 October, 10 November 1886.

126 Also, see Crouse, "Revivalism for the Working Class?" 21–37.

CHAPTER FOUR

1 Marshall, *Secularizing the Faith*.

2 Airhart, *Serving the Present Age*, 69–70. The Plymouth Brethren believed that those whose faith has "grounded in intellectual assent to

biblically derived propositions" could be assured salvation. This was unlike the Methodist's "witness of the Spirit" understanding of conversion, which provided no such assurance.

3 A similar argument is made by Christie and Gauvreau, *The Full-Orbed Christianity*, especially chapter 2.

4 Airhart, "Ordering a New Nation and Reordering Protestantism 1867–1914," 115–16.

5 Palmer, *Working Class Experience*, 144–7.

6 Airhart, "Ordering a New Nation and Reordering Protestantism 1867–1914," 117–18. On the cooperation of progressives and conservatives in United States, see Heinrich, "The Last Great Awakening."

7 Charles Alexander to A.P.F.H., 17 June 1905, Charles Alexander, drawer 34, MBIA.

8 *News*, 26 January 1906. This particular issue offers a wide selection of statistics relating to the campaign.

9 On Trotter's mission efforts, see Adair, *The Old Lighthouse*. For more on Trotter from a Canadian newspaper, see the Owen Sound *Advertiser (OSA)*, 30 January 1906. Also, see collection 47, BGCA, and drawer 51, Melvin Trotter, MBIA. Mrs Gordon also held meetings for most of January in Newmarket (Newmarket *Era [NE]*, 2 February 1906).

10 The *Paisley Advocate*, 25 January 1906, listed a number of women and men who travelled to see the "great evangelists." The Owen Sound *Sun*, 16 January 1906, reported that three hundred seats were reserved at Massey Hall for Owen Sound excursionists. According to an advertisement in the 12 January issue, the fare was $2.50 for adults and $1.25 for children under the age of twelve. On 19 January, OSA reported that an excursion from the Brantford area numbered about four hundred.

11 *TDS*, 8 January 1906. For one of several reports of people travelling to Toronto to participate in the revivals, see the *News*, 6 January 1906.

12 *TW*, 29 January 1906.

13 Ottawa *Citizen*, 7 June 1906.

14 Ibid., 9 June 1906.

15 Ibid., 7 June 1906. In addition to Campbell, the other members of the committee were the Reverend P.W. Anderson, Alderman Charles Hopewell, and Mr W.B. Garvock. Chairman of the ushers' committee was Mr R.G. Knox. Both Campbell and Knox had their pictures presented in the *Evening Journal*. The Reverend Anderson was minister of Presbyterian McKay Church.

16 Ottawa *Evening Journal (OEJ)*, 12, 16 June 1906. On Butler's conversion experience, see ibid., 20 June 1906.

17 Ibid., 19–21 June 1906. The *Citizen* reported that some evening meetings attracted 7,000 people.

18 Ibid., 22 June 1906.

19 *OEJ*, 14 June 1906; *Citizen*, 28 June 1906.

20 *Citizen*, 11 June 1906.

21 *MDS*, 5, 15 April 1907.

22 Ibid, 10 April 1907.

23 Ibid, 13, 26 April 1907.

24 *Gazette*, 4 May 1907.

25 *MDS*, 6 May 1907. In 1908 Torrey left the Moody Bible Institute and moved to the Bible Institute of Los Angeles where he also continued revival activities.

26 Fredericton *Daily Gleaner (DG)*, 19 May 1910; ibid., 13 June 1910.

27 "Great Soul-Saving Campaign Begun," Saint John *Daily Telegraph (DT)*, 7 November 1910. "Dr. Torrey Speaks on Live Questions," *Standard*, 12 November 1910; "Farewell Meetings in the Queen's Rink," *DT*, 5 December 1910.

28 Halifax *Herald (HH)*, 10 January 1911. "The Torrey Evangelistic Campaign Gaining in Influence in Windsor," ibid., 14 January 1911; "Great Interest in Evangelistic Meetings in Windsor," ibid., 24 January 1911.

29 "Why Not Have Dr. Torrey in Halifax?" ibid., 31 January 1911.

30 "Overflow Meetings Are the Order Now," *TDS*, 12 January 1906.

31 *News*, 8 January 1906. The author of the article "Women at Massey Hall," located on the women's page, was not identified.

32 *TDS*, 8 January 1906.

33 YWCA Club Minutes, 4 January 1906, MV 3522, box 6, AO. A week later, on 11 January, the club meeting was cancelled, "the girls all going to the Torrey-Alexander meetings." Mrs (J.W.?) Russel, a leader of the YWCA, was one who attended the meetings.

34 *TDS*, 2 January 1906.

35 Toronto *Saturday Night (TSN)*, 20 January 1906.

36 On the communicative effect of music as security, see Dunaway, "Music as Political Communication in the United States," 39; on Gospel songs and the "common people," see Reynolds and Price, *A Survey of Christian Hymnody*, 102; on class lines, see Routley, *Twentieth Century Church Music*, 196–8. Also, see Routley, *The Music of Christian Hymns*, 136–7.

37 *ME*, 4 January 1906.

38 *TSN*, 20 January 1906.

39 Sankey, *Sacred Songs and Solos*, no. 949.

40 *News*, 2 January 1906. Alexander was absent at the Montreal, Fredericton, Saint John, and Windsor campaigns, but the newspapers there also reported that the Gospel music played an important role in stirring the souls of revival attenders.

41 Sizer, *Gospel Hymns and Social Religion*, 135.

42 *Citizen*, 12 June 1906.

43 *DG*, 17 and 31 May and 3 June 1910.

44 "Dr. Torrey Condemns 'High Society' Gambling," *Citizen*, 13 June 1906.

45 *TDS*, 2 January 1906.

46 *Citizen*, 12 June 1906, provides a good overview of the dynamics of a Torrey-Alexander revival meeting.

47 *CB*, 18 January 1906. Only at the meeting for children and young people was there an inquiry room established.

48 These few examples are from one meeting alone. See *OEJ*, 26 June 1906.

49 *TW*, 24 January 1906.

50 Montreal *Gazette* (*MG*), 30 April 1907.

51 "Great Revival Is Bearing Fruit," *DG*, 17 May 1910.

52 *OFP*, 14 June 1906.

53 *ET*, 9 January 1906. As related in the Montreal *Gazette*, 4 May 1907, a Roman Catholic woman who was interested in joining a Protestant church asked Torrey to hear her confession. He instructed her to go to Jesus Christ instead.

54 Blumhofer, *Restoring the Faith*, 30–1.

55 *ET*, 19, 23 January 1906; *News*, 23 January 1906. Also, see Wacker, "Holy Spirit and Spirit of the Age," 46–51.

56 Heinrichs, "The Last Great Awakening: The Revival of 1905 and Progressivism," 369.

57 Bendroth, *Fundamentalism & Gender, 1875 to the Present*, 22–3.

58 "Dr. Torrey Again Declares Hell Is Fire and Brimstone," *DT*, 24 November 1910.

59 Reuben Torrey, "Writings By," "Hell: What Sort of a Place Is It and Who Is Going There," Biographical 51, MBIA. "Hell – Its Certainty and the Kind of Place It Is," *DG*, 25 May 1910; "Rev. Dr. Torrey Preached Again on Subject of Hell," ibid., 26 May 1910.

60 "Vivid Picture Drawn of Old Style Sheol", *TDS*, 17 January 1906; *OSA*, 19 January 1906.

61 Torrey, "The Bible Teaching regarding Future Punishment," 272.

62 "Just out of Prison, He Asks for Prayers," *TDS*, 9 January 1906.

63 *ET*, 16 January 1906; *TDS*, 12 January 1906; *OEJ*, 14–15 June 1906.

64 *DG*, 20 May 1910.

65 *TDS*, 15 January 1906.

66 Wacker, "Holy Spirit and Spirit of the Age," 51; Davis, *Torrey and Alexander*, 39.

67 *ET*, 5, 11 January 1906.

68 *TW*, 18 January 1906.

69 *ME*, 13 January 1906.

70 "Writes in Defence of Dr. Torrey," *News*, 19 January 1906.

71 "For and against Rev. Dr. Torrey," ibid., 23 January 1906.

72 Ibid.

73 *TDS*, 22 January 1906. It was the opinion of the Reverend Brookman that Torrey "palmed off upon his hearers the darkness of man's tradition as though it were the Light of God's Truth" (*News*, 22 January 1906).

74 "More Opinions on the Revivalists," *ME*, 23 January 1906.

75 *TSN*, 27 January 1906.

76 For example, see Almond, *Heaven and Hell in Enlightenment England*, 82–3.

77 *OEJ*, 25 June 1906. Casson saw Torrey's intellectual capacity as suspect, stating that "the waves of a century's higher thought have never reached or rippled the placid puddle of his mind."

78 Ibid., 26 June 1906.

79 *MDS*, 29 April 1907.

80 *TW*, 3 January 1906.

81 "The Chance of the Churches," *Globe*, 24 January 1906.

82 *TW*, 15 January 1906.

83 Ibid., 29 January 1906.

84 *ET*, 23 January 1906.

85 *ME*, 30 January 1906. For more on LeSueur, see Cook, *The Regenerators*, 37–46.

86 See "HAD AN ARGUMENT WITH DR. TORREY," *MDS*, 19 April 1907; ibid., 2 May 1907. For Torrey's explanation and apology, see the Montreal *Gazette* and *MDS*, 3 May 1907. At Montreal, there was a wide variety of complaints concerning his message, many of which were voiced in crank phone calls to his hotel and in the newspapers. In the *Gazette*, 30 April 1907, Torrey refers to the people who called him to make uncomplimentary remarks.

87 *TSN*, 6 January 1906. The author of the report was identified as "Canadienne."

88 Ibid., 13 January 1906.

89 Ibid., 20 January 1906. Attempts to explain revivals by psychology were not unusual at the turn of the century. For example, see Watson, "The Psychology of Revivals," and Davenport, *Primitive Traits in Religious Revivals*.

90 *TSN*, 20 January 1906.

91 Ibid.

92 *TDS*, 9 January 1906.

93 *News*, 12 January 1906.

94 *TDS*, 9 January 1906.

95 Also, see "A Criminal's Testimony" in Davies, *Twice around the World with Alexander*, 224–5.

96 Brereton, *From Sin to Salvation*, 38.

97 Alexander, *Charles M. Alexander*, 113. Alexander also wrote that "crowds of excursionists come in from day to day from all the place around ..."

98 *TDS*, 22 January 1906.

99 Oswald Smith Papers, collection 322, box 1, folder 10, Clippings, 1927–1986, BGCA; Neely, *Fire in His Bones*, 24–6.

100 DeBerg, *UnGodly Women*, 29.

101 "The Feminization of the Minister," *Wesleyan*, 16 February 1910.

102 Davis, *Twice around the World with Alexander*, chapter 22 – "Conversion of a Famous Pugilist," especially 298–300.

103 Bendroth, *Fundamentalism & Gender*, 22.

104 Long, *The Revival of 1857–58*, 40–3.

105 *Citizen*, 15 June 1906; *OEJ*, 15 June 1906.

106 *OEJ*, 20 June 1906.

107 Ibid., 19 June 1906.

108 *Citizen*, 16 June 1906.

109 *CB*, 28 December 1905; *CG*, 27 December 1905. For Methodists' desire to have revival, see ibid., 15 February 1905; *CMM*, vol. 63, January 1906; the *Presbyterian* referred to the coming Torrey-Alexander campaign several times from late October onward.

110 Grant, *A Profusion of Spires*, 182–3.

111 *CCM*, 23 November 1905. In the 14 December 1905 issue, one Anglican layman commends the work of the evangelists.

112 Ibid., 1 February 1906. Another responded in the *CCM*, 1 March 1906, stating that Soward "did not see eye to eye with the great many" Anglicans who backed Torrey.

113 *TW*, 23 January 1906; *News*, 24 January 1906.

114 "The Torrey-Alexander Mission," *Canadian Congregationalist* (CC), 25 January 1906. Other similar concerns were voiced in "Evangelism," ibid., 1 February 1906.

115 "J.B. Silcox on Dr. Torrey," ibid., 15 February 1906. "Another Estimate of Dr. Torrey in Toronto," ibid., 22 February 1906, drawer 34, MBIA. In a 17 June 1905 letter to A.P. Fitt, Charles Alexander wrote that the Reverend Hyde and Toronto Christians were planning the Torrey-Alexander campaign. For another positive appraisal of the meetings, see "Home Missionary Churches in Toronto District Association," ibid., 8 February 1906.

116 Fraser, *The Social Uplifters*; Gauvreau, *The Evangelical Century*; Marshall, *Secularizing the Faith*.

117 *Presbyterian*, 25 January 1906. The *Presbyterian Witness*, 10 February 1906, was glad to see that the work by Torrey and Alexander was recognized by the religious and secular press. The *Presbyterian*, 9 May 1907, gave a brief report of the successful Torrey meetings held at Montreal.

118 Ibid., 4, 11 January 1906.

119 Ibid., 18 January 1906. Praising the work of Torrey and Alexander were the Reverend J. McP. Scott, St John's Church; Professor T.B. Kilpatrick, Knox College; the Reverend A.B. Winchester, Knox Church; and the Reverend J.A. Turnbull, West Church.

120 "Editorial Etchings," ibid., 1 February 1906. Also, see "The Close of the Mission." For a more critical analysis of Torrey's preaching of hell, see, in the same issue, "Echoes of an Old Doctrine."

121 *Westminster*, February 1906. See the reports under "Baptist Notes," "Congregational Notes," and "Methodist Notes."

122 *CB*, 11, 18, and 25 January 1906.

123 "Torrey-Alexander Meetings," ibid., 25 January 1906. See the comments by the Reverend Alex White, Hon. John Dryden, the Reverend Jesse Gibson, Mr R.D. Warren, the Reverend J.D. Freeman, and Mr F.L. Ratcliffe.

124 Ibid.

125 "Torrey-Alexander Meetings," ibid., 1 February 1906. See the comments by the Reverend H.F. LaFlamme, Mr W.E. Robertson, the Reverend C.H. Schutt, the Reverend C.W. King, Mr William Craig, Professor P.S. Campbell, the Reverend H. Francis Perry, and the Reverend William J. Scott. The Baptists who praised the efforts of Torrey and Alexander in the *Canadian Baptist* demonstrates that Baptists in

Canada were cognizant of the themes of piety, power, and community that emerged from popular American revivalism.

126 Airhart, *Serving the Present Age*, 87, 93.

127 "What Pastors Say of the Mission," CG, 24 January 1906.

128 Ibid., 24 January 1906.

129 "The Great Revival in Toronto," ibid., 14 February 1906.

130 CMM, vol. 63, February 1906. Also, see "Revival of Religion and Higher Criticism," CG, 3 January 1906.

131 "Dr. Torrey in Montreal," CG, 15 May 1907.

132 "Dr Torrey in Montreal: An Appreciation," ibid., 22 May 1907.

133 CG, 25 May 1910; *Wesleyan*, 8 February 1911; Langille, "Torrey Meetings, Windsor."

134 *News*, 13 January 1906.

CHAPTER FIVE

1 Also, Crouse, "Great Expectations," 155–67.

2 Gordon Papers, Chapman to Gordon, 13 December 1906, UMA. Gordon also wanted Chapman for April but the latter could not commit to that date.

3 Augustine's Presbyterian Church (Fort Rouge), St Stephen's Presbyterian Church (Portage Avenue), St Andrew's Presbyterian Church (Elgin Avenue), Central Congregational Church (Hargrave and Qu'Appelle), Grace Methodist Church (Notre Dame and Ellice), and MacDougall Methodist Church (Main St North).

4 Virginia Asher Papers, Guide, collection 197, BGCA.

5 Many workers heard their message but far fewer became involved in churches. See Crouse, "They 'Left Us Pretty Much as We Were,'" 51–71.

6 MFP, 30 October 1907.

7 Prang, *N.W. Rowell*, 12. For example, Rowell attended a large Bible class at the church which was taught by J.M. Aikins, one of Winnipeg's leading lawyers.

8 MFP, 24 October 1907.

9 Gordon Papers, John Converse to Gordon, 26 November 1907, UMA.

10 *Weekly Review* (Portage la Prairie) 23 October 1907.

11 Gordon Papers, Chapman to Gordon, 12 June 1908, UMA; MFP, 12 June 1908.

12 Orillia *Times* (OT), 17, 24 September 1908; Orillia *Packet* (OP), 1 October 1908.

13 On the committee were J.J. Thompson, treasurer, R.O. Smith, secretary, the Reverend J.J. Ferguson, the Reverend W.F. Roadhouse, the Reverend D.C. MacGregor, the Reverend G.F. Saywell, Captain Knight, T.B. Mitchell, C.H. Hale, W.S. Frost, S.L. Mullett, G.H. Clark, and H.A. Croxall. See C.H. Hale, "Work of the Invitation Committee," OT, 15 October 1908.

14 Church, "Cottage Prayer-Meetings," OT, 15 October 1908. Also, see OP, 10 September 1908.

15 See Frost, "The Publicity Department," OT, 15 October 1908.

16 Gordon Papers, Chapman to Gordon, January/February 1908, UMA.

17 See Smith, "The Crowds at the Rink," OT, 15 October 1908. For one meeting, it was reported that "never before within the knowledge of the oldest resident of Orillia had there been such a large gathering under one roof." Local and regional ministers supported the campaign.

18 OT, 15 October 1908.

19 Northern Advance, 8 October 1908.

20 OP, 15 October 1908.

21 TDS, 15 October 1908.

22 News, 15 October 1908.

23 Brantford Daily Expositor (BDE), 1 October 1908.

24 Ibid., 3 October 1908.

25 Brantford Courier (BC), 23 October 1908.

26 BDE, 29 October 1908. When Chapman and Alexander arrived in Brantford for two meetings at Zion Presbyterian Church and one at Wellington Methodist Church, there was a great stir.

27 Paris Star-Transcript (ST), 4 November 1908; Presbyterian, 15 October 1908.

28 ST, 4 November 1908.

29 Gordon Papers, Chapman to Gordon, 22 March 1909, UMA. Gordon also claimed that the Chapman-Alexander duo was "a great one."

30 MFP, 22 March 1909.

31 Ottman, J. Wilbur Chapman, 137. The Regina Morning Leader, 26 March 1909, did not provide coverage of the impromptu meeting but it did print a small piece on Fanny Crosby and how she had recently attended Chapman-Alexander revival meetings held in Massachusetts.

32 Vancouver World (VW), 25 March 1909.

33 Vancouver Daily Province (DP), 25 March 1909. Another meeting attracted a "large congregation" at Central Methodist Church where Chapman workers Mr and Mrs R.B. Martin and Mr Hemminger

were in charge, and other members of the Chapman party targeted Mount Pleasant Methodist Church.

34 According to Burkinshaw, there was a deficiency of revival enthusiasm among Methodists in turn-of-the-century British Columbia. Burkinshaw, *Pilgrims in Lotus Land*, 25–6.

35 Kilpatrick and Shearer, *The Kootenay Campaign*. For other reports see *DP*, 5–10 April 1909, and the *Weekly Herald*, 29 April 1909.

36 The local newspapers provided extensive coverage of this campaign throughout February. See the Saint John *Telegraph*, the Saint John *Globe (SJG)*, and the *Sun*. In a letter to "the people of St. John," Chapman wrote: "Most of the evangelists who labor with you I know personally and I commend them without reserve. They will bring a mighty spiritual uplift to the entire community" (*Sun*, 7 February 1910).

37 *TDS*, 10 January 1911. The committee included Mrs Thomas Urquart, chair, Miss O. Culman, secretary, Miss Knox, Havergal College, Miss Thomas, Model School, Miss Grace Walker, of "Oaklands," Miss Margaret Anderson, YWCA, Miss Drummond, secretary of the YWCA, Mrs Robert Kilgour, and Miss Bessie Kilgour.

38 The eleven main churches and districts were: Westmoreland Methodist Church (Westmoreland), College Street Baptist Church (College and Baptist), Wesley Methodist Church (Dundas and Dovercourt), Victoria Presbyterian Church (West Toronto), Dunn Avenue Presbyterian Church (Parkdale), St John's Presbyterian Church (Riverdale), Euclid Avenue Methodist Church (Tecumseth), Central Methodist Church (Bloor Street East), Walmer Road Baptist Church (Spadina Road), Zion Methodist Church (Wychwood Park), and East Toronto Baptist Church (East Toronto).

39 *ET*, 6 January 1911.

40 For an example of a revival meeting for workers, see "A Great Meeting at Taylor Works," *TDS*, 6 January 1911.

41 *TW*, 5 January 1911. While the *World* did not provide extensive coverage of every meeting, its reports captured the highlights of the campaign in a positive light.

42 *TDS*, 28 January 1911. The *News*, 31 January 1911, stated that over 600,000 people had listened to the evangelists' exhortations.

43 See Miss C.B. Mackay, "The Music," *OT*, 15 October 1908.

44 *VW*, 25 March 1909.

45 *TDS*, 14 January 1911.

46 *News*, 16 January 1911.

47 *MFP*, 2 October 1907.

48 *OT*, 8 October 1908.

49 Ibid., 15 October 1908.

50 Ibid.

51 *MFP*, 29 October 1907.

52 *TW*, 18 January 1911.

53 *TDS*, 28 January 1911. On these occasions, his non-intervention allowed individuals to meditate on their relationship with God on their own.

54 Chapman did not keep statistics on how many came forward when invitations were made, but, if the newspaper reports of the meetings are reasonably reliable, the number varied from a small group of individuals to hundreds.

55 Ibid., 15 October 1908. Curiously, the sermon was not printed in this issue.

56 "An Ultra-conservative Is Evangelist Chapman," *TW*, 9 January 1911.

57 "The Only Effective Theology," *PR*, August 1909, 358–9; The Hanover *Post*, 12 January 1911. See also Chapman's *Awakening Sermons*.

58 "Men Must Believe There Is a Hell," *TM*, 21 January 1911.

59 *News*, 16 January 1911;, *TDS*, 28 January 1911. There was a hell, Chapman insisted, but "God sends no man into perdition; He has raised every possible barrier before hell"; the final decision was made by the individual.

60 Quoted in McLoughlin, *Modern Revivalism*, 383.

61 Gilling, "Revivalism as Renewal," 86.

62 For example, see Madill, "The Covenant of Service," *OT*, 15 October 1908.

63 *Presbyterian*, 19 January 1911; *TDS*, 7 January 1911.

64 *MFP*, 29 October 1907.

65 Ibid., 30 October 1907. Burwick's noon meetings appeared to attract increasingly larger numbers and it was suggested that the YMCA continue to hold noon meetings once a week in the upcoming months.

66 Ibid., 29 October 1907.

67 For an excellent sketch of the Asher's work, see *OT*, 15 October 1908.

68 *MFP*, 30 October 1907.

69 "Wonderful Revival of Religion," *OT*, 15 October 1908.

70 "The Chapman-Alexander Campaign," *CB*, 22 October 1908.

71 *BDE*, 20 October 1908; "Bar Room Meeting," *BDE*, 24 October 1908; "Are Active," *BDE*, 22 October 1908.

72 "Chapman-Alexander Evangelistic Campaign," OP, 15 October 1908.

73 "Told of Work in Slum Districts," TDS, 6 January 1911.

74 "Revival in the Shop," ET, 20 January 1911.

75 "Told of Work in Slum Districts," TDS, 6 January 1911; the Mail, 19 January 1911.

76 For more on the Ashers' work, see Crouse, "They 'Left Us Pretty Much as We Were,'" 51–71.

77 "Local Items," Voice, 18 October 1907.

78 "Police Obliged to Keep Crowds from Massey Hall," Globe, 27 January 1911.

79 Christie and Gauvreau, The Full-Orbed Christianity. See especially chapter 2.

80 OT, 15 October 1908.

81 TDS, 9 January 1911.

82 For more on social control and revivals, see Johnson, A Shopkeeper's Millennium. An insufficient amount of work has been published on this issue by Canadian labour historians. Indeed, religion in general has played a small role in most Canadian labour histories.

83 The Chapman campaigns also sought to reach the young. At the 1911 Toronto campaign, evangelist J.J. Lowe targeted a younger crowd and used techniques such as showing slides of mission work with a "lantern" which he carried with him. He had the ability to relate stories in a simple and attractive style and was acknowledged as one of the most effective evangelists "in winning young people to Christ." See Globe, 5 January 1911; Presbyterian, 2 February 1911.

84 Bendroth, "Men, Masculinity, and Urban Reivalism," 235, 239, 241. In the American scholarly literature, much of the focus is on "middle-class" participants in urban revivalism.

85 TDS, 20 January 1911.

86 News, 16 January 1911.

87 For more on the interaction of masculinity and evangelicalism, see DeBerg, Ungodly Women.

88 ET, 9 January 1911. It appears that, while they were not involved with speaking as often as Miller and Asher, Mrs Chapman and Mrs Alexander occasionally assisted with meetings for women at the 1911 Toronto campaign. Mrs Alexander also gave a discourse at the Friends' Church on the history and purpose of the Adult School movement (ET, 16 January 1911).

89 YWCA Minutes, 1897–1918, MV 3518, box 2, 1911, 251, 253, AO.

90 TDS, 10 January 1911.

91 *TW*, 15 January 1911.

92 DeBerg, *Ungodly Women*, 14.

93 Marilyn Whitely, however, does estimate that there were about thirty Methodist women working in Canada as evangelists between the years 1885 and 1910. Whitely, "Modest, Unaffected, and Fully Consecrated," 184.

94 For a list of denominations that allowed women ordination, see Hardesty, *Women Called to Witness*, 98. For Canadian Methodism leaders' resistance to grant women full laity rights, see Brouwer, "The Canadian Methodist Church and Ecclesiastical Suffrage for Women, 1902–1914."

95 *CCM*, 21 November 1907. A similar concern was expressed by another writer in ibid., 29 October 1908, during Chapman's successful revival meetings in Ontario.

96 *Presbyterian*, 21 November 1907. Roy apparently "flung himself heart and soul into the work, carrying his church with him ..."

97 It should be pointed out, however, that Anglican evangelicals in Canada between 1850 and 1920 gained significant power within the Anglican Church. By participating with other Protestants at the Chapman campaigns, Anglican evangelicals maintained a bridge between their Church and other denominations much as they had done in the late nineteenth century when they joined interdenominational ventures such as the Upper Canada Bible Society (Masters, "The Anglican Evangelicals in Toronto, 1870–1900," 51, 62–3).

98 *CB*, 22 October 1908.

99 Ibid. Roadhouse was amazed that there were meetings which drew 3,500 in a city of 6,000, especially since 1,000 of the total population were Roman Catholics and Plymouth Brethren, who, he claimed, did not attend the meetings.

100 *CC*, 8 October 1908.

101 Ibid., 15 October 1908. See also the next two issues.

102 Airhart, *Serving the Present Age*, 63.

103 *CG*, 20 November 1907.

104 Ibid., 13 November 1907.

105 Ibid., 18 December 1907.

106 Ibid., 7 October 1908.

107 Fraser, *Church, College, and Clergy*, 131.

108 Marshall, *Secularizing the Faith*, 95–6.

109 See the *Presbyterian* issues of 31 October and all of November 1907.

110 MacGregor, "The Chapman Campaign in Orillia," ibid., 29 October 1908. Also, see the 8, 15 October issues for mention of the Chapman campaigns.

111 See "Paris Notes," ibid., 29 October 1908.

112 MacBeth, "The Campaign in Paris," ibid., 12 November 1908.

113 "Evangelism," ibid., 3 December 1908.

114 *War Cry*, 21 January 1911. For more on Chapman's fondness for the Salvation Army, see "Dr. Chapman on the Salvation Army," the *War Cry*, 4 February 1911, which contains Chapman's Toronto address welcoming the new commissioner of the Salvation Army.

115 Ibid., 18 February 1911.

116 Marks, "Knights of Labor and the Salvation Army," 121. Clark, *Church and Sect in Canada*, 429.

117 *War Cry*, 11 February 1911.

118 TDS, 27 January 1911.

119 CB, 8 December 1910.

120 Ibid., 12 January 1911.

121 Ibid., 26 January 1911.

122 Ibid., 16 March 1911.

123 CC, , 5 January 1911.

124 Ibid., 9 March 1911. For some contemporary views by a Canadian Congregationalist, see Jackson, *A Hand-Book of Congregationalism*.

125 CG, 21 December 1910.

126 See CG, 11 January 1911.

127 Ibid., 18 January 1911.

128 Ibid., 25 January 1917.

129 Airhart, *Serving the Present Age*, especially chapter 3.

130 CG, 8 February 1911. Also, see Gilmour, "Pre-millennial Views," TDS, 25 January 1911.

131 Bland, "Evangelism and the Evangelistic Committee," CG, 15 February 1911.

132 Airhart, *Serving the Present Age*, 105–8.

133 CG, 12 April 1911. An earlier correspondent had suggested that Toronto adopt the old circuit system for some areas of the city (ibid., 29 March 1911). Also, see Chown and Moore, "Suggestions from the General Conference Standing Committee to Annual Conference Committees on Evangelism," ibid., 8 March 1911.

134 "What Was There in the Chapman-Alexander Campaign?" ibid., 8 March 1911. Over one-half of Toronto ministers replied to the ques-

tionnaire, with over two-thirds giving the campaign a poor grade for its results.

135 Airhart, *Serving the Present Age*, 129–39.

136 Cook, *The Regenerators*; Marshall, *Secularizing the Faith*.

137 Van Die, *An Evangelical Mind*, 167.

138 "Preaching the Gospel," *Presbyterian*, 5 January 1911. There was cordial cooperation among Anglicans, Baptists, Presbyterians, Congregationalists, and Methodists, according to the *Presbyterian*.

139 The *Presbyterian*, 19 January 1911.

140 "Chapman-Alexander Simultaneous Mission: Impressions of the Campaign," ibid., 2 February 1911.

141 *TDS*, 30 January 1911. When Chapman made this statement at an address at Metropolitan Methodist Church, Toronto ministers reportedly rose from their seats to assure Chapman that he was mistaken in his assessment of the campaign.

142 Ibid., 31 January 1911.

143 Also, see "Permanence in Evangelistic Work," *Presbyterian*, 2 February 1911. This issue will be discussed further in chapter 6.

144 "After the Campaign," CC, 9 March 1911.

145 Grant, *The Church in the Canadian Era*, 102–3.

146 Noll, *A History of Christianity in the United States and Canada*, 279.

147 MFP, 1 November 1907.

148 BDE, 26 October 1908.

149 "Men in the Church," *Voice*, 22 November 1908. Mack, "From Preaching to Propaganda to Marginalization," 138, 142.

150 Marks, *Revivals and Roller Rinks*, 34. She argues that, for some men, "conflict in the workplace may have heightened class-consciousness and led to a reluctance to worship with employers ..."

151 "The Home of the Evangelist Movement," *Voice*, 1 November 1907.

152 Aiken, MacMillan, and Gordon were listed as Winnipeg millionaires. See Artibise, *Gateway City*, 119, 125, 127.

153 On the issue of twentieth-century Protestant clergymen identifying more with the profane consumerism of modern bourgeois society than with the Christ model of assisting the needy and oppressed, more with "respectable" folk than with the labouring poor, see Rawlyk, "Writing about Canadian Religious Revivals," 220–4. For more on the divergence of worker and "middle-class" evangelical culture, see Van Die, "'The Marks of a Genuine Revival,'" 554–5.

154 This argument is presented in Gilling, "Revivalism as Renewal," 81–92.

155 Ramsay, *John Wilbur Chapman*, 65.

CHAPTER SIX

1 Thomas, *Revivalism and Cultural Change*, 78.
2 MFP, 5 November 1897.
3 "Gen. Booth and Sam Jones," *Globe*, 30 September 1886.
4 Ibid., 28 October 1886.
5 *News*, 2 January 1906.
6 Other methods included downtown missions. For example, the CMM, July to December 1885, was aware that regular church agencies could not always reach the "lower classes."
7 *Globe*, 25 September 1886.
8 Ibid., 3 December 1884.
9 Some Canadian historians have noted the discomfort that Methodists had over the fact that the Salvation Army was reaching many whom they themselves had failed to reach. See, for example, Whiteley, "Modest Unaffected, and Fully Consecrated," 187.
10 *Globe*, 25 October 1886.
11 An excellent model for careful consideration of revival and occupational status is Marks, *Revivals and Roller Rinks*.
12 See *Globe*, 5 December 1884, and EJ, 18 October 1897.
13 MDS, 8 February 1898 and 15 October 1887.
14 *Globe*, 17 November 1894, EN, 16 November 1894.
15 TDS, 23 January 1906.
16 For example, a Thomas Woodhouse stated that Sam Jones "has given the masses the advice they need, and most of those who heard him do not go to any church." See *Globe*, 28 October 1886.
17 Ibid.
18 On at least one occasion, Moody himself lumped the majority of people into a middle-class category. He characterized the attendance at one inquiry meeting as "middle class and some of the richer people." See MDS, 14 October 1887.
19 See Campbell's letter to the editor, TW, 23 November 1894.
20 Findlay, *Dwight L. Moody*, 306–7; Weisberger, *They Gathered at the River*, 225.
21 *Globe*, 24 November 1894.
22 Sawatsky, "'Looking for that Blessed Hope,'" 270.
23 TM, 23 November 1894.
24 Sawatsky, "'Looking for that Blessed Hope,'" 103–27.
25 See MDS, 10–13 October 1887.
26 Bliss, *A Canadian Millionaire*, 88–90, 97–8.

27 Marshall, *Secularizing the Faith*, 11.
28 For biographical profiles of Parson, Frizzell, and Mutch, see
   Sawatsky, "'Looking for that Blessed Hope,'" 89–94. Other Toronto
   so-called proto-fundamentalist clergymen who supported Moody
   included the Reverend Thomas Cutler DesBarres, rector of St Paul's
   Church, the Reverend Samuel John Hunter, a Methodist, and the
   Reverend John Salmon, a founder of the Christian Missionary Alliance (ibid., 86–8, 98–102).
29 The *Toronto Empire* figure quoted in HS, 26 November 1894.
30 Membership two years before and three years after Moody's 1894
   Toronto Campaign (Methodist figures are taken in June and Presbyterian numbers at the end of the year):

	1892	1893	1894	1895	1896	1897
Metropolitan Church	489	599	620	611	596	575
Walmer Road Baptist	378	410	467	505	519	575
Cooke's Presbyterian	1,145	1,184	1,330	1,375	1,375	1,379
St Andrews	598	595	595	561	561	–
Knox	772	716	700	654	622	569
Queen St	226	261	252	268	279	294
Chalmers	428	452	470	505	547	531
Total Presbytery of Toronto	16,677	15,275	16,420	16,180	17,477	16,990
Total Toronto District (Meth.)	13,913	13,509	14,163	14,207	14,829	15,268

Source: *Methodist Minutes*, 1892–97, UCA; *Baptist Year Book*, 1892–97, MDA;
Presbyterian Acts, 1892–97, QUSL.

31 On the relationship of revivalism and cultural expression, see Van
   Die, *An Evangelical Mind*, 10–12.
32 Airhart, *Serving the Present Age*, 4.
33 "Methodism in Cities," CMM, July-December, 1885; "Revivals," ibid.,
   February 1886; "Evangelism," ibid., September 1886.
34 On moral tone, see Van Die, *An Evangelical Mind*, 10–11.
35 Jones, *Sam Jones and Sam Small in Toronto*, ii.
36 For the positive appraisals of the campaign by Methodist clergymen
   and lay people, see "Good-Bye to the Sams," *Globe*, 28 October
   1886; "Sam Jones and His Work," ibid., 30 October 1886; and, for
   Sheppard's praise of the meetings, "Good-bye Sam: What We Think
   of You and Your Work," TEN, 28 October 1886. In an encouraging
   letter to Jones, I.B. Aylesworth, a Methodist minister, wrote that
   "there is no class of men who need prodding ... more than Methodist
   preachers; and every right thinking one will approve and profit by it"

(Reverend I.B. Aylesworth to Reverend Sam Jones, 20 October 1886, Sam Jones Papers, box 6, folder 1, UGL).

37 *Globe*, 20 October 1886.

38 *TW*, 19 October 1886.

39 Ibid, 23 October 1886.

40 Membership in the years before and after the October 1886 Jones-Small campaign (the figures were tallied in the month of June of each year):

	1885	1886	1887	1888
Parkdale	153	181	225	343
Metropolitan	684	700	750	780
Elm Street	610	680	760	640
Sherbourne	387	398	400	684
Berkely	408	431	457	435
Richmond	312	299	303	216
Spadina	355	435	431	478
Dundas	312	361	415	505
St Paul	177	190	228	302
King	20	50	50	148
Agnes	208	290	442	613
Carlton	321	344	460	514
Total, Toronto District	6,943	7,801	8,956	9,952
Difference	–	+858	+1,155	+996

Source: Methodist Minutes, 1884–88, UCA

41 *MG*, 14 March 1887.

42 See *Globe*, 19 September 1887, for the coverage of the first meeting held by Munhall. According to *TW*, 23 September 1887, he was invited by several ministers – three Methodist, two Presbyterian, two Baptist, and one Episcopalian. *TW*, 3 October 1887, reported that "so great was the crush for admission that the doors [of the Granite Rink] were closed about half an hour before the advertised time." For more on Munhall, see Sandeen, *The Roots of Fundamentalism*.

43 Letter to Reverend Sam Jones, 16 October 1886, Sam Jones Papers, box 6, folder 1, UGL. There is no indication that this letter was solicited.

44 *Grip*, 30 October 1886. Ramsay Cook has argued that Bengough was a Protestant moral reformer who was open to various religious prescriptions for society's ills (Cook, *The Regenerators*, 123–51).

45 Clark, *Of Toronto the Good: A Social Study*, 172. Throughout his book, Clark made numerous criticisms of Christianity and Canadian clergymen, such as his statement that "all kinds of chicanery and infidelity are practised by the leaders under the cloak of ecclesiastical and religious duty" (164).

46 Morgan, *The Canadian Men and Women of the Time*, 1016.
   Shenstone was a prominent manufacturer and president of the Canada Cycle and Motor Company. These ministers are designated "conservative evangelicals" to make the point they were not progressives.
47 Reverend Thomas Hyde, Biographical Drawer 42, MBIA.
48 *TW*, 17 January 1906.
49 *TDS*, 29 January 1906. *NE*, on 2 February, reported that "about 1600"
   converts had assembled at the Cooke's Presbyterian Church alone.
   Conversions reported in *TDS* for the Torrey-Alexander Campaign in
   January 1906:

DECEMBER			
31 (Sunday)	46		
JANUARY			
1	54	15	97
2	47	16	69
3	5	17	97
4	48	18	77
5	34	19 (Children's and evening)	372
7 (Sunday)	207	21 (Student's and Men's)	181
8	57	22	107
9	88	23	138
10	72	24	76
11	75	26	127
12	775	27	154
14 (Sunday)	218	28 (Sunday)	764
Total	4,413		

Source: Toronto *Daily Star*, 29 Jan. 1906.

50 J.B. Kennedy, "Evangelists and Evangelism," *CB*, 25 April 1907. Arthur
   Brown, ibid., 16 May 1907, wrote a letter in defence of Torrey.
51 Memberships before and after Torrey's January 1906 Toronto
   Campaign:

	1903	1904	1905	1906	1907	1908
Metropolitan Methodist	807	841	1,018	1,159	1,210	1,193
Cooke's Presbyterian	1,104	1,225	1,283	1,442	1,446	1,090
Jarvis Street Baptist	920	879	1,006	1,044	1,047	1,058
Toronto District (Meth.)	17,205	17,718	19,153	20,892	21,942	23,299
Presbytery of Toronto	19,256	20,799	21,825	24,053	25,573	26,297

Source: Methodist Minutes, 1903–08, UCA; *Baptist Year Book*, 1903–08, MDA;
Presbyterian Acts, 1903–08, QUSL.

52 *Citizen*, 11 June, 1906.

53 *OEJ*, 21 June 1906; W.S. Jacoby, drawer 42, MBIA.

54 Alexander to A.P. Fitt, n.d., Charles Alexander, drawer 34, MBIA.

55 *OEJ*, 30 June 1906. In the 18 June 1906 issue, it was recorded that 7,000 children at the meeting was a conservative estimate.

56 Ibid., 29 June 1906.

57 Methodists: 1904/5,603, 1905/5,784, 1906/6, 032, 1907/6,055. Presbyterians: 1904/7,245, 1905/7,672, 1906/8,072, 1907/8,542. *Methodist Minutes*, 1904–07, UCA; *Presbyterian Acts*, 1904–07, QUSL.

58 "Torrey Revival Has Closed with about 800 Conversions," *DG*, 13 June 1910; *Minutes of the NB and PEI Conference*, 13, UCA.

59 Memberships before and after Torrey's 1910 Fredericton campaign:

	1907	1908	1909	1910	1911	1912
St Paul's (Presbyterian) Fredericton	237	221	240	323	331	333
Methodist	335	345	340	465	392	404
Presbytery of St John	5,797	5,947	5,998	6,446	6,401	6,413
Fredericton District (Meth).	1,813	1,836	1,796	1,879	1,770	1,763

Source: Methodist Minutes, 190–12, UCA; *Presbyterian Acts*, 1907–12, QUSL.

60 *Fredericton City Directory*.

61 MC225, MS11 A2, St Paul's Communion Registrar, March 1889 to October 1913, PANB.

62 "Dr. Torrey, in Able Sermon, Declares Hell Is Certain," *DT*, 23 November 1910; "More Than 7,000 Heard Torrey Yesterday, ibid., 14 November 1910; "Dr. Torrey Closes Mission of Month," *Standard*, 5 December 1910.

63 "News of the Churches," *SJG*, 14 November 1910.

64 *Maritime Baptist*, 15 February 1911.

65 Fraser, *The Social Uplifters*.

66 MFP, 11 November 1907. According to one journalist, "the head of the procession was away out of sight and hearing before the rear half of the multitude could fall into line."

67 *Voice*, 1 November 1907.

68 Ibid., 3 January 1908.

69 *Presbyterian Church in Canada, Acts and Proceedings of the General Assembly*, 1908–14, QUSL.

70 *Presbyterian*, 19 January 1911.

71 Memberships three years before and after Chapman's 1911 Toronto Campaign (of the churches where simultaneous meetings were held):

	1908	1909	1910	1911	1912	1913	1914
METHODIST CHURCHES							
Central	696	765	805	799	825	758	752
Euclid	578	550	540	535	467	482	553
Wesley	1,180	1,200	1,185	1,311	1,347	1,430	1,167
Westmoreland	624	699	785	880	920	935	880
PRESBYTERIAN CHURCHES							
Parkdale	1,203	1,249	1,266	1,402	1,485	1,600	1,605
St John's	738	804	852	939	977	1,003	1,109
Victoria	816	819	909	1,000	1,108	1,205	1,250
BAPTIST CHURCHES							
College Street	767	826	799	869	914	847	700
East Toronto	115	125	121	136	144	148	160
Jarvis Street	1,058	1,069	1,003	1,055	1,105	1,367	1,397
Walmer Road	869	927	1,043	1,075	1,167	1,256	1,277

Source: Methodist Minutes, 1908–14, UCA; Baptist Year Book, 1908–14, MDA; Presbyterian Acts, 1908–14, QUSL.

72 Membership three years before and after Chapman's 1911 Toronto campaign (Presbytery of Toronto and Toronto District)

	1908	1909	1910	1911	1912	1913	1914
Presbytery of Toronto	26,297	26,587	28,847	30,566	32,067	33,860	35,067
Toronto District (Meth.)	23,277	24,229	24,856	25,494	26,887	28,199	29,701

Source: Methodist Minutes, 1908–14, UCA; Presbyterian Acts, 1908–14, QUSL.

73 Piva, The Condition of the Working Class in Toronto, 1900–1921, 15.

74 Ibid., 69–70.

75 "Pray for Canada," the Wesleyan, 17 January 1906.

76 "Religious Campaign for Halifax," HH, 2 February 1911.

77 Cook, The Regenerators; Marshall, Secularizing the Faith; Airhart, Serving the Present Age; Gauvreau, The Evangelical Century.

78 TW, 29 January 1906.

79 On opponents pressing "theists" to surrender their influence, see Smith, The Seeds of Secularization, 2–3.

80 Charles Gordon Papers, box 17, folder 6, Torrey to Gordon, 28 May, 1906, UMA. Other Torrey correspondence shows the evangelist to be uncompromising on relatively petty issues.

81 "Torrey Mission Leaders Give Campaign Details," Standard, 14 November 1910.

82 A letter to E.G. Chapman from Gordon caused the former to consider not assisting with the Kootenay meetings at all. Gordon Papers, telegram from E.G. Chapman to Gordon, 27 February 1909, UMA: "Great disappointed and chagrined your letter twenty third I will be very glad to be relieved of the responsibility and necessity of the Kootenay work which I was undertaking at great personal cost and wholly without compensation except that received in the work." Gordon was dissatisfied with the selection of Mr D.S. Toy, Mr James O. Buswell, and Dr Frank Granstaff. J. William Chapman to Gordon, 24 February 1909; E.G. Chapman to Gordon, 26, 27, 28 February and 6 March 1909; E.G. Chapman to Reverend J.G. Shearer, 27 February 1909.

83 Ibid., Letter from Chapman to Reverend J.G. Shearer, 5 March, 1909.

84 Moir, "The Canadian Baptist and the Social Gospel Movement, 1879–1914," 155.

85 Burkinshaw, *Pilgrims in Lotus Land*, 49.

86 Airhart, *Serving the Present Age*, 130, 132.

87 Quoted in Martin, "Billy Sunday and Christian Manliness," 815.

88 Dynes, "Billy Sunday in New York," CG, 13 June 1917. Gordon Thompson believed that one of Sunday's strengths was that he had "a good strong temper" in an era when "very few preachers ... get really mad about anything" (Thompson, "Billy Sunday and New York," ibid., 4 July 1917).

89 Sinclair-Faulkner, "Theory Divided from Practice," 323–5.

90 Marks, *Revivals and Roller Rinks*; Christie and Gauvreau, *The Full-Orbed Christianity*. On Marks's spirited defence of the place of religion in Canadian labour and social history, see Marks, "Heroes and Hallelujahs," 169–86

91 Palmer, however, disagrees with Marks's claim that there was a strong connection between the Knights of Labor and the Salvation Army. See Palmer, "Historiographic Hassles," 133.

92 "The Church and the Working Class," *Eastern Labor News (ELN)*, 1 February 1913.

93 "The Church and the Working Class," ELN, 1 February 1913.

94 "A House Divided," ibid., 15 May 1909.

95 For a sample, see "Labor and the Church," *Saskatchewan's Labor Realm*, 16 August 1907; "Labor's Champion," *Tribune*, 10 February 1906; "In Pulpit and Platform," *Voice*, 27 September 1907; "Christianity," ELN, 9 October 1909.

96 "Protest and Appeal," *Western Clarion*, 27 March 1909.

97 Marshall, *Secularizing the Faith*, 3.

98 "Churchless People in Our Cities and Towns," *Wesleyan*, 3 January 1912.

99 "The Christianization of Christianity," ibid., 22 May 1901.

100 *VDC*, 4 November 1888.

101 Bland, *James Henderson*, 327–31.

102 *OP*, 8 October 1908; *BDE*, 1 October 1908. A serious problem, according to Chapman, was that the Hamilton committee's failure to make adequate preparations, especially the organization of prayer meetings to be held before the arrival of the evangelists. Each side was "not slow in placing the responsibility on the other side."

103 Baskerville, "Did Religion Matter?" 74.

104 On social status, Steve Bruce uses the terms poor and the wealthy. See Bruce, "Born Again," 109.

105 Before the 1894 Hamilton campaign, Moody stated: "I do not know how much I am to get. I will get just what they give me; there is no stipulated amount." See "Evangelist Moody Arrives," *HS*, 26 November 1894.

106 Victoria *Daily Colonist* (*VDC*), 6 November 1888.

107 "Large Attendance – Sudden Conversion, One Thousand Dollars Wanted," *MDS*, 15 October 1887.

108 See "Preparing for Moody," The *Globe*, 3 November 1894; "The Subscription List," *TM*, 6 November 1894; "Moody Subscription Lists," ibid., 16 November 1894.

109 *HS*, 26 November 1894.

110 "Six Hundred Souls," The *Globe*, 20 October 1886. Also, *PL*, 13 November 1886.

111 "Revival Committee Would Welcome Cash," *TDS*, 23 January 1906.

112 *NE*, 2 February 1906.

113 *Citizen*, 30 June 1906.

114 "Appeal for Funds for Evangelists," *MFP*, 8 November 1907.

115 "Short of Cash in Evangelism," *TDS*, 1 February 1911.

116 *SJG*, 12 November 1910.

117 Johnson, *A Shopkeeper's Millennium*. Tucker, "Class and Culture in Recent Anglo-American Religious Historiography," 161.

118 For Emery, one's definition of secularization is crucial. He upholds the evolutionist interpretation because it fits his understanding of how tradition works. For more, see Emery, *The Methodist Church on the Prairies*, xvii–xix.

119 Marshall, *Secularizing the Faith*.
120 Abrams, *Selling Old-Time Religion*.
121 Marshall, *Secularizing the Faith*, 71.
122 On the American experience, see Gilbert, *Perfect Cities*, 181.

CONLUSION

1 MDS, 21 October 1887.
2 "The Air Was Filled with Religious Fire," TDS, 22 January 1906.
3 Christie and Gauvreau, *The Full-Orbed Christianity, 1900-1940*.
    Christie and Gauvreau, "'The World of the Common Man Is Filled
    with Religious Fervour.'" Also, see Knowles, "Christ in the
    Crowsnest."
4 Christie and Gauvreau, *The Full-Orbed Christianity*, 63.
5 "Saloons Needs Attention," TDS, 30 January 1911.

Bibliography

ABBREVIATIONS

Archives

AO   Archives of Ontario
BGCA   Billy Graham Center Archives
MBIA   Moody Bible Institute Archives
MDA   McMaster Divinity Archives
PANB   Provincial Archives of New Brunswick
QUSL   Queen's University, Stauffer Library
RHPL   Richmond Hill Public Library
UCA   United Church Archives
UGL   University of Georgia Libraries
UMA   University of Manitoba Archives

Newspapers

BC   Brantford *Courier*
BDE   Brantford *Daily Expositer*
BW   [Kingston] *British Whig*
CB   *Canadian Baptist*
CC   *Canadian Congregationalist*
CCM   *Canadian Churchman*
CG   *Christian Guardian*
CMM   *Canadian Methodist Magazine*
CT   Chicago *Tribune*

DC   *Dominion Churchman*
DFP   [Ottawa] *Daily Free Press*
DG   [Fredericton] *Daily Gleaner*
DME   [Toronto] *Daily Mail and Empire*
DN   [Kingston] *Daily News*
DNA   [Vancouver] *Daily News Advertiser*
DP   [Vancouver] *Daily Province*

DT	[Saint John] *Daily Telegraph*	ODFP	Ottawa *Daily Free Press*
DW	[Kingston] *Daily Whig*	OEJ	Ottawa *Evening Journal*
EC	*Evangelical Churchman*	OFP	Ottawa *Free Press*
EJ	[Ottawa] *Evening Journal*	OP	Orillia *Packet*
ELN	*Eastern Labour News*	OSA	Owen Sound *Advertiser*
EN	[Toronto] *Evening News*	OT	Orillia *Times*
ET	[Toronto] *Evening Telegram*	PL	*Palladium of Labour*
GR	Galt *Reporter*	PR	*Presbyterian Record*
HDS	Hamilton *Daily Spectator*	SJG	Saint John *Globe*
HH	Halifax *Herald*	ST	[Paris] *Star Transcript*
HS	Hamilton *Spectator*	TDS	Toronto *Daily Star*
LA	London *Advertiser*	TEN	Toronto *Evening News*
MDS	Montreal *Daily Star*	TM	Toronto *Mail*
ME	*Mail and Empire*	TN	Toronto *News*
MFP	*Manitoba Free Press*	TSN	Toronto *Saturday Night*
MG	Montreal *Gazette*	TW	Toronto *World*
NE	Newmarket *Era*	VDC	Victoria *Daily Colonist*
NYT	New York *Times*	VW	Vancouver *World*

PRIMARY SOURCES

Archives

ARCHIVES OF ONTARIO, TORONTO, ONT.
YWCA Club Minutes, 1902–1907
YWCA Minutes, 1897–1918

BILLY GRAHAM CENTER ARCHIVES, WHEATON COLLEGE, ILL.
Collection 77 John Wilbur Chapman Papers
Collection 197 Virginia Asher Papers
Collection 322 Oswald Smith Papers

MCMASTER DIVINITY ARCHIVES, HAMILTON, ONT.
Baptist Year Book, 1884–1914

Biographical Files

Peter S. Campbell

Jones Hughes Farmer
J.D. Freeman
Jesse Gibson
Joseph Leeming Gilmour
Elmore Harris
Charles Widden King
Herbert Fenwick Laflamme
C.E. MacLeod
Henry Francis Perry
Charles H. Schutt
A.T. Sowerby
Albert George Upham
Thomas Urquhart

MOODY BIBLE INSTITUTE ARCHIVES, CHICAGO
D. L. Moody Papers
Charles Alexander Letters
J. Wilbur Chapman Letters
Rev. Thomas B. Hyde Biographical Material
W.S. Jacoby Biographical Material
Moody and Sankey Folder
Reuben Torrey Letters 1905–6, 1907–8;
Reuben Torrey "Writings By"
Letters Concerning Torrey-Alexander;
Melvin Trotter Biographical Material
Sam Jones Biographical File

PROVINCIAL ARCHIVES OF NEW BRUNSWICK
St Paul's Communion Registrar

RICHMOND HILL PUBLIC LIBRARY, LOCAL HISTORY ROOM,
RICHMOND HILL, ONT.
Lecture Broadsides Scrapbook

UNITED CHURCH ARCHIVES, TORONTO.
Methodist Minutes of Conferences, 1884–1914

Biographical Files

Rev. T.E. Bartley

Rev. George Brown
Rev. John Fitzpatrick
Rev. John F. German
Rev. W.E. Hassard
Rev. William Hincks
Rev. Charles Johnston
John Thomas Morris
Rev. Edwin A. Pearson
Rev. Marmaduke L. Pearson
Rev. James A. Rankin
Rev. John V. Smith
Rev. William F. Wilson

Personal Papers

Salem Bland
D.J. Macdonnel

UNIVERSITY OF GEORGIA LIBRARIES, SPECIAL COLLECTIONS
DIVISION, ATHENS, GA.
Sam Jones Papers

UNIVERSITY OF MANITOBA ARCHIVES, WINNIPEG.
Charles W. Gordon Papers

WYCLIFFE COLLEGE ARCHIVES, TORONTO.
O'Meara Papers, 1910–11

Newspapers and Periodicals

Aurora *Banner,* 1906
Baltimore *American,* 1886
Brantford *Courier,* 1897, 1908
Brantford *Expositor,* 1897, 1908
Burlington *Free Press and Times,* 1908
Busy Man's Magazine, 1905–06
Canada Christian Advocate, 1875, 1877
Canadian Baptist, 1887, 1890, 1894, 1897, 1905–06, 1911
Canadian Churchman, 1886, 1890, 1894, 1905–11
Canadian Congregationalist, 1911
Canadian Independent, 1886

Canadian Methodist Magazine, 1885–1906
Canadian Methodist Review, 1895
Canadian Statesman (Bowmanville), 1894
Canadian White Ribbon Tidings, 1906–1909
Catholic Register, 1906
Chatham *Banner-News*, 1901
Christian Guardian, 1884–87, 1894–97, 1905–11
Chicago *Tribune*, 1886
Citizen (Ottawa), 1906
Congregationalist and Canadian Independent, 1894, 1897
Daily Colonist (Victoria), 1888
Daily Examiner (Peterborough), 1897
Daily Free Press (London), 1887, 1890
Daily Gleaner (Fredericton), 1910
Daily News (Kingston), 1887
Daily News-Advertiser (Vancouver), 1888
Daily Province (Vancouver), 1909
Daily Telegraph (Saint John), 1910
Daily Whig (Kingston), 1887, 1897
Eastern Labor News, 1909, 1913
Evangelical Churchman, 1884–1897
Evening Journal (Ottawa), 1897, 1906
Evening Telegram (Toronto), 1886–87, 1908, 1911
Galt *Reporter*, 1887
Gazette (Montreal), 1887, 1907
Globe (Toronto), 1884, 1886, 1887, 1894, 1897, 1906, 1911
Grip (Toronto), 1886–87
Halifax *Herald*, 1911
Hamilton *Daily Spectator*, 1887, 1894
Hanover *Post*, 1911
Irish Canadian, 1884–86
London *Advertiser*, 1887, 1890
Mail and Empire (Toronto), 1906
Mainland Guardian (Vancouver), 1888
Manitoba Free Press, 1897, 1907, 1909
Maritime Baptist, 1911
Methodist Recorder, 1899–1900
Montreal *Daily Star*, 1886–87, 1897–98, 1907
Morning Leader (Regina), 1909
Nation, 1876

Newmarket *Era*, 1906
News (Toronto), 1884, 1886–87, 1894, 1906, 1908, 1911
New York *Times*, 1875
Northern Advance (Barrie), 1908
Orillia *Packet*, 1908
Orilla *Times*, 1908
Ottawa *Free Press*, 1897
Owen Sound *Advertiser*, 1906
Owen Sound *Sun*, 1906
Owen Sound *Times*, 1911
Paisley *Advocate*, 1906
Palladium of Labor, 1884, 1886
Presbyterian, 1905–11
Presbyterian Record, 1884–87, 1891, 1893–97, 1900, 1903, 1906–09
Presbyterian Witness, 1906, 1911
Review (Portage la Prairie), 1907
Saint John *Globe*, 1910
Saint John *Telegraph*, 1910
Saskatchewan's Labor Realm, 1907
Standard (Ridgetown, Ont.), 1889
Star-Transcript (Paris), 1908
Stratford *Beacon*, 1887
Toronto *Daily Mail*, 1884, 1886–87, 1894, 1897, 1911
Toronto *Daily Star*, 1906, 1908, 1911
Toronto *Saturday Night*, 1906
Toronto *World*, 1884, 1886–87, 1894, 1906
Tribune (Toronto),1906
Vancouver *World*, 1909
Voice (Winnipeg), 1907
War Cry, 1886–1911
Week (Toronto), 1884, 1886
Weekly Herald (Calgary), 1908–09
Weekly News-Advertiser (Vancouver), 1909
Weekly Review (Portage la Prairie), 1907
Wesleyan, 1901, 1906, 1910–11
Western Clarion (Vancouver), 1909–11
Western Sun, 1897
Westminster, 1896–97, 1906–11

Printed Primary Sources

Alexander, Helen C., J. Kennedy Maclean. *Charles M. Alexander: A Romance of Song and Soul-Winning*. London: Marshall Brothers 1920.

Bland, Salem. *James Henderson, D.D*. Toronto: McClelland and Stewart 1926.

Chapman, J. Wilbur. *Awakening Sermons*. New York: Fleming H. Revell 1922.

– *The Ivory Palaces of the King*. Chicago: Fleming H. Revell 1893.

– *Revival Sermons*. New York: Fleming H. Revell 1911.

Clark, C.S. *Of Toronto the Good, a Social Study: The Queen City of Canada As It Is*. Montreal: Toronto Publishing 1898.

Conrad, Rev. Arcturus, ed. *Boston's Awakening: A Complete Account of the Great Boston Revival under the Leadership of J. Wilbur Chapman and Charles M. Alexander*. Boston: King's Business Publishing Company, 1909.

Daniels, W.H., ed. *Moody: His Words, Work and Workers*. New York: Nelson and Phillips 1877.

Davenport, Frederick Morgan. *Primitive Traits in Religious Revivals: A Study in Mental and Social Evolution*. New York: Macmillan 1905.

Davis, George T.B. *Torrey and Alexander: The Story of a World-Wide Revival*. New York: Fleming H. Revell 1905.

– *Twice around the World with Alexander: Prince of Gospel Singers*. New York: *Christian Herald* 1907.

Finney, Charles Grandison. *Lectures on Revivals of Religion*. Cambridge, Mass.: Belknap Press of Harvard University Press 1960.

Fredericton City Directory. Fredericton: H.M. McAlpine Directory 1910.

Grant, Rev. G.M. "Laon on Messrs. Moody and Sankey and Revivalism." *Canadian Monthly*, 8 September 1875.

Jackson, Samuel N. *A Hand-Book of Congregationalism*. Toronto: Congregational Publishing 1894.

Jones, Laura. *The Life and Sayings of Sam P. Jones*. Atlanta: Franklin-Turner 1907.

– *Sam Jones and Sam Small in Toronto: A Compilation of the Best Sermons Preached by Rev. Sam Jones and Rev. Sam Small at the Great Revival in Toronto, as Reported in the Columns of the Globe, together with Short Sketches of Their Lives*. Toronto: Rose Publishing 1886.

Laon. "Messrs. Moody and Sankey and Revivalism." *Canadian Monthly*, 7 June 1875.

Moody, William R. *The Life of Dwight L. Moody*. Chicago: Fleming Revell 1900.

Morgan, Henry James. *The Canadian Men and Women of the Time*. Toronto: William Briggs 1912.

Morrow, Abbie Clemens. *Best Thoughts and Discourses of D.L. Moody*. Toronto: J.B. Magurn 1876.

Ottman, Ford C. *J. Wilbur Chapman: A Biography*. Garden City, N.J.: Doubleday, Page 1920.

Sankey, Ira D. *Sacred Songs and Solos: Twelve Hundred Hymns*. London: Marshall, Morgan and Scott, n.d.

Smith, George Adam. *The Life of Henry Drummond*. Toronto: Fleming H. Revell 1899.

Torrey, R.A. "The Bible Teaching regarding Future Punishment." In Reuben Torrey, ed., *The Higher Criticism and the New Theology*. New York: Gospel Publishing House 1911.

Watson, A.D. "The Psychology of Revivals." *Canadian Methodist Review*, vol. 7, no. 5 (September-October 1895).

Youman, Harriet. *Grimsby Park: Historical and Descriptive with Biographical Sketches of the Late President Noah Phelps and Others*. Toronto: William Briggs 1900.

Secondary Sources

Abrams, Douglas Carl. *Selling Old-Time Religion: American Fundamentalists and Mass Culture, 1920–1940*. Athens, Ga.: University of Georgia Press 2001.

Adair, James R. The Old Lighthouse: The Story of the Pacific Garden Mission. Chicago: Moody Press 1966.

Airhart, Phyllis. "Ordering a New Nation and Reordering Protestantism, 1867–1914." In George Rawlyk, ed. *The Protestant Experience 1760–1990*. Burlington, Ont.: Welch Publishing 1990.

– *Serving the Present Age: Revivalism, Progressivism and the Methodist Tradition*. Montreal and Kingston: McGill-Queen's University Press 1992.

Allen, Richard. "Salem Bland: The Young Preacher." *Bulletin (Committee on Archives of the United Church of Canada)*, no. 26 (1977): 75–93.

– *The Social Passion: Religion and Social Reform in Canada, 1914–1928*. Toronto: University of Toronto Press 1971.

Almond, Philip C. *Heaven and Hell in Enlightenment England*. Cambridge, U.K.: Cambridge University Press 1994.

Artibise, Alan, ed. *Gateway City: Documents on the City of Winnipeg, 1873–1913*. Winnipeg: University of Manitoba Press 1979.

Baskerville, Peter. "Did Religion Matter? Religion and Wealth in Urban Canada at the Turn of the Twentieth Century: An Exploratory Study." *Histoire sociale/Social History*, vol. 34, no. 67 (May 2001): 61–96.

Beckert, Sven. *The Monied Metropolis: New York City and the Consolidation of the American Bourgeoisie, 1850–1896*. Cambridge, U.K.: Cambridge University Press 2001.

Bendroth, Margaret Lamberts. *Fundamentalism & Gender, 1875 to the Present*. New Haven, Conn.: Yale University Press 1993.

– "Men, Masculinity, and Urban Revivalism: J. Wilbur Chapman's Boston Crusade, 1909." *Journal of Presbyterian History* vol. 75, no. 4 (winter 1997): 235–46.

Bliss, J. Michael. *A Canadian Millionaire: The Life and Times of Sir Joseph Flavelle, Bart. 1858–1939*. Toronto: Macmillan 1978.

– *Plague: A Story of Small-pox in Montreal*. Toronto: Harper Collins Publishers 1991.

Blumhofer, Edith. *Restoring the Faith: The Assemblies of God, Pentecostalism, and American Culture*. Chicago: University of Illinois Press 1993.

Blumhofer, Edith, and Randall Balmer, ed. *Modern Christian Revivals*. Chicago: University of Illinois Press 1993.

Boone, Kathleen C. *The Bible Tells Them So: The Discourse of Protestant Fundamentalism*. Albany, N.Y.: State University of New York Press 1989.

Boyer, Paul. *Urban Masses and Moral Order in America, 1820–1920*. Cambridge, Mass.: Harvard University Press 1978.

Bradford, Gamaliel. *D.L. Moody: A Worker in Souls*. New York: Doubleday, Doran 1928.

Brereton, Virginia. *From Sin to Salvation: Stories of Women's Conversions, 1800 to the Present*. Bloomington, Ind.: Indiana University Press 1991.

– *Training God's Army: The American Bible School, 1880–1940*. Bloomington, Ind.: Indiana University Press 1990.

Brouwer, Ruth Compton. "The Canadian Methodist Church and Ecclesiastical Suffrage for Women, 1902–1914." *Canadian Methodist Historical Society Papers*, vol. 2, n.d.

Bruce, Steve. "Born Again: Conversion, Crusades and Brainwashing." *Scottish Journal of Religious Studies* vol. 3, no. 2 (autumn 1982): 107–23.

Burkinshaw, Robert K. *Pilgrims in Lotus Land: Conservative Protestantism in British Columbia*. Montreal and Kingston: McGill-Queen's University Press 1995.

Bush, Peter George. "James Caughey, Phoebe and Walter Palmer and the Methodist' Revival Experience in Canada West, 1850–1858." MA thesis, Queen's University 1985.

Caldwell, Thekla Ellen Joiner. "Women, Men and Revival: The Third Awakening in Chicago." PHD thesis, University of Illinois 1991.

Christie, Nancy, and Michael Gauvreau. *The Full-Orbed Christianity: The Protestant Churches and Social Welfare in Canada, 1900–1940*. Montreal and Kingston: McGill-Queen's University Press 1996.

– "'The World of the Common Man Is Filled with Religious Fervour': The Labouring People of Winnipeg and the Persistence of Revivalism, 1914–1925." In George Rawlyk, ed., *Aspects of Canadian Evangelicalism*. Montreal and Kingston: McGill-Queen's University Press 1997.

Clark, S.D. *Church and Sect in Canada*. Toronto: University of Toronto Press 1948.

Clarke, Brian. *Piety and Nationalism: Lay Voluntary Association and the Creation of an Irish-Catholic Community in Toronto, 1850–1895*. Montreal and Kingston: McGill-Queen's University Press 1993.

– "Religion and Public Space in Protestant Toronto, 1880–1900." In Marguerite Van Die, ed. *Religion and Public Life in Canada: Historical and Comparative Perspectives*. Toronto: University of Toronto Press 2001.

Cook, Ramsay. *The Regenerators: Social Criticism in Late Victorian English Canada*. Toronto: University of Toronto Press 1985.

Cook, Sharon Anne. "Evangelical Moral Reform: Women and the War against Tobacco, 1874–1900." In Marguerite Van Die, ed., *Religion and Public Life in Canada: Historical and Comparative Perspectives*. Toronto: University of Toronto Press 2001.

– *"Through Sunshine and Shadow": The Woman's Christian Temperance Union, Evangelicalism, and Reform in Ontario, 1874–1930*. Montreal and Kingston: McGill-Queen's University Press 1995.

Costigliola, Frank. "The Creation of Memory and Myth: Stalin's 1946 Election Speech and the Soviet Threat." In Martin J. Medhurst and H.W. Brands, ed. *Critical Reflections on the Cold War: Linking Rhetoric and History*. College Station, Texas: Texas A & M University Press 2000.

Crouse, Eric. "American Revivalists, the Press, and Popular Religion in Canada, 1884–1914." PHD thesis, Queen's University 1996.

- "Great Expectations: J.Wilbur Chapman, Presbyterians, and Other Protestants in Early Twentieth-Century Canada." *Journal of Presbyterian History*, vol. 78, no. 2 (summer 2000): 155–167.
- "'The Great Revival': Evangelical Revivalism, Methodism, and Bourgeois Order in Early Calgary." *Alberta History*, vol. 27, no. 1 (winter 1999): 18–23.
- "Methodist Encounters: Confronting the Western and Urban Frontiers of 19th-Century America." *Methodist History*, vol. 40, no. 3 (April 2002): 157–67.
- "Revivalism for the Working Class? American Methodist Evangelists in Late-Nineteenth-Century Urban Ontario." *Ontario History*, vol. 91, no. 1 (spring 1999): 21–37.
- "They 'Left Us Pretty Much as We Were': American Saloon/Factory Evangelists and Canadian Working Men in the Early-Twentieth Century." In Bruce L. Guenter, ed., *Historical Papers 1999*. Canadian Society of Church History 2000 51–71.
DeBerg, B.A. *UnGodly Women: Gender and the First Wave of American Fundamentalism*. Minneapolis, Minn.: Fortress Press 1990.
Denning, Michael. *The Cultural Front: The Laboring of American Culture in the Twentieth Century*. New York: Verso 1996.
Dorsett, Lyle W. *Billy Sunday and the Redemption of Urban America*. Grand Rapids, Mich.: William Eerdmans 1991.
- *A Passion for Souls: The Life of D.L. Moody*. Chicago: Moody Press 1997.
Douglas, Ann. *The Feminization of American Culture*. New York: Doubleday 1977.
Dunaway, David King. "Music as Political Communication in the United States." In James Lull, ed., *Popular Music and Communication*. California: Sage Publications 1987.
Ellis, Walter E. "Gilboa to Ichabod: Social and Religious Factors in the Fundamentalist-Modernist Schisms among Canadian Baptists, 1895–1934." *Foundations* vol. 20 (1977): 16–41.
Emery, George. *The Methodist Church on the Prairies, 1896–1914*. Montreal and Kingston: McGill-Queen's University Press 2001.
Evensen, Bruce J. "'Expecting a Blessing of Unusual Magnitude': Moody, Mass Media, and Gilded Age Revival." *Journalism History* vol. 24, no. 1 (spring 1998): 26–36.
- "'It Is a Marvel to Many People': Dwight L. Moody, Mass Media, and the New England Revival of 1877." *New England Quarterly*, vol. 72, no. 2 (June 1999): 251–74.

Findlay, James Jr. *Dwight L. Moody: American Evangelist, 1837–1899*. Chicago: University of Chicago Press 1969.

Forbes, David Bruce, and Jeffrey H. Mahan, ed. *Religion and Popular Culture in America*. Berkeley, Calif.: University of California Press 2000.

Frank, Douglas. *Less Than Conquerors: How Evangelicals Entered the Twentieth Century*. Grand Rapids, Mich.: Eerdmans 1986.

Fraser, Brian J. *Church, College, and Clergy: A History of Theological Education at Knox College, Toronto, 1844–1994*. Montreal and Kingston: McGill-Queen's University Press 1995.

– *The Social Uplifters: Presbyterian Progressives and the Social Gospel in Canada, 1875–1915*. Waterloo, Ont.: Canadian Corporation for Studies in Religion 1988.

Freeman, Joshua, et al. *Who Built America? Working People and the Nation's Economy, Politics, Culture, and Society*. Vol. 2. New York: Pantheon Books 1992.

French, Goldwin. "The Evangelical Creed in Canada." In W.L. Morton, ed., *The Shields of Achilles: Aspects of Canada in the Victorian Age*. Toronto: McClelland and Stewart 1968.

Gauvreau, Michael. *The Evangelical Century: College and Creed in English Canada From the Great Revival to the Great Depression*. Montreal and Kingston: McGill-Queen's University Press 1991.

– "Beyond the Half-Way House: Evangelicalism and the Shaping of English Canadian Culture." *Acadiensis*, vol. 20 (1990/91): 158–177.

Gilbert, James. *Perfect Cities: Chicago's Utopias of 1893*. Chicago: University of Chicago Press 1991.

Gilling, Bryan D. "Revivalism as Renewal: J. Wilbur Chapman in New Zealand, 1912–1913." *American Presbyterians*, vol. 70 (summer 1992): 81–92.

Grant, John W. *The Church in the Canadian Era: The First Century of Confederation*. Toronto: McGraw-Hill Ryerson Ltd., 1972.

– *A Profusion of Spires: Religion in Nineteenth-Century Ontario*. Toronto: University of Toronto Press 1988.

Hall, Peter Dobkin. "Moving Targets: Evangelicalism and the Transformation of American Economic Life, 1870–1920." In Larry Eskridge and Mark A. Noll, ed., *More Money, More Ministry: Money and Evangelicals in Recent North American History*. Grand Rapids, Mich.: William B. Eerdmans 2000.

Hambrick-Stowe, Charles E. "'Sanctified Business': Historical Perspectives on Financing Revivals of Religion." In Larry Eskridge and Mark A.

Noll, ed., *More Money, More Ministry: Money and Evangelicals in Recent North American History*. Grand Rapids, Mich.: William B. Eerdmans 2000.

Hardesty, Nancy. *Women Called to Witness: Evangelical Feminism in the 19th Century*. Nashville, Tenn.: Abingdon Press 1984.

Hatch, Nathan O. *The Democratization of American Christianity*. New Haven, Conn.: Yale University Press 1989.

Heinrichs, Timothy Jacob. "The Last Great Awakening: The Revival of 1905 and Progressivism." PHD thesis, University of Washington 1991.

Hogg, Michael A., and Dominic Abrams. *Social Identifications: A Social Psychology of Intergroup Relations and Group Processes*. London: Routledge 1988.

Hutchison, William R. *The Modernist Impulse in American Protestantism*. Cambridge, Mass.: Harvard University Press 1976.

Johnson, Paul. *A Shopkeeper's Millennium: Society and Revivals in Rochester, New York, 1815–1837*. New York: Hill and Wang 1978.

Johnston, Charles M. *McMaster University: Volume 1 / The Toronto Years*. Toronto: University of Toronto Press 1976.

Johnstone, Barbara. *Discourse Analysis*. Malden, Mass: Blackwell, 2002,

Katerberg, William H. *Modernity and the Dilemma of North American Anglican Identities, 1880–1950*. Montreal and Kingston: McGill-Queen's University Press 2001.

Kealey, Gregory. *Toronto Workers Respond to Industrial Capitalism, 1867–1892*. Toronto: University of Toronto Press 1991.

Kealey, Gregory S., and Bryan D. Palmer. *Dreaming of What Might Be: The Knights of Labor in Ontario, 1880–1900*. Toronto: New Hogtown Press 1987.

Kee, Kevin. "Heavenly Railroad: Ernest Crossley, John Hunter and Canadian Methodist Revivalism, 1884–1910." MA thesis, Queen's University 1994.

– "Revivalism: The Marketing of Protestant Religion in English-Speaking Canada, with Particular Reference to Southern Ontario, 1884–1957." PHD thesis, Queen's University 1999.

Kiesler, Charles A., and Sara B. Kiesler. *Conformity*. Reading, Mass.: Addison-Wesley 1969.

Knowles, Norman. "Christ in the Crowsnest: Religion and the Anglo-Protestant Working Class in the Crowsnest Pass, 1898–1918." In Michael D. Behiels and Marcel Martel, ed., *Nation, Ideas, Identities: Essays in Honour of Ramsey Cook*. Toronto: Oxford University Press 2000.

Lakoff, George, and Mark Johnson. *Metaphors We Live By*. Chicago:
   University of Chicago Press 1980.
Long, Kathryn Teresa. *The Revival of 1857–58: Interpreting an American
   Religious Awakening*. New York: Oxford University Press 1998.
Lumsden, Ian, ed. *Close the 49th Parallel etc: The Americanization of
   Canada*. Toronto: University of Toronto Press 1970.
Mack, Barry. "From Preaching to Propaganda to Marginalization: The
   Lost Centre of Twentieth-Century Presbyterianism." In George Rawlyk,
   ed., *The Evangelical Impulse: Aspects of Canadian Evangelicalism*.
   Montreal and Kingston: McGill-Queen's University Press 1997.
Magney, William. "The Methodist Church and the National Gospel,
   1884–1914." *The Bulletin*, no. 20 (1968): 3–95.
Maldonado, Luis. "Popular Religion: Dimensions, Levels & Types." In
   Norbert Greinacker and Norbert Mette, ed. *Popular Religion*.
   Edinburg: T. & T. Clark 1986.
Marks, Lynne. "Heroes and Hallelujahs - Labour History and the Social
   History of Religion in English Canada: A Response to Bryan Palmer."
   Histoire Sociale/ Social History vol. 34, no. 67 (May 2001): 169–86.
– "The Knights of Labor and the Salvation Army: Religion and
   Working-Class Culture in Ontario, 1882–1890." *Labour*, vol. 28 (fall
   1991): 89–127.
– *Revivals and Roller Rinks: Religion, Leisure, and Identity in
   Late-Nineteenth-Century Small-Town Ontario*. Toronto: University of
   Toronto Press 1996.
Marsden, George. *Fundamentalism and American Culture: The Shaping
   of Twentieth-Century Evangelicalism, 1870–1925*. New York: Oxford
   University Press 1982.
Marshall, David B. *Secularizing the Faith: Canadian Protestant Clergy
   and the Crisis of Belief*. Toronto: University of Toronto Press 1992.
Martin, Robert F. "Billy Sunday and Christian Manliness." *Historian*, vol.
   58, no. 4 (1996): 811–23.
Masters, D.C. "The Anglican Evangelicals in Toronto 1870–1900."
   Canadian Church Historical Society Journal, vol. 20
   (September-December 1978): 51–66.
McCarraher, Eugene. *Christian Critics: Religion and the Impasse in
   Modern American Social Thought*. Ithaca, N.Y.: Cornell University
   Press 2000.
McDannell, Colleen. *The Christian Home in Victorian America,
   1840–1900*. Bloomington, Ind.: Indiana University Press 1986.

McKillop, A.B. "Culture, Intellect, and Context." *Journal of Canadian Studies*, vol. 24, no. 3 (autumn 1989): 7–31.

McLoughlin, William G. *Modern Revivalism: Charles Grandison Finney to Billy Graham.* New York: Ronald Press 1959.

– *Revivals, Awakenings, and Reform: An Essay on Religion and Social Change in America, 1607–1977.* Chicago: University of Chicago Press 1978.

Minnix, Kathleen. *Laughter in the Amen Corner: The Life of Evangelist Sam Jones.* Athens, Ga.: University of Georgia Press 1993.

Moir, John S. "The Canadian Baptist and the Social Gospel Movement, 1879–1914." In Jarold K. Zeman, ed. *Baptists in Canada: Search for Identity Amidst Diversity.* Burlington, Ont.: Welch 1980.

Moore, R. Laurence. *Selling God: American Religion in the Marketplace of Culture.* New York: Oxford University Press 1994.

Moyles, R.G. *The Blood and Fire in Canada: A History of the Salvation Army in the Dominion, 1882–1976.* Toronto: Peter Martin Associates 1977.

Neely, Lois. *Fire in His Bones: The Official Biography of Oswald J. Smith.* Wheaton, Ill.: Tyndale House 1982.

Nelson, Bruce C. "Revival and Upheaval: Religion, Irreligion, and Chicago's Working Class in 1886." *Journal of Social History*, vol. 25 (1991): 233–53.

Noll, A. Mark. "George Rawlyk's Vision from the Periphery and the Study of American History: A Preliminary Probe." In Daniel C. Goodwin, ed., *Revivals, Baptists & George Rawlyk: A Memorial Volume.* Wolfville, N.S.: Acadia Divinity College 2000.

– *A History of Christianity in the United States and Canada.* Grand Rapids, Mich.: Eerdmans 1992.

Noll, Mark A., David Bebbington, and George Rawlyk, ed., *Evangelicalism: Compartive Studies of Popular Protestantism in North America, the British Isles, and Beyond, 1700–1990.* New York: Oxford University Press 1994.

Opp, James. "Revivals and Religion: Recent Work on the History of Protestantism in Canada," *Journal of Canadian Studies*, vol. 32, no. 2 (summer 1997): 183–193.

Owram, Doug. "Writing about Ideas." In John Schultz, ed., *Writing About Canada: A Handbook of Modern Canadian History.* Scarborough, Ont.: Prentice-Hall 1990.

Palmer, Bryan D. *A Culture in Conflict: Skilled Workers and Industrial Capitalism in Hamilton Ontario, 1860–1914.* Montreal and Kingston: McGill-Queen's University Press 1979.

- "Historiographic Hassles: Class and Gender, Evidence and Interpretation." *Histoire sociale/Social History*, vol. 33, no. 65 (May 2000): 105–44.
- *Working-Class Experience: The Rise and Reconstitution of Canadian Labour, 1800–1980*. Toronto: Butterworth 1983.

Pals, Daniel L. *Victorian Lives of Jesus*. San Antonia, Texas: Trinity University Press 1982.

Pedersen, Diana. "'Keeping Our Good Girls Good': The YMCA and the Girl Problem, 1870–1930." *Canadian Woman Studies*, vol. 7, no. 4 (winter 1986): 20–4.

Phillips, W., et al. *Mass Media: Systems and Effects*. New York: Holt, Rinehart and Winston 1976.

Pierard, Richard V. *The Unequal Yoke: Evangelical Christianity and Political Conservatism*. Philadelphia: J.B. Lippincott 1970.

Piva, Michael. *The Condition of the Working Class in Toronto, 1900–1921*. Ottawa: University of Ottawa Press 1979.

Prang, Margaret. *N.W. Rowell: Ontario Nationalist*. Toronto: University of Toronto Press 1975.

Putney, Clifford. *Muscular Christianity: Manhood and Sports in Protestant America, 1880–1920*. Cambridge, Mass.: Harvard University Press 2001.

Ramsay, John C. *John Wilbur Chapman: The Man, His Methods, and His Message*. Boston: Christopher Publishing, 1962.

Rawlyk, George. "A.L. McCrimmon, H.P. Whidden, T.T. Shields, Christian Higher Education, and McMaster University." In George Rawlyk, ed., *Canadian Baptists and Christian Higher Education*. Montreal and Kingston: McGill-Queen's University Press 1988.
- *The Canada Fire: Radical Evangelicalism in British North America, 1775–1812*. Kingston and Montreal: McGill-Queen's University Press 1994.
- "Writing about Canadian Religious Revivals." In Edith Blumhofer and Randall Balmer, ed., *Modern Christian Revivals*. Urbana, Ill.: University of Illinois Press 1993.

Rawlyk, George A., ed. *The Canadian Protestant Experience*. Burlington, Ont.: Welch Publishing 1990.

Reimer, Chad. "Religion and Culture in Nineteenth-Century English Canada." *Journal of Canadian Studies*, vol. 25, no. 1 (spring, 1990): 192–203.

Reimer, Samuel. "A Generic Evangelicalism? Comparing Evangelical Subcultures in Canada and the United States." In David Lyon and

Marguerite Van Die, ed., *Rethinking Church, State, and Modernity: Canada Between Europe and America*. Toronto: University of Toronto Press 2000: 228–42.

- "A More Irenic Canadian Evangelicalism?: Comparing Evangelicals in Canada and the U.S." In Daniel C. Goodwin, ed. *Revivals, Baptists & George Rawlyk: A Memorial Volume*. Wolfville, N.S. Scotia: Acadia Divinity College 2000.

Reynolds, William J., and Milburn Price. *A Survey of Christian Hymnody*. Carol Stream, Ill.: Hope Publishing 1987.

Rottenberg, Dan. *The Man Who Made Wall Street: Anthony J. Drexel and the Rise of Modern Finance*. Philadelphia: University of Pennsylvania Press 2001.

Routley, Eric. *The Music of Christian Hymns*. Chicago: GIA Publications 1981.

- *Twentieth Century Church Music*. New York: Oxford University Press 1964.

Rudy, Jarrett. "Unmaking Manly Smokes: Church, State, Governance, and the First Anti-Smoking Campaigns in Montreal, 1892–1914." *Journal of the Canadian Historical Association*, vol. 12 (2001): 95–114.

Rutherford, Paul. *A Victorian Authority: The Daily Press in Late Nineteenth-Century Canada*. Toronto: University of Toronto Press 1982.

Sandeen, E. *The Roots of Fundamentalism: British and American Millenarianism, 1800–1930*. Grand Rapids, Mich.: Eerdmans Publishing 1970.

Sawatsky, Ronald George. "'Looking for that Blessed Hope:' The Roots of Fundamentalism in Canada, 1878–1914." PHD thesis, University of Toronto Press 1985.

Schmidt, Leigh Eric. *Consumer Rites: The Buying & Selling of American Holidays*. Princeton, N.J.: Princeton University Press 1995.

Sinclair-Faulkner, Tom. "Theory Divided from Practice: The Introduction of the Higher Criticism into Canadian Protestant Seminaries." *Studies in Religion*, vol. 10 (1981): 321–43.

Sizer, Sandra. *Gospel Hymns and Social Religion: The Rhetoric of Nineteenth-Century Revivalism*. Philadelphia: Temple University Press 1978.

Smith, Gary Scott. "Evangelicals Confront Corporate Capitalism: Advertising, Consumerism, Stewardship, and Spirituality, 1880–1930." In Larry Eskridge and Mark A. Noll, ed., *More Money, More Ministry: Money and Evangelicals in Recent North American History*. Grand Rapids, Mich.: William B. Eerdmans 2000.

– *The Search for Social Salvation: Social Christianity and America,
  1880–1925*. Lanham, Md.: Lexington Books 2000.
– *The Seeds of Secularization: Calvinism, Culture, and Pluralism in America,
  1870–1915*. Grand Rapids, Mich.: Christian University Press 1985.
Staggers, Kermit L. "Reuben A. Torrey: American Fundamentalist,
  1856–1928." PHD thesis, Claremont University 1986.
Stark, Rodney, and Roger Finke. *Acts of Faith: Explaining the Human
  Side of Religion*. Berkeley, Calif.: University of California Press 2000.
Stout, Harry. *The Divine Dramatist: George Whitefield and the Rise of
  Modern Evangelicalism*. Grand Rapids, Mich.: William B. Eerdmans
  1991.
Sutherland, Neil. *Children in English-Canadian Society: Framing the
  Twentieth-Century Consensus*. Toronto: University of Toronto Press
  1976.
Szasz, Ferenc Morton. *The Divided Mind of Protestant America,
  1880–1930*. Tuscaloosa, Ala.: University of Alabama Press 1982.
Thomas, George M. *Revivalism and Cultural Change: Christianity,
  Nation Building, and the Market in the Nineteenth-Century United
  States*. Chicago: University of Chicago Press 1989.
Tucker, Bruce. "Class and Culture in Recent Anglo-American Religious
  Historiography: A Review Essay." *Labour/Le Travailleur,* vol. 6
  (autumn 1980): 159–69.
Van Die, Marguerite. *An Evangelical Mind: Nathanael Burwash and the
  Methodist Tradition in Canada, 1839–1918*. Montreal and Kingston:
  McGill-Queen's University Press 1989.
– "'The Marks of a Genuine Revival': Religion, Social Change, Gender,
  and Community in Mid-Victorian Brantford, Ontario." *Canadian
  Historical Review,* vol. 79, no. 3 (September 1998): 524–63.
Veltmeyer, Henry. *The Canadian Class Structure*. Toronto: Garamond
  Press 1983.
Wacker, "Holy Spirit and Spirit of the Age." *Journal of American
  History,* vol. 72, no. 1 (June 1985): 45–62.
Weisberger, Bernard. *They Gathered at the River: The Story of the Great
  Revivalists and Their Impact upon Religion in America*. Chicago:
  Quadrangle Books 1958.
Westfall, William. *Two Worlds: The Protestant Culture of Nineteenth
  Century Ontario*. Montreal and Kingston: McGill-Queen's University
  Press 1989.
Whitely, Marilyn. "Modest, Unaffected, and Fully Consecrated: Lady
  Evangelists in Canadian Methodism." In Elizabeth Gillan Muir and

Marilyn Whitely, ed., *Changing Roles of Women within the Christian Church in Canada*. Toronto: University of Toronto Press 1995.

Williams, Peter. *Popular Religion in America: Symbolic Change and the Modernization Process in Historical Perspective*. Englewood Cliffs, Calif.: Prentice Hall 1980.

Zuckermann, Michael. "Holy Wars, Civil Wars: Religion and Economics in Nineteenth-Century America." *Prospect*, vol. 16 (1991): 205–40.

Index